'An excellent read from a deeply knowledgeable author. This lively, often funny social history guides readers through Helsinki's past, never losing sight of the bigger picture. The city's story is skilfully interwoven with the dramatic wars and geopolitics of Finnish history.'

— Patrick Salmon, Chief Historian, UK Foreign, Commonwealth & Development Office

'Rich in historical detail and full of colour, this is a wonderful book for anybody wanting to understand how Helsinki grew from a little sixteenth-century village by the river mouth into a modern, globally networked Nordic metropolis.'

— Kristina Spohr, Professor of International History, London School of Economics, and author of *Post Wall, Post Square*

'Helsinki is one of those places simultaneously on the edge and in the middle of things. Meinander weaves a highly readable tale of this fascinating city of hidden depths.'

— Dan Kaszeta, Fellow of the Royal Historical Society and author of *The Forest Brotherhood*

'An absorbing, well-researched and immensely enjoyable introduction, full of vim and vigour. Helsinki is a fluent, pleasurable read for anyone wishing to explore the city; or to discover its history, and its important place in the Nordic and European story.'

— David Kirby, author of *A Concise History of Finland and Britain*, 1947

'[With this book,] Meinander has answered an eternal challenge. He is known as a master of the grand tapestry, his works elegantly combining the broad strokes of history with the world of lived experience as captured in the moment by eyewitnesses. Now, he has shifted his gaze closer and taken up the history of his own hometown ... A vivid and diverse tale of Helsinki.'

— Helsingin Sanomat

'An engaging story of Helsinki from its foundation in 1550, through Swedish domination, Russian expansion and Baltic sea trade to the forging of a new country, the archetypal Cold War border state, and today's modernising Eastern Baltic hub.'

— Charles Clarke, former UK Home Secretary and editor of *Understanding the Baltic States*

'The history of Helsinki has finally found a worthy author. Meinander talks about [the city] and its past with the sure hand of a professional historian, but also with warmth and empathy— as if telling a story about a friend.'

— Kulttuuritoimitus

HELSINKI

HENRIK MEINANDER

Helsinki

The History of a Nordic City

Translated by
Richard Robinson

HURST & COMPANY, LONDON

Published originally in Swedish by Schildts & Söderströms
Published by agreement with Helsinki Literary Agency

First published in the United Kingdom in 2025 by
C. Hurst & Co. (Publishers) Ltd.,
New Wing, Somerset House, Strand, London, WC2R 1LA
© Henrik Meinander, 2025
Translated by Richard Robinson
All rights reserved.

A Cataloguing-in-Publication data record for this book
is available from the British Library.

ISBN: 9781805264583

EU GPSR Authorised Representative
Easy Access System Europe Oü, 16879218
Address: Mustamäe tee 50, 10621, Tallinn, Estonia
Contact Details: gpsr.requests@easproject.com, +358 40 500 3575

Published with the support of FILI – Finnish Literature
Exchange

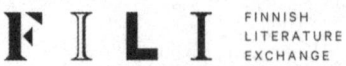

www.hurstpublishers.com

Printed and bound in Great Britain by Bell and Bain Ltd, Glasgow

CONTENTS

Maps   ix

List of Illustrations   xv

Preface   xix

1.   The Harbour   1

2.   In the Glow of Suomenlinna   41

3.   The Capital City   77

4.   Industry and Independence   121

5.   The Heart of the Republic   165

6.   Cold War Climates   209

7.   The Northern European Metropolis   251

Bibliography   271

Index   285

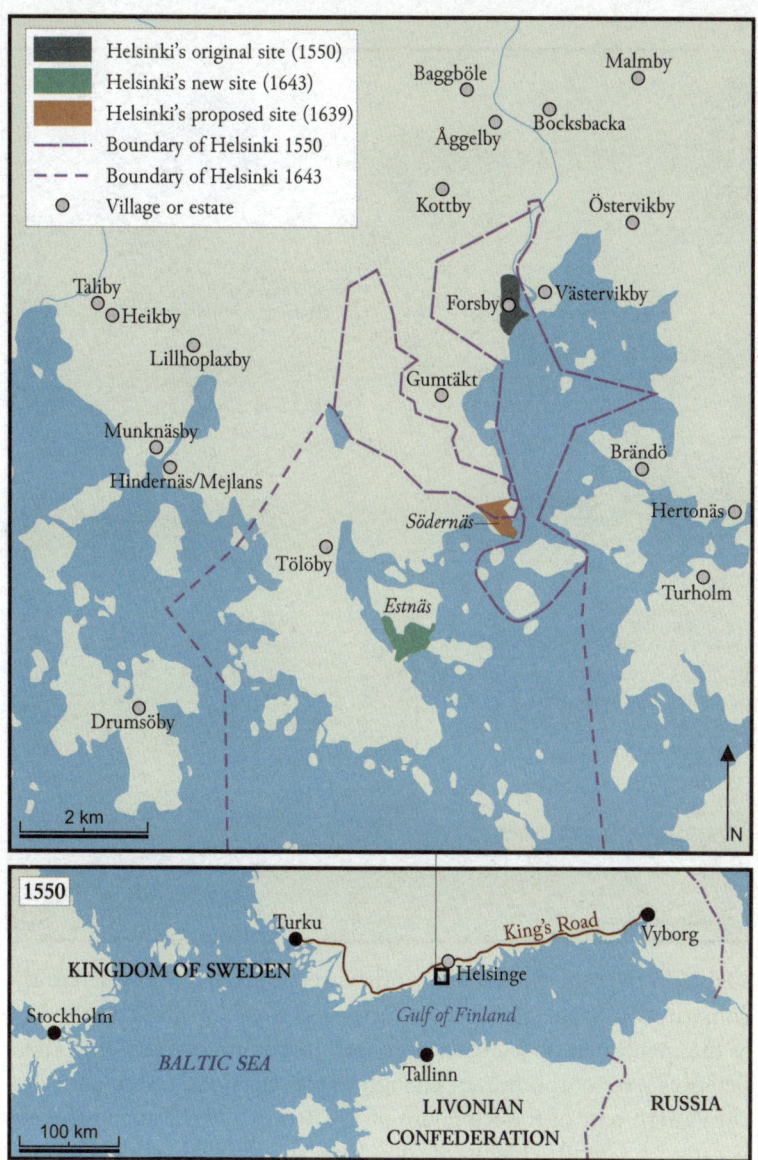

Legend:
- Helsinki's original site (1550)
- Helsinki's new site (1643)
- Helsinki's proposed site (1639)
- Boundary of Helsinki 1550
- Boundary of Helsinki 1643
- ○ Village or estate

Baggböle · Malmby · Åggelby · Bocksbacka · Kottby · Östervikby · Forsby · Västervikby · Taliby · Heikby · Lillhoplaxby · Gumtäkt · Munknäsby · Hindernäs/Mejlans · Brändö · *Södernäs* · Hertonäs · Tölöby · *Estnäs* · Turholm · Drumsöby

2 km

N

1550

Turku · King's Road · Vyborg

KINGDOM OF SWEDEN · Helsinge

Stockholm · *Gulf of Finland*

BALTIC SEA · Tallinn

LIVONIAN CONFEDERATION · RUSSIA

100 km

Map 1 The town was founded in 1550 by the rapids of the Vantaa River in the Parish of Helsinge, on the northern coast of the Gulf of Finland. Although it was relocated in 1640, the town kept its original Swedish name of Helsingfors, meaning "the rapids of Helsinge". This is also the root of its Finnish name: Helsinki.

Map 2 In the mid-eighteenth century, geopolitical tensions led to the construction of the Swedish sea fortress of Sveaborg (later Fennicised as Suomenlinna) on a cluster of islands just south of Helsinki. These defences were not, however, enough to prevent Russia from annexing the eastern part of the Kingdom of Sweden in 1809. Finland thereby became a Grand Duchy of the Russian Empire, with Helsinki appointed its administrative capital in 1812. By the 1840s, the city centre had been totally rebuilt in the Empire style under the inspired direction of architect C. L. Engel.

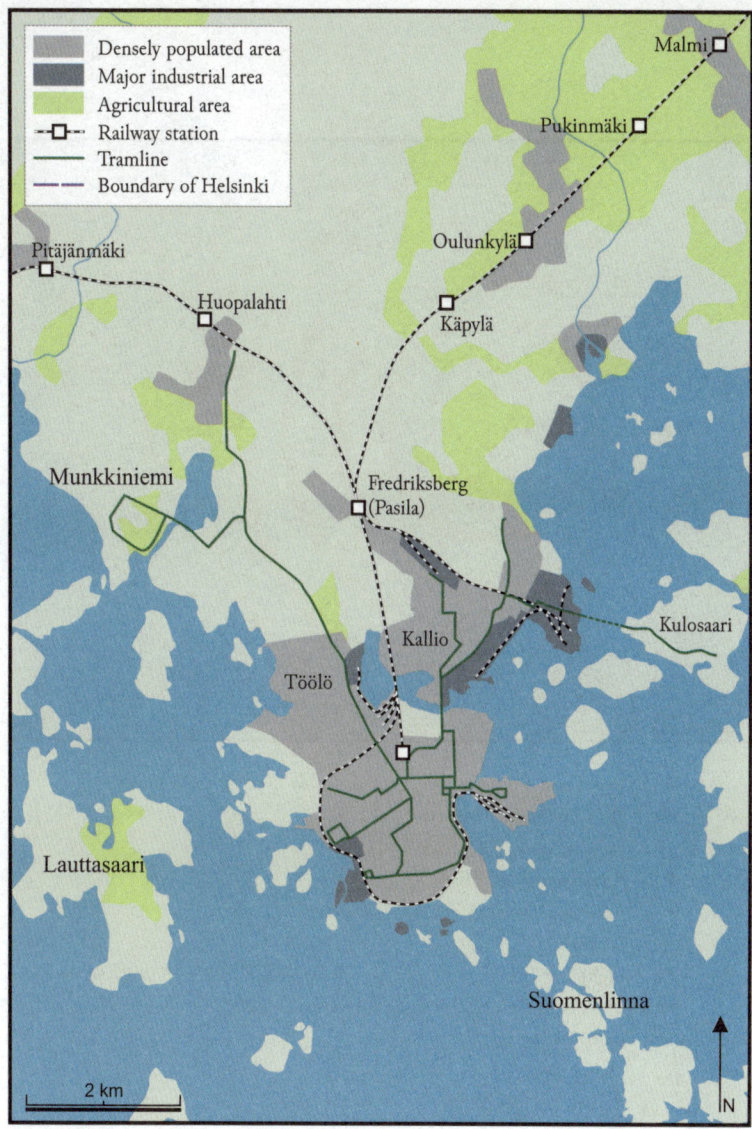

Map 3 By the turn of the twentieth century, Helsinki had grown into a thriving industrial city with good transport links, modern infrastructure and a vibrant urban milieu. The development of Finland's railway network in the late nineteenth century had helped transform the city, connecting it more directly to other parts of the country and to the huge Russian markets. The rise of rail traffic had also turned the port of Helsinki into Finland's leading import harbour.

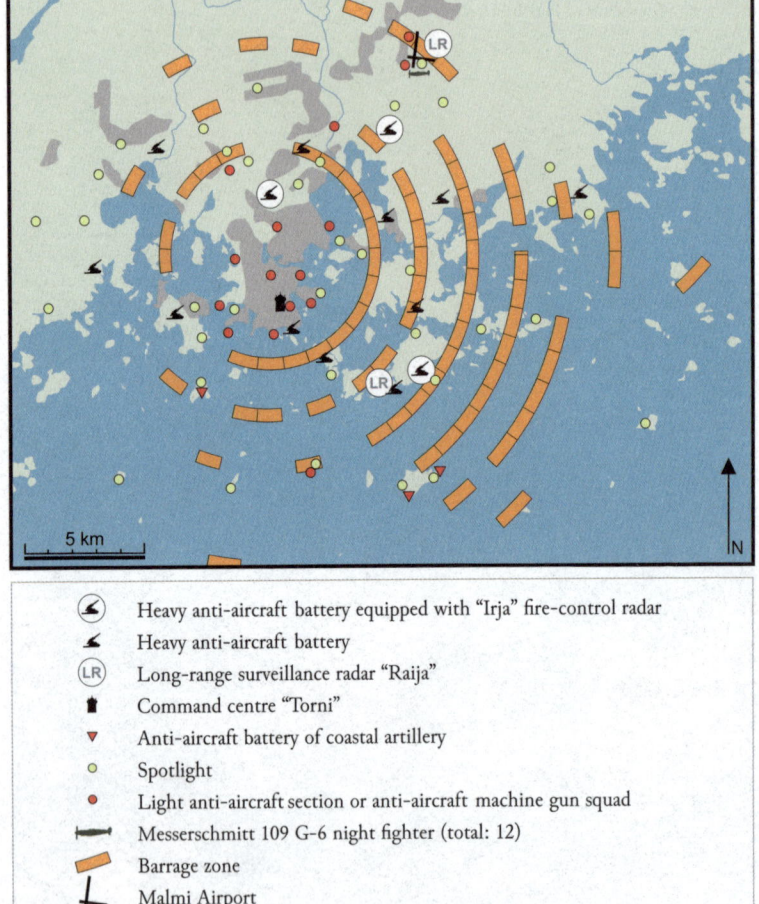

Legend:

- ⬟ Heavy anti-aircraft battery equipped with "Irja" fire-control radar
- ⬟ Heavy anti-aircraft battery
- (LR) Long-range surveillance radar "Raija"
- ⬟ Command centre "Torni"
- ▼ Anti-aircraft battery of coastal artillery
- ○ Spotlight
- ● Light anti-aircraft section or anti-aircraft machine gun squad
- ⊢ Messerschmitt 109 G-6 night fighter (total: 12)
- ▬ Barrage zone
- ⊥ Malmi Airport
- ▨ Densely populated area

Map 4 In 1943, Helsinki's air defences were strengthened considerably with modern German anti-aircraft technology. As a consequence, only six per cent of the city's building stock was destroyed during the three large Soviet air raids in February 1944.

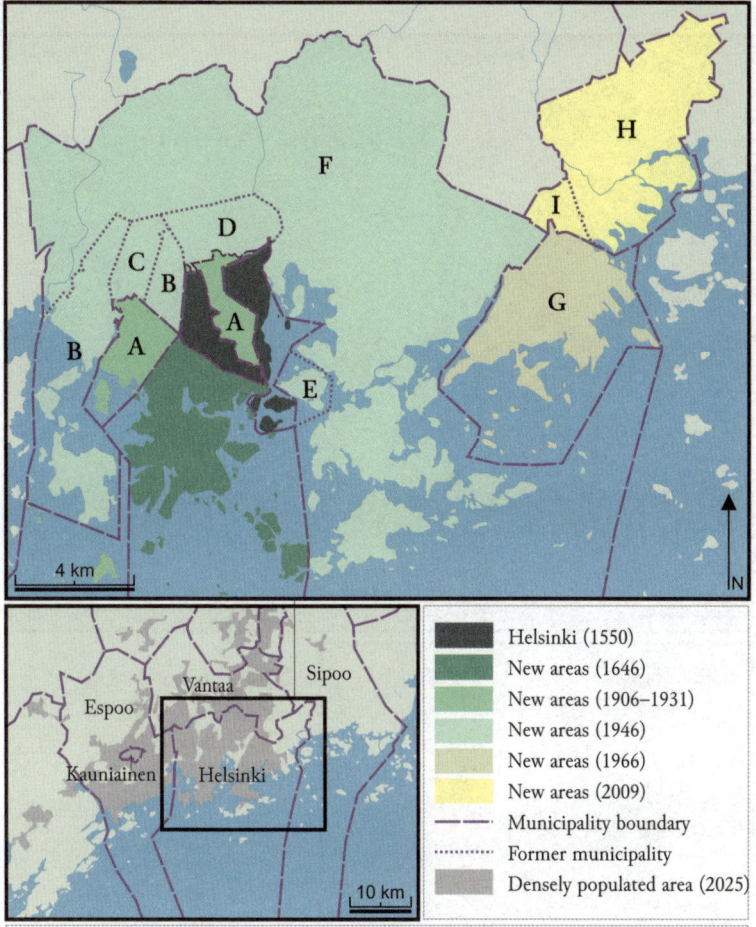

Map 5 After expanding in the mid-seventeenth century, Helsinki's geographical boundary went unchanged for hundreds of years. It was only in the first half of the twentieth century that the city's limits began to broaden again, culminating in the great incorporation of 1946. This brought a lot of the surrounding countryside and smaller urban centres under Helsinki's administrative control. Further incorporations took place in 1966 and 2009, as the surrounding municipalities became increasingly urbanised.

A Meilahti and Kumpula (Incorporated from Helsinki Rural Municipality), B Huopalahti Municipality, C Haaga Borough, D Oulunkylä Municipality, E Kulosaari Municipality, F Incorporated from Helsinki Rural Municipality, G Vuosaari (incorporated from Helsinki Rural Municipality), H Incorporated from Sipoo, I Incorporated from Vantaa (formerly Helsinki Rural Municipality)

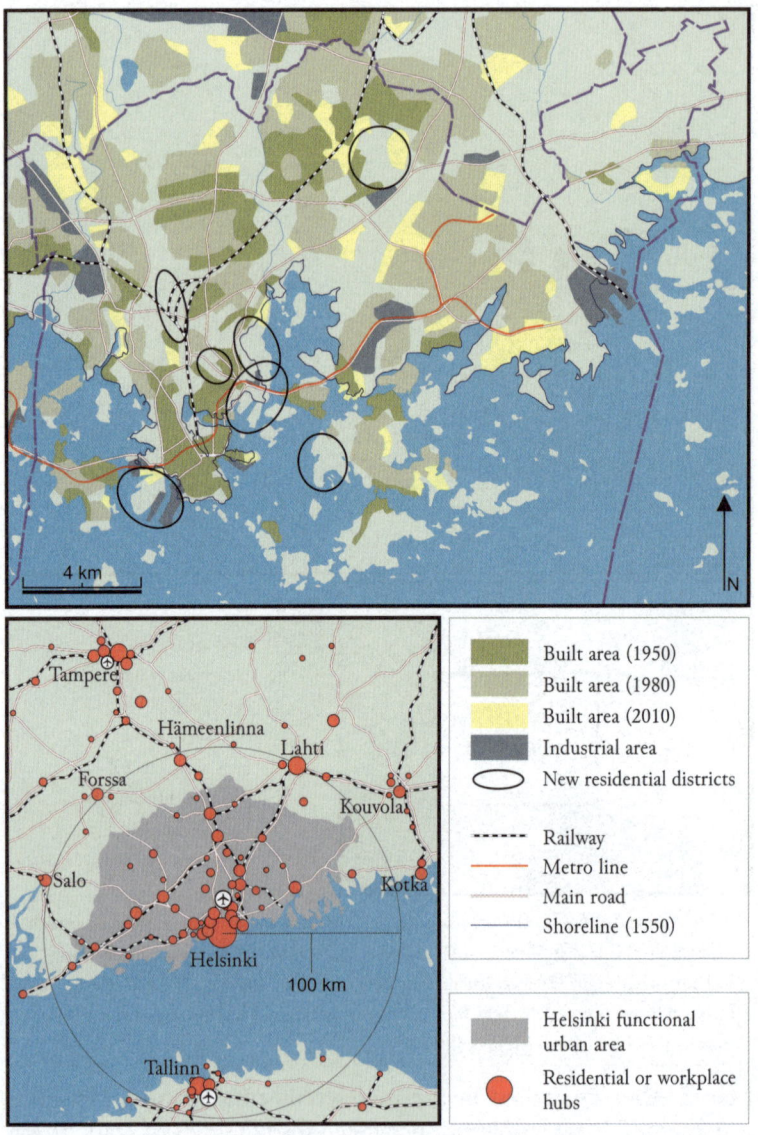

Built area (1950)
Built area (1980)
Built area (2010)
Industrial area
New residential districts

- - - - Railway
—— Metro line
~~~~ Main road
—— Shoreline (1550)

Helsinki functional
urban area

Residential or workplace
hubs

Map 6 Since the 1980s, many of Helsinki's new residential districts have been built on former harbours or at other regenerated industrial sites on the shoreline. In the modern day, both Helsinki's metropolitan region and its functional urban area have close connections to the Estonian capital of Tallinn. This flourishing exchange has breathed new life into a centuries-old relationship between the two cities.

LIST OF ILLUSTRATIONS

1. Gustav Vasa, King of Sweden 1523–60. Portrait by an unknown artist c. 1557–8. Nationalmuseum, Stockholm, Wikimedia Commons.

2a. The town's shoreline and topography during the seventeenth and eighteenth centuries. Map by B. Aminoff. Eirik Hornborg, *Helsingfors stads historia II*, Helsinki: City of Helsinki, 1950, p. 591.

2b. Torsten Burgman's house, the first-ever stone building in Helsinki, was constructed in the late 1690s. Architectural plan from 1748. The Military Archives of Sweden, Stockholm / Jere Jäppinen (ed.), *Burgman: Helsingin ensimmäinen kivitalo*, Helsinki: Helsinki City Museum, 2007.

3. The Russian Navy's siege of Helsinki in May 1713. Copy of Russian map. Historical Picture Collection of the Finnish Heritage Agency.

4a. The construction of Suomenlinna's shipyard. Copper engraving by Elias Martin, 1782. Historical Picture Collection of the Finnish Heritage Agency.

4b. Dancing on Suomenlinna in 1764. Wash drawing by Elias Martin. Nationalmuseum, Stockholm, Wikimedia Commons.

5. Helsinki, Suomenlinna and their environs in 1808, just as Finland's time under Swedish rule was coming to an end. Map by N. G. Werming. The National Library of Finland.

6a. The view looking south towards Helsinki from the Häme customs house at Pitkäsilta. Watercolour by Magnus von Wright, 1837. Picture Collections of Helsinki City Museum.

6b. The sights of Senate Square in 1838. Lithograph by F. Tengström. Historical Picture Collection of the Finnish Heritage Agency.

7a. Kaivohuone—the well house—and its baths opened for business in Kaivopuisto in 1838. Lithograph by Fredrik Liewendal, 1848. Picture Collections of Åbo Akademi.

7b. *Bombardement de Sweaborg* (The Bombing of Suomenlinna). Contemporary French woodcut by Trichon. Historical Picture Collection of the Finnish Heritage Agency.

8. Nyländska Jaktklubben (The Nyland Yacht Club) in the South Harbour. Oil painting by Albert Edelfelt, 1899. The Finnish National Gallery.

9a. The working-class street scene on Hämeentie in 1908, looking down towards Hakaniemi Square. Photo: Signe Brander. Picture Collections of Helsinki City Museum.

9b. Crowds of demonstrators packed onto Pohjoisesplanadi during the General Strike in Helsinki in early November 1905. Photo: Picture Collections of Helsinki City Museum.

10a. Russia's Baltic Sea Fleet lay anchored in the North Harbour until the German Army wrested control of Helsinki from the Reds in April 1918. Photo: Picture Collections of Helsinki City Museum.

10b. German soldiers assembled at the Stone of the Empress monument on the Market Square in April 1918. Photo: Eino W. Seppänen. Picture Collections of Helsinki City Museum.

11. *Havis Amanda*, Ville Vallgren's statue and fountain by the Market Square. Photo: Fred Runeberg, 1933. Picture Collections of Helsinki City Museum.

12a. Stockmann department store in 1932, two years after its long construction process had finally come to an end. Photo: Siiri Suo. Historical Picture Collection of the Finnish Heritage Agency.

12b. Emil Zátopek, the Czechoslovakian long-distance runner, on his way to victory in the 10,000m at the Helsinki Olympics in 1952. Photo: Vilho Uomala. Picture Collections of the Finnish Heritage Agency.

13a. Traffic at a standstill where Keskuskatu intersects with Aleksanterinkatu, which was then being trialled as a pedestrianised street. Photo: Eeva Rista, 1970. Picture Collections of Helsinki City Museum.

13b. Fashionable and spirited youths at the Potato Square— as the plaza in front of Old Student House is known in city slang—in 1968. Photo: Ismo Hölttö. Helsinki Art Museum (HAM) Collection.

14. President of the United States Gerald Ford (second from right) and Secretary of State Henry Kissinger (third from

right) in the main auditorium of Finlandia Hall. Photo: US National Archives and Records Administration.

15a. Once Kalasatama's construction is complete in 2035, the city district will be home to an estimated 25,000 residents and 10,000 jobs. Mock-up picture: Oiva Anttinen, Voima Graphics Oy.

15b. Architect Pauli E. Blomstedt's plans for Helsinki's future expansion in 1932. "Helsingin tulevaisuus I – yleisasemakaava", *Arkkitehti* 4/1932, pp. 49–55.

16a. The new faces of Helsinki. Photo: Mika Ranta. *Helsingin Sanomat*, 3.12.2017.

16b. A memento of the Ice Age. Photo: Raisa Ranta. Picture Collections of Helsinki City Museum.

PREFACE

I have a deep affinity for Helsinki. It is where I was born and raised, and, when my time eventually comes, it is where I hope to see out my final days. My connection to the city is such that it was no easy task to start writing this book. For a long time, Helsinki's history felt far too personal and subjective, inseparable from my own past. When, at last, I resolved to try to tell its story a few years ago, it was only after I had come up with three good justifications for doing so.

To begin with, I wanted to fill a gap in the literature on Helsinki. While there is a growing corpus of well-researched studies detailing specific topics and trends in the city's past, there was not an up-to-date, popular history of its full 475 years. Not, at least, one that was both concise and empirically grounded. My approach to documenting the development of Finland's capital was inspired by the brilliance and lucidity of the histories of world-renowned cities like London and Jerusalem.

Secondly, Helsinki's history shines a fascinating light on how the Baltic Sea region as a whole has continuously been influenced and formed by the twin forces of geopolitics and the global economy. The city was founded in 1550 for the purpose of a attracting a share of the trade between Central Europe and Russia over to the southern coast of Finland, which had been a part of the Kingdom of Sweden since the twelfth century. Although this economic gambit did not pay off in the short term, as the centuries passed

Helsinki developed into a dynamic trade hub. Its shipping routes stretched out into the world's oceans, and its railway connections extended, via St Petersburg, across the entirety of the Russian Empire. They brought with them unparalleled economic benefits, both for Helsinki and the whole of Finland. The city might still be a long way from the centre of the world, but its history provides an illustrative example of how peripheral markets have gradually been entwined with the world economy, and shaped by its globalising influence.

Far more than any other Nordic capital, Helsinki has also been the stage for a number of dramatic events in the great power politics of Northern Europe. The reason, of course, is that its geographical location on the Gulf of Finland has been—and remains—on the very edge of Western civilisation. The juxtaposition between East and West intensified after 1703, when St Petersburg was founded on the same gulf, at the mouth of the Neva River. It is not for nothing that this year has been characterised as a decisive one in the history of Finland.

Since then, every single great-power war fought by Russia has impacted Helsinki, in one way or another. During the Napoleonic Wars, Russia seized the eastern part of the Swedish realm— that is to say, Finland—and turned it into a Grand Duchy of the Russian Empire in 1809.

Helsinki thereby became the new administrative centre and received a complete architectural facelift that befitted its new status. As the First World War caused old empires to crumble, Helsinki came to play a prominent role in the Russian Revolution, out of which emerged the newly independent Finland. And when the Second World War broke out, Helsinki was one of the first European cities to come under aerial bombardment.

Last but by no means least, my third justification for embarking on this book was that Helsinki's history is worth capturing in an accessible account for the sake of posterity. Its development from a small harbour town to a Northern European metropolis encompasses a rich tapestry of social, cultural and economic elements that can be best appreciated when viewed as a whole. Thanks to its sea-centric setting—built on a series of islands and peninsulas extending into the Baltic—Helsinki has welcomed a steady stream of new inhabitants, both from within Finland and further afield. As a result, its linguistic character has undergone a number of transformations over the centuries and will doubtless continue to evolve in the future.

In my efforts to describe how structural forces have influenced the lives of Helsinki's residents, I have brought, where possible, the stories and snapshots of specific individuals to the fore. Even if the past is inevitably a foreign country, it is the historian's task to serve as the intermediary and attempt to articulate how contemporaries saw and experienced their city. Alongside the inhabitants' language use and everyday existence, I have paid relatively close attention to Helsinki's spatial profile and sense of place. In other words, to its architecture, city planning and geographical expansion, but also to the urban milieu and the public art that form part of Helsinki's collective memory.

I am naturally pleased that this book has been published almost concurrently in Finnish, Swedish and English, the three leading languages in Helsinki today. In respect of this English edition, I would like to give special thanks to the translator, Dr Richard Robinson, whose discerning judgement, cultural knowledge and keen eye for language I can always count on. Likewise, I am as usual in debt to my trusted cartographer,

PREFACE

Dr Hannu Linkola, producer of the six maps on the preliminary pages of the book. I am also very grateful to the editor, Mei Jayne Yew, for her efficient cooperation and nuanced revisions. Finally, I wish to extend my warm thanks to Michael Dwyer, the Managing Director of Hurst Publishers, who has now helped three of my books reach an English audience.

Henrik Meinander
Helsinki, July 2025

THE HARBOUR

Gustav Vasa's Fixed Idea

Helsinki—a city shaped by the sea, a city best seen from the sea. Approaching from the water, we can already catch a glimpse of the city's church towers on the outskirts of its archipelago. First, the double spire of St John's Church, then the domes of the Lutheran Helsinki Cathedral and the Orthodox Uspenski Cathedral, with Kalasatama's new skyscrapers now vying for the eye's attention in the background. After our ferry has carefully navigated the Kustaanmiekka Strait at the historic sea fortress of Suomenlinna, we put in at the South Harbour. Here our gaze is drawn to the Market Square and the light-coloured facades of the row of Empire-style buildings that stand grandly behind it.

Helsinki's proximity to the sea has been key to so much of its growth. Even nowadays, when the city stretches tens of kilometres inland, it is still defined by its coastal connections. In fact, no other capital in the Baltic Sea region has a centre that extends as far out into the sea, as can be felt by its climate and seen by its views. Wherever you are in Helsinki's inner city, you will always be close to the water. The further we look back through the centuries, and even through the millennia, the more we come to comprehend how the city's location has dictated its fate, for better and for worse.

To best appreciate how Helsinki came into being, we need to start by zooming all the way out. Let us begin with a broad statement of fact: humankind is not equally distributed all over the globe. Today, more than half of the eight billion people in the world live in the southern and eastern parts of Asia, and fewer than a tenth live in Europe. This demographic disparity is even greater between the southern and the northern halves of the European Union. Only a little over seven per cent (33 million) of the EU's 450 million inhabitants live north of the Baltic Sea's south coast. And the further back we go in time, the smaller the proportion of the European population that resided around the Baltic Sea.

Climate and geography are, of course, the two primary reasons for this, and they were even harsher when the first humans moved into the region. During the most recent ice age, the whole of northern Europe was covered by a glacier that was more than one kilometre thick. It was only once this had melted, around 10,000 years ago, that the Baltic Sea region was first populated. The northern climate, with its persistent winters, meant that the residents' lives were long impacted by food scarcity, and occasionally cut short by severe famines. Most of the area's hardy inhabitants were located along the sea's coastline and the inland waterways.

Although the Roman Empire never reached the Baltic Sea, its size and influence were such that it did help stimulate trade relations with regions beyond its dominion. In this way, Northern Europe became more economically and culturally interconnected with the Continent during antiquity. After the empire's fall and the Arabic invasion of the Mediterranean coast, a power vacuum emerged in Europe, which, together with a warming climate and a growing population, shifted many European trade routes further north. This was the first time that sizeable trading posts appeared along the Baltic coast, but the Scandinavian Viking chieftains would soon add to their number. The Viking Age (800–1050) is not typically known for its mercantile developments, such is its strong association with plundering and barbarism, yet these chieftains were able to maintain peaceful trade relations both over the North Sea and far into Russia and Ukraine.

The most decisive epoch in the whole of Europe's economic and political history came, however, after the Black Death in the mid-fourteenth century. A series of structural misfortunes lay behind the humanitarian catastrophe. The population increase had led to the over-exploitation and subsequent impoverishment of farmland. In tandem with the cooler climate of the period, this had caused a number of famines—not least the Great Famine of 1315–17—which had a deleterious effect on immune systems at a population level. This ultimately culminated in the rapid spread of the plague and the death of at least 50 million Europeans. The most affected were the densely populated areas of Western and Southern Europe; the least were East Sweden and Finland.

As the pandemic subsided in Western Europe, it was replaced by a glaring shortage of labour power. Wages increased, the value of land sank, and the feudal system with its autonomous lords began to break apart. The labour-intensive grain cultivation had to be partly replaced with animal husbandry, particularly of cattle and sheep. This, in turn, required a greater area of farmland for pasture and the importation of more grain, not least from the Baltic Sea region. Together with the first shoots of a monetary economy and a growing interest in extracting resources from other parts of the globe, this laid the foundation for the capitalist world order that reigns supreme today.

What has all this got to do with Helsinki and its origin story? Well, a network of so-called Hanseatic towns was formed in the wake of the increasing trade around the Baltic Sea's and North Sea's coasts. This was controlled from northern Germany by the Hanseatic League, who used these towns to keep an iron grip on mercantile activities across the region. As time went by, the Nordic royal powers mounted an increasingly hostile challenge to the league's dominance, for they wanted a bigger share of the profitable trade, particularly that which took place between Bruges (in modern Belgium) and Novgorod (in modern Russia).

The Hanseatic League's most important junction in its trade with Russia became the town of Reval on the north coast of Estonia, which now goes by the name of Tallinn. The town had been founded in the 1230s by Hanseatic merchants who fast established a firm hold on trade with southern Finland. Their swift success was a consequence of Estonia—and the Baltic region as a whole—being much more densely populated than Finland, a far larger territory that had been an integrated part of the kingdom of Sweden since the 1100s. By the mid-1500s, at the very time of Helsinki's founding, both Finland and Estonia had a population of around 250,000. The latter may have been smaller in size, but it had the more favourable southern climate and the more fertile land. It also benefitted from the Russian trade that not only flowed through Reval, but also through the smaller outposts further east, Narva and Dorpat.

A clear indication that the Estonian towns were flourishing in the mid-sixteenth century is their size. Reval alone had 6,000-7,000 inhabitants, or as many as all seven towns in Finland put together. As a result, Sweden's province of Nyland (hereafter referred to by its Fennicised name, *Uusimaa*), on the north coast of the Gulf of Finland, served as an economic hinterland for Reval and the surrounding region. Cistercian monks from Padise Abbey, west of Reval, were also active in Finland, for they possessed extensive agricultural land and fishing rights on the coast of Uusimaa.

Until the fifteenth century, the abbey had fishing rights at Helsinga rapids. These were found at the mouth of the Vantaa River in central Uusimaa, and were one of the best spots on the southern Finnish coast to catch salmon. In the 1430s, these rights were handed over to the local peasantry, but this did not reduce the trade connections between the Uusimaa coast and Reval. On the contrary, mercantile activity over the Baltic Sea was on the rise in this period, with the Uusimaa fishermen, peasants and landowners all keen to benefit from being in the orbit of Hanseatic Reval and its environs. This growing flow of goods did not go unnoticed by the Swedish Crown.

For as long as the Hanseatic League retained control over Russian trade, their economic resources afforded them a sizeable influence on power politics in the Nordic kingdoms. In the late 1300s, the rulers of Sweden, Norway and Denmark formed a loosely connected elective monarchy—the Kalmar Union—to reduce the Hanses' dominance, but the initiative fell apart in a series of internal power struggles. These culminated in the Swedish War of Liberation (1521–3), during which Gustav Vasa severed Sweden's ties with Denmark and ascended to the Swedish throne. Little by little, he set about challenging the Hanseatic League's control of both the lucrative Russian trade and his own realm, since Sweden had, to a large extent, come into existence as a result of the mercantile exchange over the Baltic Sea. The country's inhabitants also continued to be highly dependent on it for their livelihood.

As with many other European countries at this time, Sweden was transformed into a powerful sovereign state during Gustav Vasa's thirty-seven-year-long reign, which ended when he died of natural causes in 1560. One part of this consolidation was the transition to the Lutheran religion: through the confiscation of the church's property, the crown bolstered its coffers and turned the clergy into compliant followers of the King. Another was the switch to a hereditary monarchy in the 1540s. These developments alone were not enough for Sweden to hold its own against the other main actors in the Baltic Sea region: it also needed to strengthen its economy and military. As such, the King invested a great deal of effort into collecting more taxes, customs duties and trade revenues. As elsewhere in Europe, the administrative process behind this was increasingly concentrated in the kingdom's towns.

In the mid-1530s, the increasingly powerful sovereign states of Sweden and Denmark won a short-lived war against the town of Lübeck, known as the Queen of the Hanseatic League. Their victory served to loosen the Hanseatic stranglehold on the Baltic Sea trade, although goods from Russia continued to pass through the league's established mercantile centres in the region. This prompted Gustav Vasa to adopt a new strategy: in the summer of 1547, he resolved to found an entirely new town somewhere on the southern Finnish coast. This would compete against the Baltics for its share of the trade, which was burgeoning in this period as new markets developed in Western Europe.

Finland only had two port towns of any note at the time: Turku and Vyborg. The King was dissatisfied by just how little Russian mercantile traffic went through them, and even toyed with the idea of transferring the entire population of Turku to his planned new settlement. However, there was a wider issue in southern Finland that he found extremely vexing: the unregulated seaborne trade taking place between Finnish peasants and the Baltic towns. Exchanging goods in this way was an established practice, and it had been vital to the Finns' livelihood over the past centuries, as it had ensured they had a ready supply of salt and grains. It was, however, illegal, since it meant that the Swedish Crown received no excise duty on a significant portion of the region's foreign trade. In an effort to curtail the practice, Gustav Vasa introduced harsher punishments in the 1540s, but these had little effect.

This, then, was another driving force behind the King's decision to establish a new town in southern Finland. Administrators were tasked with finding a suitable site for a new port, one which would be a more attractive prospect for Russian and Dutch merchants. After his officials had finished surveying the region, in January 1548, Gustav Vasa decreed that the town be founded on the shore of Santahamina, an island in the Civil Parish of Helsinki. It had been a popular anchorage point since Viking times.

From a seafaring and naval perspective, Santahamina had lots of advantages, not least that it was a natural harbour, with a deep fairway. It was also protected by a chain of islands, behind which lay a coastal channel, the open sea and, due south, Reval. Yet Santahamina was, itself, an island, one that was not connected to the mainland. Moreover, in this period it was situated a long way from the Civil Parish of Helsinki's established settlement. The Finnish noblemen were acutely aware of these issues, and those that enjoyed Gustav Vasa's trust sought to dissuade him from his choice. After some skilful negotiating, they managed to convince him that the town should be built instead to the west of the Vantaa River's rapids. At this time, the river's mouth was called Helsinki River. The rapids were intersected by the King's Road, which ran west to east across Finland, connecting the castle in Turku to that in Vyborg. They were also significantly closer to the fertile ground that formed the civil parish's core. The peasant farmers who resided here had kept up the long tradition of trading with Reval that the King so desired to clamp down on.

Even in this improved location, the decision to build an entirely new town from scratch was foolhardy, to put it mildly, and not just because the King had never actually visited the site himself. Up to this point, the mercantile towns of the Baltic Sea had all grown up around existing trading posts, strategically important fortresses or ecclesiastical sites, such as monasteries or places of pilgrimage. In addition, the Uusimaa coast offered few exports to get excited about: it had tar and timber, but, beyond those, its best options were salmon, butter and other foodstuffs. However, it was not worth anyone's while opposing Gustav Vasa in the late 1540s. He had become increasingly obstinate and fickle as the years had gone by, and he now held such power that he could pursue his whims almost as he pleased.

On 12 June 1550, the King dictated a short letter to Uusimaa's senior officials. He demanded that the burghers of the four other southern coastal towns—Ulvila, Rauma, Tammisaari and Porvoo—be forced to migrate to Helsinki and build the new settlement. These residents were promised the same privileges as the kingdom of Sweden's other merchants, but if they refused to comply with the King's orders then they were "to be punished as disobedient subjects". This letter stands, in all its unabashed brutality, as the only evidence of the King's decision to found the town, which is why this date is considered to be the city's birthday. The annual celebration of Helsinki Day has been held on 12 June since 1959.

The Village at the River Mouth

If the letter marked the start of Helsinki's history, what can we say about the region's pre-history? Archaeologists have found that the rapids' first settlement, built close to the river's mouth, dates to circa 5,000 years ago (3,000 BC). Before this time, both Helsinki as we currently know it and its surrounding coastal regions had spent tens of thousands of years below sea level, due to the isostatic depression caused by the last ice age. As the land began to rise, small communities of hunters took up residence on the islands and coasts that were slowly emerging from the water. They would only stay on these at certain times of the year, hunting seals and other animals. Gradually, these early societies started to adopt more agricultural practices, such as burn-beating and cattle farming, but it was not until the thirteenth century that a more permanent settlement was established in the region. In this period, there was a population increase in modern-day Sweden that pushed a number of peasants to cross the Baltic Sea and seek new lives for themselves on the Gulf of Finland's coastline. These fresh arrivals brought with them more advanced ploughs, which meant that, for the first time, the region's clay soils could be cultivated.

Although there is no concrete proof of where the place name *Helsinge socken* (the Civil Parish of Helsinki) comes from, researchers presume that it, too, was brought by these new settlers. The peasants who made their homes on both sides of the Vantaa River's mouth most likely hailed from Helsingeland in Middle Norrland. As the centuries passed, the civil parish grew to become one of the richest and most densely populated communities on the south coast, prospering from the fertile plains and the excellent sea connections, which enabled a lively trade over the Gulf of Finland with Reval. The parish's centre was about five kilometres to the north of the rapids, and it was here that a handsome grey stone church was constructed in the 1400s: the Church of St Lawrence.

The arrival of the Swedish-speaking migrants had an impact on the Finnish-speaking Tavastians, who, until then, had fished and burn-beaten in the region around the Vantaa River's rapids. They either moved further north, or assimilated with the newcomers. This had an additional knock-on effect, in that Swedish became the dominant language of the region. Even today, after many centuries of twists and turns in language relations, Finland's biggest Swedish-speaking population is still to be found in the area. The Swedish Crown, of course, contributed to this linguistic shift, as it gradually increased its influence in southern Finland. Under Gustav Vasa's uncompromising stewardship, the territory was incorporated more directly into Sweden's burgeoning centralised state.

In the summer of 1550, when the first of the forcibly displaced burghers arrived on the west shore of the Helsinki rapids, they were not met by much of a settlement. The only buildings seem to have been a few granaries, which had been constructed in anticipation of the King's eventual decree. The residents of Porvoo and Tammisaari had loyally complied with his orders, but those in the small west-coast towns of Rauma and Ulvila were less willing to be uprooted. It took several more royal threats before they finally upped sticks to the Uusimaa coast over the next two summers. As such, it took a while for the town to get going, even if the Crown had aggressively acquired land on both sides of the river's mouth and had started to build a royal estate (*kungsgård*) on the island between the two branches of the rapids. Its construction gave a much-needed status boost to the new settlement, which was having difficulty attracting Russian and Dutch merchants to its shores.

In order to help Helsinki develop into the Crown's pre-eminent trading centre and naval base on the Gulf of Finland, Gustav Vasa also had plans to build a stone fortress. This was to be situated on the same island as the royal estate, since its location between the rapids would make it a challenge for an enemy army to breach. It was to protect the town on the western side of the rapids against an attack from the east. The island, however, was low-lying, with high hills rising on the land on either side of it, so considerable earthworks would be required to avoid enemy troops raining cannon fire down upon it.

This topographical weakness ultimately meant that there would be no fortress. Nevertheless, the King appointed his trusted official Erik Spåre as bailiff of the royal estate and put considerable resources at his disposal, so some additional construction did still take place on the island. A number of buildings were erected, as were some defensive works, all of which served to signal the Crown's presence in the area. When Gustav Vasa twice visited the town in the autumn of 1555, the royal estate was fortified with solid defensive ramparts and twelve cannons. This was not dissimilar to how the bastions were equipped on the approach to Stockholm. Although, unlike with the Swedish capital, the King would not make a habit of returning to Helsinki: these two trips marked the first and the last occasions he stopped by the town.

By this time, the King had already concentrated central Uusimaa's administrative power in Helsinki. During his stay there in 1555, he permitted the royal estate to further strengthen its economy and influence by expanding its land holdings and increasing its taxation rights. This was not the primary reason for his visit, however. A protracted border dispute with Russia had escalated into a full-blown war in the summer of 1555, meaning that Helsinki and its waters were required to function as the assembly point for the Swedish troops and naval fleet. In anticipation of the conflict, these had been transported to Finland the previous winter.

The town's citizens were initially duty-bound to quarter the troops, but this led to so many complaints that Gustav Vasa eventually decided to dispatch them closer to the border. While this restored calm to Helsinki itself, the ongoing war had a paralysing effect on the town's trade relations. Not only that, now that the King had finally laid eyes on the place, he found that its location and waterways did not meet his expectations in the slightest. In the last few years of his life, he would spend a long time pondering over the possibility of moving the town to another harbour, one that would have deeper waters and lie closer to the open sea. Gustav Vasa's disappointment was perhaps also reflected by his decision to allow those forcibly displaced from the other coastal towns to leave Helsinki and return to their old places of residence.

In the spring of 1557, Sweden struck a peace deal with Russia that resulted in a clear and unambiguous border being drawn between the two countries. At the same time, however, their struggle for supremacy over the Baltic Sea trade increased in intensity. Helsinki's seaborne trade, therefore, was buffeted by the capricious winds of this struggle until 1561, when Reval and its hinterland in northern Estonia voluntarily attached itself to the Swedish Crown in order to avoid being captured by the Russians. This fundamentally transformed living conditions in Helsinki, and not only because customs duties between it and Reval were abolished. Sweden aimed to strengthen its military control over the Baltics, which meant that Helsinki became the Crown's most important transit and service harbour for dispatching troops and weaponry over to Reval.

The new throughflow of soldiers benefitted a small band of Dutch and German merchants whom the Crown had convinced to come to Helsinki, partly through offers of trade privileges and contracts. Together with a handful of mercantile families from Porvoo, they were so prosperous that, according to tax records from the early 1570s, they had amassed a far greater fortune than the average owned by the burghers of any other town in Finland. Although the wealth was far from evenly distributed: no other town in Finland at this time had so many impoverished merchants per capita as Helsinki.

This stark disparity was brought about by three catastrophes that struck Helsinki in the years 1570 and 1571, hitting the less well-off townsfolk the hardest. From the few surviving sources from this period, we know that a significant portion of the town burned down sometime in 1570. During the winter that followed, inhabitants were ravaged by the plague. Last but not least, a new Swedish war against "our old Sworn Enemy" meant that the beleaguered town was subject to a number of Russian raids in early 1571, as were the other settlements in Uusimaa. The upshot was that, over the course of just two years, the population of Helsinki fell by a quarter, from circa 800 to 600 people.

It was unfortunate timing that this series of calamities came immediately after the town had been granted new privileges in 1569. Any short-term economic boost they could have given to Helsinki was lost in the turmoil, but, in the long term, the town still benefitted from the Crown's need to establish it as a transport harbour for Swedish military campaigns in the Baltics. It also enjoyed good connections to inland Finland, so timber exports became another secure source of income. Moreover, Helsinki had developed into a key port for tar exports, due in part to the demands of the Dutch and German merchants that the Tavastians' product adhere to Continental quality standards.

The cumulative effect of these various factors was that Helsinki neither decisively grew nor shrank over the next half century. The Crown's tax rolls from the 1610s record the town as then having around 500 inhabitants, so a hundred fewer than after the disasters of the early 1570s. Once the Crown's interest in the town had waned, it was not long before the royal estate on the rapids began to fall into disrepair. The town's centre shifted all the more clearly towards the river mouth's western bank. Here, a stone's throw or so from the harbour and the shoreline storehouses, the town hall stood at the head of the main square, around which low log houses with courtyards had gradually been built. Similar dwellings had been erected along the main roads into the town. In the north-west, near the King's Road, a relatively modest wooden church had been constructed, although its position on the brow of a hill still allowed it to tower over the settlement. Archaeological studies have found that, for a long time, it only had a dirt floor, and that it was probably only fitted out with benches—as was the Lutheran custom—in the early 1600s. With one eye on their own afterlife, the local nobility and well-to-do had, however, ensured that the interior was lavishly decorated with expensive fabrics, extravagant chandeliers and silver communion chalices. The first Finnish equivalent of *memento mori* was published in Priest Jaakko Finno's hymnbook in 1583; at that time, it was an adage that no one could afford to forget.

Information about the town's early clergy is fragmentary. Two clergymen who have gone down in the historical record are Bertil Christophori and Samuel Savonius. The former periodically took up the role of town pastor alongside his work as Helsinki's first schoolmaster, while the latter is reported to have served as reverend for at least thirty years (until 1629), which is an exceptionally long time, especially considering the post's meagre wages. As his surname suggests, Savonius originated from Savonia, a historical province of Sweden in eastern Finland. During his early years in office, he was twice sent across the Gulf of Bothnia to represent the estate of the clergy at meetings of the Riksdag, the Swedish parliament.

As for the rest of the town's inhabitants, we can only get faint clues as to their lives from archaeological finds. There were a small number of rich merchants and officials who employed servants, although many of these elites actually lived outside of the town itself. Besides them, the majority of the residents were poor artisans and manual labourers, who scarcely owned more than their clothes and their tools. Their daily existence was clearly a world away from life in Reval, which had a population ten times that of Helsinki. The centuries-old Hanseatic hub continued to be a bustling commercial centre, its grand main square dominated by the town hall and surrounded by ornate stone buildings, its skyline crowded with tall church spires, its citizens protected by the imposing medieval castle on Toompea

Hill. The scene must have left quite an impression on the many Helsinki residents who visited the town during their lifetimes. Compared to Reval, their home must have seemed like a sleepy fishing village, set far back in a nondescript bay on the other side of the Gulf of Finland.

One of these travellers to Reval was Sigfrid Aronus Forsius (circa 1560–1624), who would go on to gain renown across the whole Nordic region as an astronomer. Since he sometimes went by the name Helsingforsius, it is assumed that he hailed from Helsinki. The earliest surviving record of his life and career is from the 1590s, when he worked as a clergyman and schoolteacher at the Finno-Swedish Cathedral in Reval. Forsius was extremely well-read, but not content to sit on his laurels, so he would go on to hold many leading positions at the Crown's seats of learning and dioceses. He is best-known to posterity for his work *Physica*, in which he displays his extensive knowledge of the principal Continental studies of natural philosophy and physics. Plenty more could be written about Forsius' dramatic life story, but, for the purposes of outlining Helsinki's destiny, it is sufficient to note that he served as military chaplain for the troops of Duke Charles (later King Charles IX of Sweden) in Finland. As such, he might well have witnessed first-hand when the Duke had nine people beheaded after capturing Helsinki in 1599; they were supporters of King Sigismund, against whom Charles was embroiled in a bloody struggle for the Swedish throne.

Sweden developed into a formidable force.in the Baltic Sea region under the rule of Gustav Vasa's two eldest sons, Eric XIV and John III. With power, however, came vicious family feuds. Eric XIV was king for only nine years (1560–9) before he was deposed by his brother, John, who would also eventually have him poisoned in captivity. John III would remain head of the realm until his death in 1592, after which his son Sigismund ascended to the throne. This provoked another bout of infighting, for Sigismund was already the King of Poland, and a Catholic to boot. His uncle, Charles, led a rebellion against him, with much of the ensuing fighting taking place in Finland, where the nobility remained loyal to Sigismund the longest. The beheadings in Helsinki in September 1599 were just the start of Charles's revenge. Two months later, he had around fifty nobles executed in Turku for their support of Sigismund, before travelling back to his home country to carry out a similarly bloody retribution there. With his enemies quashed, Charles was appointed regent by the Riksdag, although he would have to wait until 1604 to be formally declared King of Sweden.

Charles XI's period of rule was short (he died in 1611), but certainly not sweet for Finland or Helsinki. Under his forebearers, Finland had often been at the centre of events, as can be seen, for example, by the founding of Helsinki itself. King Charles, however, had very little trust in the Finnish nobility, and his focus was undoubtedly elsewhere, namely on the Baltics, where he continued his fight against Sigismund, who was still King of Poland. While it is true that Charles renewed Helsinki's trade privileges on three occasions, the town's commercial activities took a backseat to its new role as shipping port for the troops and equipment that he sent across the Gulf of Finland. The town's peace was also shattered by this influx of soldiers, since they were prone to fighting and theft. The Crown tried to combat the disorder with threats of severe punishments and strict prohibitions, but its efforts were in vain. The badly behaved troops were certainly an unwelcome distraction for the town's merchants, who were then engaged in a running battle with Porvoo, Helsinki's eastern neighbour, for control over the trade between the region's interior and Reval.

When Gustav II Adolf succeeded his father in 1611, Sweden was still mixed up in wars in various parts of the Baltic Sea region.

As a result, between 1614 and 1616, the new King travelled back and forth across the Gulf of Finland, making two trips to Helsinki in the process. The town might have been neither bustling nor booming, but it was logistically important. In the spring of 1614, he spent ten days there and took the opportunity to renew its town privileges. In January 1616, he summoned many of the kingdom's elite and representatives from Finland's estates to an assembly in Helsinki. As in Sweden, Finland's four estates represented different sections of its population: the nobility, the clergy, the burghers and the peasants. Gustav wanted to reach an agreement with them on two matters, above all else: the first was a new war tax, the second an unwavering support for his protracted war against Sigismund. He was continuing the conflict started by his father, and so no doubt realised that the Finns' loyalty could not be taken for granted, especially after Charles had mercilessly executed so many Finnish noblemen on Sigismund's side.

The ten-day-long meeting of the estates was, without question, the biggest event in the town's history since Gustav Vasa's visit in 1555. Both had markedly similar catalysts: an ongoing war and the need to retain control over the eastern part of the realm. On this occasion, the meeting and its negotiations took place in the town hall, the only two-storey building in Helsinki. It was also the setting for King Gustav II Adolf's welcome speech, which was a long-winded defence of his and his father's sustained fight against the power-hungry Sigismund and his expansionist aspirations for Poland and Catholicism.

This would, ultimately, be the only time under Swedish rule that all the representatives of the Finnish estates converged for an assembly to discuss matters of the realm with the monarch. An older work of history, imbued with more nationalistic sentiment, has gone so far as to declare the meeting "the *Diet* [parliament] of Helsinki". This is, of course, an overstatement, but it touches on how vital the eastern part of the kingdom was to Sweden's rulers in this period, especially their political manoeuvring in the Baltic Sea region. In the early seventeenth century, however, their attention was slowly starting to be diverted further south by the war with Poland. This shift in focus would soon come to influence the direction of Helsinki's development.

The New Helsinki

Sweden's eternal warmongering needed financing. This could not be done effectively without a complete overhaul of the Crown's decision-making processes, its taxation system and its ability to mobilise troops. The solution was a systematic centralisation of the kingdom's administration. This played a crucial role in Sweden emerging victorious from its thirty-year war with Poland, and in its transformation into Europe's strongest unitary state. This new state apparatus was the ingenious creation of Lord High Chancellor Axel Oxenstierna and was built around a series of centralised government branches. He also established administrative counties who exercised their authority through a standardised judicial system. In Finland, the reforms were implemented through the establishment of a special office of governor-general. The third holder of this post, Count Per Brahe, founded a number of port towns on Finland's west coast (Ostrobothnia) and, in 1640, Finland's first university, the Royal Academy of Turku. Most relevant to our story, however, was his decision in 1639 to move Helsinki further south, so that it would stand face-to-face with the Baltic Sea.

There were certainly justifiable reasons for doing so. Neither Helsinki nor Porvoo had shown any notable commercial success since 1617, when they obtained their staple rights, which permitted them to trade directly with foreign ports. By the mid-1630s, the Council of the Realm in Stockholm, functioning as Queen Christina's regency, had started to lose patience with the towns. The council members contemplated stripping them of their rights and building instead a new staple town on Santahamina, the same island on the outer edge of the archipelago where Gustav Vasa had originally wanted to found Helsinki. However, after Per Brahe had acquainted himself with the site, he realised that its shores were ill-suited to the requirements of a port town. In the spring of 1639, Brahe proposed an alternative to the Council of the Realm: the cape of Sörnäinen, a few kilometres to the south, along the shoreline from the town's existing location at the rapids.

Sörnäinen had, Brahe asserted, a number of features in its favour. The cape lay near the open sea but was sheltered by a chain of islands. Its channel was clearly deeper than that of the current harbour at the rapids, where land uplift was causing the water to become increasingly shallow, at a rate of 30 centimetres per century. Sörnäinen also had a hill at its south-eastern tip, which was tailor-made for a fortress. On 30 May 1639, the Council of the Realm accepted Brahe's proposal and sent over an engineer to draw up a plan for the new staple town. Besides wanting to improve trade, the council also had great administrative expectations for this endeavour, having just agreed to split the vast county of Uusimaa and Häme in two. Uusimaa, as a result, needed a new county town, and the council intended for Sörnäinen to take on the role.

In this epoch in Europe, orderly, systematic urban planning was in vogue, and Sörnäinen's grid design adhered closely to this trend. The town was to have a spacious square at its centre, and a bastion furthest out on the tip of the cape. Comparable plans were sketched out in this period for Gothenburg and Nyenschantz (the site of modern St Petersburg), the Swedish Crown's new towns at the western and eastern limits of its realm. On the west coast of Finland, in Ostrobothnia, harbour towns were also built in the 1640s with a similar rectilinear layout. When

Brahe inspected Sörnäinen during "the new town's foundation" in January 1640, the forest had already been cleared away and the buildings' plots marked out with sticks. Consequently, in his report to Oxenstierna, the Governor-General was able to state with satisfaction that "there is now nothing more to be done than to move there and build."

As it happens, this freshly staked-out town was located right where the city began to build the new district of Kalasatama in the early 2010s. And, interestingly enough, Kalasatama's main square is situated in almost the very same place as that sketched out for Sörnäinen. This underlines the importance of topological factors in town development; centuries might pass, but the nature of the terrain can inspire similar urban planning solutions. While Brahe's Sörnäinen would, ultimately, never be realised in the 1600s, in the late 1800s the cape was turned into a major port for the city's rapidly growing industries. A century later, as Helsinki's commercial life advanced in leaps and bounds, much of the freight shipping moved east to Vuosaari, and the city began the process of rebuilding that would give the area its modern identity of Kalasatama.

As for Sörnäinen's early modern identity, its planned development was curtailed because the noblemen endowed with the surrounding lands refused to exchange them. Without these, the town had absolutely no space to expand in the future. This was something of a secondary concern, since those lands had no bearing on the initial construction plans for Sörnäinen, but it was enough to deter Brahe, who did not want to end up in a dispute with his noble brethren. He instructed his engineers to resume their survey of the nearby coastline and, in the summer of 1640, they came across a suitable alternative site. It was a peninsula a couple of kilometres to the south of Sörnäinen, and thereby closer to the archipelago encircling the mainland and the open sea beyond. Moreover, its northern bay had already been used as a landing place in the 1630s by the military and freight ships that were too large to put in at Helsinki's shallow estuary.

On 29 October 1640, the Council of the Realm decreed that Helsinki should be moved down from the Vantaa River to this new location, instructing officials to carry out the order without delay. The town was permitted to keep its existing name, but its future home would be on Estnässkatan, the eastern peninsula of Estnäs (hereafter referred to as Vironniemi). Almost four centuries later, in modern-day Helsinki, this area is better known as the districts of Kruununhaka and Katajanokka. The latter district translates to "Juniper Cape" in English, and its etymology is a fascinating example of how Helsinki's present identity is intrinsically bound to its geographic and linguistic history. The "skata" part in Estnässkatan means a narrow cape in Uusimaa's Swedish dialect, which is exactly what Katajanokka was until the mid-1840s, when a channel was dug to separate it from the rest of the peninsula. This original topography is reflected in Katajanokka's Swedish name "Skatudden" ("the narrow cape's tip"), which existed long before the Finnish was coined. So where, then, did the "Juniper" come from in the Finnish name? Well, it is actually a mondegreen of "skata", which, over the centuries, turned into "kataja" in the mouths of Helsinki's Finnish speakers.

The move to Estnässkatan did not proceed quite as quickly as the Council of the Realm might have hoped. It was no doubt fresh in the memory of Helsinki's residents that the plans for both Santahamina and Sörnäinen had come to nothing. In both cases, the landowners had been ordered to clear away the forests unnecessarily. The pace of the move was certainly also impacted by the fact it was voluntary; unlike in 1550, the Crown did not demand a forced relocation. Moreover, Estnässkatan's climate likely served as a deterrent for some: its sea air was fresher than at Helsinki's current home by the rapids, but it was also often harsh and biting. If that were not enough, Helsinki was then locked in an interminable dispute with Porvoo over the two towns' trade privileges. However, in spite of various setbacks, the town finally started to take shape on Estnässkatan in the late 1640s, thanks in no small part to Per Brahe's concerted efforts.

It had been Brahe, in 1640, who had pushed for Helsinki to be made county town for Uusimaa in tandem with the latter's separation from Häme. Only eight years later, he scrapped the division and reunited the regions as a single county, but he permitted Helsinki to remain the county town. This was naturally a status boost to the County Governor residing there and increased his influence among Stockholm's political elite. This made it easier for Helsinki to get financing for the construction of its church and town hall, as well as the bridges necessary to connect it to the main road running north through the Civil Parish of Helsinki all the way to Häme. The County Governor's residence was to be found by the town's wharf, and it was apparently nothing to brag about. Its shortcomings became a real bugbear for the first long-term holder of the office, Ernst Johan Creutz, after he arrived in the town in the autumn of 1653.

Creutz belonged to one of the most pre-eminent noble families in the kingdom of Sweden. He had at his disposal the large Malmgård Manor in Pernaja, a little to the east of Porvoo along the Finnish coast, as well as sizeable fiefdoms in the Baltics and elsewhere. His promising career in Stockholm had, however, ground to a halt due to his violent temper and undiplomatic remarks. In an effort to protect him, Per Brahe, Creutz's long-time champion, saw to it that he was appointed County Governor far away from the Swedish capital, in Helsinki. Creutz's conduct does not seem to have improved in this role: indeed, there were countless occasions when he upset the town's administrative and economic elite. On the other hand, his autocratic and, at times, downright brutal, reign as County Governor had a positive effect on the town as a whole. He demanded unfailing loyalty from his officials, and he clamped down on the big merchants who openly flouted the Crown's trade restrictions. One of his main targets was the illegal trade between Uusimaa and Reval, which he made a concerted effort to stamp out by allowing confiscated goods to be redistributed, as had once been the custom. Not all his methods were so judicious: one summer night in 1659, he finished off a wild evening's drinking by opening fire on the mayor's house with cannons. The target of his ire had proved to be insufficiently servile, and this was Creutz's gentle reminder that he should toe the line.

Unsurprisingly, the mayor pressed charges for this bombardment, and the case went all the way to the Turku Court of Appeal before a settlement was reached. Perhaps more surprisingly, it did not mark the end of Creutz's career, since the Crown's leadership in Stockholm valued his robust approach to imposing its authority, in spite of his myriad indiscretions. He had, after all, only just shouldered responsibility for the upkeep and defence of Finland when Karl X Gustav, preoccupied by his wars against Poland and Denmark, had left the eastern part of the realm to its own devices. There was one thing, however, that Creutz was unable to change. Try as he might, he could not direct more of the profitable tar trade to Helsinki. Stockholm and Vyborg would retain their dominant positions over its export throughout the second half of the seventeenth century, with the Crown keeping a tight rein on the market via a tar company with monopoly privileges it had set up for this very purpose.

According to current research, tar was an important export for Helsinki, but the town's prosperity was not solely dependent on the number of barrels of the black viscous liquid shipped from its port. The tar market experienced various dramatic ups and downs during Helsinki's first fifty years, yet the population still grew from around 600 to almost 2,000 inhabitants. Moreover, there are many indications that its fortunes were affected far more by becoming the county town and developing as a port for troop and timber shipments to the Baltics. The fact that tar's bookkeeping records have been exceptionally well-preserved has, most likely, led to its importance to the town being overstated in the academic literature.

There is no doubt, however, that the tar trade did have an indirect influence on the development of Helsinki and the whole of Finland. It was more profitable to turn the Finnish forests into tar than it was to export them as lumber or sawn timber to Western Europe. During the seventeenth century, Finland was responsible for three-quarters of all the tar made in the kingdom of Sweden. The Age of Sail was then in full swing, and the increase in shipping over the Earth's oceans and seas had led to a steep rise in demand. This meant that, for the first time, Finland was the main producer of a global raw material, for the thick-flowing, black liquid was needed to waterproof the decks and hulls of seafaring vessels the world over. So great was the tar trade in the Swedish-controlled Baltic Sea in the seventeenth century that it gave a noticeable boost to the movement of all capital across the region, which obviously also benefitted the nascent Helsinki and its inhabitants.

How did the town look around the time of its hundredth birthday? Well, it was in the 1650s that Helsinki's centre started to take shape on its new home of Vironniemi, with urban development focusing on the southern half of the one-square-kilometre peninsula. In the east lay the North Harbour, with its large wharf in its southern corner, which lay up against the narrow strip of land out to Katajanokka in the south-east. In the south, the town's natural limit was the bay of Kaupunginlahti, which would gradually be developed into the South Harbour. In the west and south-west lay the shallow and reedy Kluuvi, which was, until the mid-1800s, an offshoot of Töölönlahti, a bay to the north-west of Vironniemi.

All that is to say, Helsinki was not far from being an island at this time. Its only connection to the mainland was a thin strip of ground in the south-west, little more than one hundred metres wide, between Kaupunginlahti and Kluuvi. Today, it is the eastern half of Esplanadin Puisto. The whole of the peninsula had, until this point, stood desolate, barren and uninhabited—the only farm in the vicinity was the Töölö homestead, which was located on the same spot as the modern-day Opera House. The Crown recognised that it needed to improve access to the town, so one of its first investments was the construction of two bridges to the mainland, north of Töölönlahti, where a road ran up towards the rapids, today called Hämeentie. The western approach to the town became known as Turuntie, and largely followed the same route as the current Mannerheimintie.

Until the end of the eighteenth century, the wharf and the customs house remained the logistical heart of the town, while its commercial, administrative and spiritual centre emerged a few blocks to the west, around the Great Square (*Suurtori*). This was situated in the same spot as the eastern half of Senate Square today, so with a little bit of imagination we can picture how Helsinki would have looked in the 1600s. Suurkatu stretched west from the wharf to the Great Square and the church grounds. It was this main street that would later become Aleksanterinkatu, the only difference being that, at this time, it came to an end one block west of the graveyard, at Kluuvi's muddy shoreline.

The town's grid pattern had been carefully delineated by engineers in Stockholm to extend over much of the peninsula. It did not, however, take into account the challenges posed by the topography, namely the terrain's great fluctuations in height in the north, and the awkward shoreline in the west. As a result, only the blocks closest to Suurkatu were actually built as intended, while the rest of the low wooden houses fit themselves around the terrain and the agricultural land that was gradually cleared on the town's outskirts. Helsinki's development was far from straightforward in other respects, too: over the decades to come, it would be assailed by economic downturns, wars and famines. No less of an impediment to its growth were the chronic quarrels of its citizens and the destructive fires that repeatedly raged through its streets.

The first and the worst of these blazes ravaged the town in early August 1654. A fire quickly spread in the blocks south of the Great Square, and, in just three hours, two-thirds of Helsinki's sixty houses had burned to the ground. Most severely hit were the wealthy townhouses and the administrative quarter, although not everyone mourned what had gone up in smoke. The demanding County Governor Creutz made the most of the demise of his old residence: he ensured that a magnificent new property was built, at the Crown's expense, on an extensive plot of land just north of the town's wharf. When the imposing administrative and residential building was finished, replete with its high gate and large garden, it was very evident who ruled the roost in Helsinki.

Trades and Town Houses

By the mid-1690s, Helsinki's population had risen to 2,100 people, but this was still a drop in the ocean compared to Stockholm, Reval and Riga, the great cities of the Swedish Empire's Baltic Sea region. Nonetheless, the new Helsinki had achieved a considerable amount in barely a half-century: it had established itself as county town of Uusimaa and Häme, and had emerged as a crucial transit point in the supply of raw materials, manpower and troops to the bigger Baltic Sea towns and cities. Its expansion can be seen in a map of the town from 1696, which was updated eleven years later with a list of all the plot owners. From this detailed source, it is evident that new buildings had been constructed in multiple directions. Land had been cleared for cultivation along both main roads out of town, as well as on any other relatively flat and fertile earth that could be found among the peninsula's crags, hollows, marshy pools and sandy ground.

The map shows that two small jetties had been built on the western shore of Kaupunginlahti, today South Harbour, and includes a number of vessels moored in their vicinity. This indicates that the town's shipping activities were developing in a promising direction. To the north-east of the North Harbour, the tar company had built some warehouses on a small island, which subsequently got the name Tervasaari, literally "Tar Island". The most prestigious properties were still the residence of the County Governor and the big townhouses south of Suurkatu and around the Great Square. All the public buildings of note were also found in the plaza's immediate proximity, including the town hall, the mayor's house and the church with its cemetery.

This was the wooden Church of the Holy Spirit, which had been hastily built to replace the similarly wooden Christina Church that burned down in the fire of 1654. The new place of worship quickly became dilapidated, but neither the Crown nor the town's well-to-do citizens were particularly keen to finance its renovation. The local elite were, however, willing to make expensive, showy donations to its interior, so the church's shabby appearance on the outside belied the opulence within. When they died, they were laid to rest under the floor of the church itself. While this was a sign of the esteem in which the deceased were held, it did come with a downside for the living, since churchgoers had to endure the fetid stench of rotting corpses, particularly in the heat of the summer. The rest of the parishioners were buried outside in the little churchyard, until the famine of 1696–7 forced residents to set up another cemetery to the west of the town. Today, this is officially known as Old Church Park, now found in the dead centre of Helsinki. Among locals, however, it is still better known as Plague Park (*Ruttopuisto*), being where the victims of successive epidemics were buried. It is officially the "old" park because a new cemetery was established in the early 1800s by the sea in Hietaniemi, which is on the western edge of Helsinki's modern centre.

Artisans, seamen and manual labourers typically resided on the outskirts of the town. The wealthy households needed servants, however, which meant that the well-heeled quarter in the very centre was home to people from all echelons of society. The town's elite spoke either Swedish or German, but a significant portion of the rest of the inhabitants came from Finland's interior and had, therefore, grown up in Finnish-speaking or bilingual communities. This caused a degree of friction, especially when it came to the church services; since the clergymen usually did not know Finnish, they could not preach in a language comprehensible to many of their flock, even though the Crown formally required them to do so. In the late 1680s, the congregation finally got a pastor who spoke excellent Finnish: Andreas Ignatius, the town's schoolmaster. Unfortunately, however, his linguistic abilities were marred by his disagreeable character, which meant that he was regularly embroiled in legal disputes and other assorted power struggles.

In a cruel twist of fate, Helsinki's congregation began to sing perhaps the most-beloved psalm of the Lutheran Church, "Den blomstertid nu kommer" ("Here Comes the Summertime"), just as Ignatius embarked on his twenty-year reign as pastor. His combative temperament aside, it was to prove a wretched period in the town's history. The whole Swedish realm was struck by a famine in 1696 and 1697, brought on by cold temperatures and crop failures. This led to a shockingly large number of people succumbing to starvation and epidemics. In Finland, a quarter of the population was killed (117,000 of 444,000 people), and the relative death toll in Helsinki was higher still, probably because hordes of beggars, many of whom were likely carrying disease, made their way to the town in search of food.

Almost a third of Helsinki's inhabitants died, that is 640 residents out of 2,100 in total. The situation reached its nadir in early 1697, when 540 corpses had to be buried in the new cemetery outside of town. Six decades later, the town's first chronicler, Henrik Forsius, recorded the gruesome recollections of the older residents who had witnessed how the starving and terminally ill had dragged themselves to their pre-dug graves in Plague Park: "They themselves saw the place where their weary bones would rest." Their demise was apparently brought about by a variety of viral diseases and bacterial infections, but those of the next epidemic had a more clear-cut cause: the recurrence of the Black Death, or, rather, the Bubonic plague. This tore through the town in 1710, hot on the heels of war, and, in line with the previous epidemic in the town, it killed a third of all inhabitants (roughly 650 out of 2,000 people). It also took the lives of nearly as many non-residents who had streamed into the town from other regions around that time. As with the victims of the previous epidemic, their remains now lie under the verdant Old Church Park in the centre of Helsinki, its nickname ensuring their tragic fate is passed down from one generation to the next.

With these sombre death tolls, it is easy to forget that daily life in late-seventeenth-century Helsinki was not merely a succession of epidemics and wars. Nor was it merely a succession of the legal disputes and power struggles that have been well-preserved in the historical record. It was a place of opportunity for many, as can be seen by the steady arrival of new and enterprising migrants from across the Swedish realm. There was a ceaseless demand for goods and services, and any vacancies that opened up in the town's labour market were filled fast. Fresh faces also joined the ranks of the Crown's highest officials and the town's prosperous merchants. The consumption habits and lifestyles among these groups created new employment opportunities for some migrants, while indirectly offering the rest a better standard of living than they had experienced in the countryside.

Among the new blood that flowed into Helsinki in the late 1680s were the three Burgman brothers—Torsten, Hans and Petter—who hailed from Vyborg. Their father had seen success as a merchant in the tar trade, and had married into one of Vyborg's most influential families. His sons, however, decided to go in search of new challenges to Helsinki, where they took advantage of their Vyborg contacts and an apparently plentiful supply of seed capital to make a name for themselves. Over the next two decades, they occupied leading positions in Helsinki's economic and public life. As burgher tradition dictated, they all married into well-connected families in the town, and each developed their commercial interests to complement those of their siblings.

The eldest brother, Torsten, followed in his father's footsteps and became a central figure in the town's tar trade. Hans, the middle brother, took on important positions in Helsinki's ecclesiastical life alongside his mercantile activities, while the youngest, Petter, grew wealthy through trading in timber, and other products besides. Over time, the two older brothers were appointed aldermen in the town, which gave them considerable administrative influence that they could deploy to bolster their business interests. Both acquired sizeable plots of land on Suurkatu for their trading houses and large families, while Petter's home was on the north-west corner of the Great Square.

Torsten Burgman and his wife Ebba Westman had seven children, of whom five survived to adulthood, a rare feat in this period. In addition to a handful of servants, their household also consisted of the seamen's families that they put up for the winter, who could amount to almost ten additional residents. In order to accommodate such a multitude, Torsten had the town's very first stone house constructed on his plot in the late 1690s. It would stand proud on Suurkatu until the great fire of 1808 turned it to ash, along with many of the other buildings in the south-eastern quarter of the centre.

Before its fiery demise, the Burgman's single-storey brick house would come to be owned by many other prominent Helsinki citizens, and, after a large extension, would ultimately function as the County Governor's residence. It is, nonetheless, worth paying particular attention to Torsten Burgman's time there, since we can gather some clues as to his family's everyday existence via a detailed inventory of his estate that was made upon his death in 1711. The most public part of the house's interior was the shop, with its two sales counters and various storage cupboards, containing everything from textiles, twine and buttons to cutlery, curtain rings and wagon nails. There was also an eye-catching variety of dyes, illustrative of the enthusiasm with which the seventeenth-century residents of Helsinki coloured their clothes and furniture. The selection includes the intriguingly named "lead yellow" and a deep red called "dragon blood".

In the property's private living quarters, the estate inventory records items of precious metal, ornaments, expensive articles of clothing and a fine stock of linen. Together, they demonstrate how Ebba Westman, as housewife, was able to take charge of the family's fortune and use it to procure conspicuous status symbols. That said, by the time the contents of the house were catalogued, it is likely that a number of high-value items were more conspicuous by their absence. Even though Torsten himself was a successful moneylender, he had recklessly pledged the stone house as collateral, which meant that neither his widow nor his children would inherit any vast wealth. As such, they seem to have, one way or another, emptied out much of the property before the estate inventory was drawn up. There are plenty of signs that point to this, not least that Torsten did not, according to the list, own a single piece of clothing at the time of his death.

It is rare to be given such a snapshot, blurry as it may be, into the lives of Helsinki's inhabitants in this era. The existence of the vast majority of people was only documented in court proceedings and church records, which can give an unduly negative picture of their everyday experience. If they managed to survive their early childhood years, enter into the family trade and go on to establish their own household, then their lives were likely not half bad. Moreover, even if they did appear in court documents, it was usually to help ensure that justice was served, which goes to show that the community, as a whole, did not tolerate wrongdoings and transgressions. Alongside criminal cases, defamation claims and economic disputes, the town's magistrates' court also dealt with sexual offences. These were, namely, pre-marital and extra-marital relations, which the Swedish Crown tried to stamp out during the fervour of Caroline absolutism in the late seventeenth century. It was not very successful in this endeavour, and, if anyone suffered as a result, it was typically the unmarried woman, since her partner in crime was seldom honourable enough to accept the consequences of his actions.

The usual punishment in such cases were fines and "church duty", which involved separating the guilty party from the rest of the congregation by keeping them in a pillory at the church gate for the duration of the service. Under canon law, it was taken for granted that everyone would attend worship, and it was considered an especially serious offence to miss a morning service. However, in practice, the clergies' attitude towards attendance was more relaxed: it was enough for someone to come to just a few weekend services each year, so long as they still participated religiously in the High Sabbaths. The churchgoers' powers of concentration were not only tested by the pastor's interminable sermons, but also by the noisy conversations and bouts of snoring that emanated from their fellow parishioners in the pews. The congregation's seating hierarchy was so strict that it regularly provoked squabbles and occasionally even serious quarrels that degenerated into verbal abuse and fisticuffs.

Life in late-seventeenth-century Helsinki certainly had its drawbacks, but these did not differ dramatically from those in other parts of the Swedish Empire. Besides which, Sweden's development into a Great Power and its increased control of the Baltic Sea region had led to myriad improvements to living conditions in the town. Helsinki's trade and transit activities had expanded, its municipal administration had become more effective and, last but not least, its geographical position had been strengthened after Sweden's victory in the Ingrian War with Russia in 1617. This resulted in the redrawing of the eastern border, which gave Sweden a large chunk of territory in Karelia and Ingria, and provided a bigger buffer between Helsinki and any potential onslaught from Russia.

Ruin and Rebirth

Geopolitical supremacy can only last for so long, and the first cracks began to emerge in Sweden's imperial dominance in the early 1700s. The country had, under Charles XI, enjoyed a period of peace lasting over two decades, but this all changed after his teenage son rose to the throne in 1697. Only three years later, an alliance of neighbouring states launched an attack on the Swedish Empire, one that would slowly grow into the most destructive war that the eastern part of the realm, and Helsinki in particular, had ever experienced. Initially, there was little to suggest this would happen: on the contrary, everything went deceptively well for the foolhardy warrior king. After several months of fighting, he forced Denmark to make peace, and, in late November 1700, the Swedish Army won a brilliant victory over Russia at the

Battle of Narva. These successes distorted the autocratic Charles XII's judgement and led to a conflict that would drag on for more than twenty years, pulling Sweden into increasingly dire straits in the process. It is for good reason that the war has gone down in Swedish and Finnish history as The Great Strife (*Stora Ofreden*) and The Great Wrath (*Isoviha*), respectively. In English, it typically goes by the more prosaic name, The Great Northern War. When a peace deal was finally signed in Uusikaupunki in 1721, Sweden was forced to cede large regions of Karelia to Russia, as well as the whole of Ingria, Estonia and Livonia.

As so many times before, it was Finland that bore the brunt of Sweden's deteriorating fortunes on the battlefield. King Charles XII and his Swedish Army suffered a catastrophic defeat to Russia in the Battle of Poltava in 1709, and over the following year Russian forces captured the Swedish fortress towns of Vyborg, Riga and Reval. From this point on, Russian Emperor Peter the Great set his sights on conquering the rest of Finland. His aim was not to incorporate the whole land with Russia, but rather use it as a base from which to launch raids against Stockholm, in order to pressure the Swedes into a quick peace. However, he was forced to put his planned invasion on ice, due to both the plague that ran rampant across the Baltic Sea region in 1710 and the new war that Russia began with the Ottomans that same year. It was not until the spring of 1713 that a large Russian army disembarked in eastern Uusimaa, from where it swiftly launched a seaborne assault on Helsinki and other key sites in southern Finland. Since the Swedish defeat in Poltava, Charles XII had stayed in the Ottoman Empire plotting his next move, but his long absence had left the Council of the Realm in Stockholm completely paralysed. Its inaction caused Russia's occupation of Finland to continue all the way until 1721, when peace was finally agreed.

Prior to 1713, Helsinki's inhabitants had followed the war's progress over the years with increasing disquiet. They had taken in ever-larger crowds of refugees from the towns that had already been seized by the Russians, with the first wave arriving back in the autumn of 1702. These evacuees came from the Swedish fortress town Nyen, on the mouth of the Neva River, which was almost the exact same location where Peter the Great would found St Petersburg a year later, in 1703. The advance of Russian forces across Karelia and the Baltics displaced more and more people, with some of them finding their way to Helsinki. The city was already bulging at the seams, having been full of soldiers and sailors ever since the war began. The quartering of the military had, as ever, been a source of disharmony, but it was, above all, a source of income, as the Crown covered the cost of the troops' victuals. Moreover, the armed soldiers were the only protection the town had against the approaching Russian forces, whose barbarity had already become the subject of wild rumours.

Some of these rumours would prove to be disturbingly accurate depictions of the atrocities the Russians would carry out, especially in Ostrobothnia, where communities were routinely tortured and slaughtered en masse. The first dark clouds of the impending storm appeared on the horizon in September 1712, when a Russian galley fleet landed on the archipelago east of Helsinki and opened fire with cannons on the town. As luck would have it, a Swedish squadron was just about to call on Helsinki with a delivery of provisions, so it was able to chase the Russians away. The experience, however, struck fear in the heart of many residents, and led to a number of the affluent merchants making a hurried escape from the town, bundling their possessions onto any available vessel and departing for Stockholm with their families.

As dawn rose on 8 May 1713, the townsfolk's worst nightmares became reality: sailing in through the inlets and bays around Helsinki was a huge Russian fleet. The enemy troops wasted no time beginning their siege of the town, bombarding it with artillery fire and disembarking on its outskirts. The undermanned Swedish forces simply did not have the capacity to fend off the Russians, who were descending on them from almost every direction. From the safety of a Russian warship on Kruunuvuorenselkä, the body of water between Helsinki's eastern archipelago and its mainland, none other than Peter the Great himself stood watching the fierce fighting. His forces' vast numerical superiority quickly began to tell: among other strategic positions, they gained control of the highest rocks on Katajanokka—where Uspenski Cathedral stands today—and proceeded to rain cannon fire down on the very centre of the town.

By the onset of night on 10 May, the situation appeared bereft of hope for the Swedes. As such, the commander of the Swedish forces, Major-General Carl Gustaf Armfeldt, together with the Crown's highest officials, resolved to evacuate all who remained to the north before burning the entire town to the ground. They would later face stinging criticism for this decision, since a Swedish squadron would arrive in Helsinki the very next day, forcing the Russian troops to retreat eastwards towards Porvoo. However, Armfeldt followed the orders he had received to the letter: upon undertaking such a retreat, all Swedish commanders were supposed to adhere to a scorched earth policy. When Peter the Great disembarked on the morning of 11 May in a still-burning Helsinki, he could hardly have been any less satisfied. His objective had been to use Helsinki as a supply and shipping harbour for the occupying Russian Army. It now lay, like the town, in ruins. Of the few buildings left standing among the smouldering rubble were Torsten Burgman's deserted stone house and the bell tower amidst the charred remnants of the Church of the Holy Spirit.

The town might have gone up in smoke, but its advantageous location—directly across the Gulf of Finland from Reval—remained unchanged. Over the subsequent eight years, therefore, a significant part of Russia's 30,000-strong occupying army was chiefly supplied with provisions through Helsinki. Large ramparts, fortified with six bastions, were built around the old town centre. Within these, the Russians constructed accommodation for their administration and merchants. Outside of the ramparts, five extensive barracks were established, along with a number of storehouses, granaries and slaughterhouses. As a counterpart to the old wharf at the North Harbour, a similar-sized loading dock was erected to the south of the centre, around which the South Harbour would start to take shape after the war.

Much more could be said about the long Russian occupation, under which Finland endured all manner of trials and tribulations. At the more minor end of the scale was the widespread felling of the forests belonging to the local population on the outskirts of Helsinki. Most of the timber was transported to the mouth of the Neva, where vast quantities of beams and boards were needed to feed the frenzied development of St Petersburg. Far more grievous was the Russians' enslavement of thousands of Finns, many of whom were also sent east to the vast construction project, where they were put to work building the boulevard that would become the new capital's great parade route: Nevsky Prospekt. There is every chance that former Helsinki residents numbered among those forced labourers.

The emergence of St Petersburg as Russia's capital came to have a monumental impact on Finland. It is for good reason that 1703, the date of its founding, has been characterised as the most important year in Finland's history. Only half a century later, the metropole would boast a population of almost 100,000 people: with its physical size and symbolic importance, it would fundamentally reshape the geopolitical landscape in the northern half of the Baltic Sea region. It would also have an increasingly significant impact upon Finland's economic development. Of course, none of this was written in the stars when the first Helsinki residents returned to their hometown in the autumn of 1721, although the large ramparts, storehouses and barracks the Russians had left behind offered an indication of which way the wind was blowing.

There were plenty of lessons to be learned from the calamitous war. Above all else, it demonstrated to the Swedish political elite, in no uncertain terms, the acute need to fortify Helsinki, especially as they considered that a new war was soon likely to break out. The town's Russian defences were, therefore, left intact for a number of years, and a new grid plan was drawn up in 1723 with space reserved for fortifications on its edges. This proposal was on the table for barely a year before it was shelved owing to a glaring lack of resources. The incoming residents were consequently allowed to rebuild the town as they saw fit, which meant that they largely replicated the structure it had prior to its destruction in 1713. Circumstances were so straitened that people were forced to disregard the authorities' demand that all new houses be made of stone. Bricks were in such short supply that no one moving to the town could afford them.

As a consequence, the new incarnation of Helsinki was built, in the manner of its forebears, out of wood. Not only was it much cheaper to do so, but it also enabled people to get a roof over their heads far more quickly and easily. Those who returned lived, initially, in the dwellings, storehouses and granaries abandoned by the Russians, but, as the town's trade and county administration started to regain some of its former vigour, so, too, did the reconstruction process begin to pick up steam.

Bringing Helsinki back from the ashes was a laborious process, one that does not seem to have appealed to the significant proportion of its former merchants who never returned. Among those that did come back was the enterprising Abraham Wetter, who was chosen as the town's new mayor and became by far the most influential resident over the next two decades, thanks largely to his formidable wealth. In early 1724, he purchased Torsten Burgman's stone house on Suurkatu at auction, and swiftly had it restored.

Three years later, the town's new place of worship, the Ulrika Eleonora Church, stood tall on almost the exact same spot as its two predecessors, that is at the north-west corner of modern-day Senate Square. The church was named in honour of King Charles XII's sister, who briefly reigned as queen after her brother's death in 1718, before handing over the crown to her husband, Frederick I, in 1720. The red-painted cruciform building had a lofty tower at its centre and space for a hundred worshippers inside. It would stay standing until 1827, when it was demolished to make room for the new Senate Square, which functioned as an unambiguous demonstration of the Russian Empire's power. A hundred years thereafter, a plaque would be unveiled in memory of the church on the square's stone paving. In a sign of how comprehensively Helsinki has forgotten its pre-Russian days, this is currently the only memorial to anything from the Swedish era that is to be found in the modern city centre.

In the decade after the Ulrika Eleonora Church was completed in 1727, a number of other new public buildings were constructed at the inhabitants' own expense, including a town hall, a schoolhouse and a customs house. Despite these commendable efforts to breathe new life into Helsinki, in the late 1730s the town must have seemed like a pale imitation of that which was lost to the flames in May 1713. The population was still half of what it had been prior to the war, having fallen from circa 2,000 to 1,000 people, and the County Governor's residence was a travesty when compared to Creutz's former showpiece building.

There was little support forthcoming from Stockholm: the Swedish realm's financial strength and military force was only a fraction of what it had been during its time as a Great Power, when the Baltic had been, in essence, an inland sea of Sweden. And Helsinki's situation was particularly dire compared to the other towns on Finland's south coast, as none of them had been quite so ravaged by the war. While its arduous reconstruction was underway, the more fortunate merchants in Porvoo and Hamina succeeded in capturing a substantial share of the economic hinterland, privileges and markets that had previously been controlled by Helsinki's residents. In the late 1720s, the town's representative at Sweden's Riksdag, Sven Silcke, sent a bitter missive to Stockholm, in which he stated that Helsinki's inhabitants were, due to these injustices, "little more than crofters of Hamina".

2

IN THE GLOW OF SUOMENLINNA

The Fortune of the Fortress

Cities rise and grow, collapse and wither, and are ripped apart and revitalised in a constant interplay with both their immediate surroundings and the world at large. Sometimes their fate is dictated by dramatic economic shifts, as was the case with Amsterdam. The city expanded at an explosive pace during the seventeenth century, thanks to Holland's central role in the development of the capitalist world economy. Over the next couple of centuries, however, it wilted and languished as the British gained the upper hand in global trade, squeezing the Dutch out of the picture. Sometimes the driving force shaping a city is geopolitics, as was the case with St Petersburg. Without Peter the Great's goal of transforming Russia into a maritime power in Europe, the city would never have been founded, become the capital of the empire, nor later have been allocated such a wealth of resources.

Helsinki was, for its part, also a geopolitical creation. The town had been established by Gustav Vasa to gain more control over the Baltic Sea trade, yet the Swedish Crown's often-faltering resources had stunted this ambition. After the town's obliteration and laboured recovery in the first half of the 1700s, its fortunes took a decisive turn for the better, however. This sea change was one that would also, in the long run, have a positive impact on the whole of Finland. And, like so many times previously in the town's history, the development was part of a chain reaction caused by a series of shifts in Great Power politics.

The most obvious of these was Russia's incremental conquest of the eastern parts and provinces of the Swedish Empire. After the Great Northern War (1700–21), there followed three further conflicts, each of which ended in ignominy for Sweden. After the third, in 1809, it was forced to hand over its eight Finnish provinces to Russia. These became an autonomous Grand Duchy of the Russian Empire, their territory comprising, to a large extent, that of modern Finland. In the late 1730s, no one in Sweden— neither the King nor any decision-maker in Stockholm—could have ever imagined that their tussle for power with Russia would produce such an outcome. On the contrary, at this point in time, many Swedes had become consumed by the desire for revenge. The expansionist "Hats" were now dominant in the Riksdag— the Swedish parliament—and legislative changes enacted in the 1720s had empowered the estates to govern the country. This allowed the Hats to make secret plans to recapture the parts of the empire that had been lost.

The so-called War of the Hats began in the summer of 1741, and quickly became an unmitigated catastrophe. The Swedish Army was a pale imitation of its former self, ineffective and lacking a cutting edge. In late August 1742, the few Swedish troops defending Helsinki surrendered, after which the Russian Army was able to occupy the rest of southern and central Finland without serious resistance. In the peace treaty struck a year later, in the late summer of 1743, Sweden was forced to cede additional territory to Russia, this time a sizeable chunk of south-east Finland. Moreover, the country bound itself to pursue a foreign policy that was non-aggressive and Russia-oriented.

Older Helsinki residents still remembered all the misery and wretchedness that had been wrought upon the town by the previous war three decades earlier. It is no surprise, then, that this time around they took a sceptical attitude towards Sweden's military campaign. Many inhabitants, including the social elite, had fled before the Russian troops encircled the town in August 1742, but the poorer residents had stayed put. An indication of their indifference towards the conflict was the absence of violent disturbances in the late summer, when the Russians, following the Swedes' surrender, marched triumphantly on the town and occupied all its public buildings. The prevailing calm was also a consequence of the Russian command keeping its troops under strict supervision, and its decision to quarter the majority of them in camps outside the town. When word spread that the town was not being subject to any sort of terror, a number of residents made the decision to return. The mercantile elite kept their distance, but in their stead came merchants from Reval, who saw an opportunity to capture the freshly vacated markets.

The year-long occupation imposed several obligations on Helsinki's residents, not least in respect of providing lodgings and supplies to the Russians. However, when the town's leading merchants started to move back after the peace treaty, the building stock was found to be in relatively good condition, in spite of everything. The merchants from Reval were ordered to leave, and, slowly but surely, the town's authorities re-established themselves. They knew that Helsinki's defences needed to be fortified—and fast. Their ardent demands to this effect were presented before the Riksdag in Stockholm in 1746–7, sparking some heated political machinations that also involved diplomats from the Great Powers. It was eventually decided that a deputation would be set up to examine how the defences and economy of Finland as a whole could best be strengthened.

This course of action was made possible by the Franco-Swedish alliance that the Hats had forced through in the same Riksdag session. Besides securing better defences for Finland, their aim was to put an end to Russia's extortion of Sweden. As part of the terms of the alliance, Sweden would receive significant financial support from France on an annual basis, the principal purpose of which was to fortify Finland. The defence plan was similar to that which had been drawn up back in the 1720s, after the previous war: both stipulated that Finland's central fortification was to be built in Helsinki. If it had seemed like Helsinki's location was strategically important twenty years ago, the most recent conflict had only reinforced the point, for the town had again been used as a supply base by the Russian occupiers. In addition to strengthening Helsinki, a border fortification was to be constructed on an island further east: Svartholm Sea Fortress. This was directly to the south of the coastal town of Loviisa, which had just been founded to serve as a trading centre near the new border with Russia.

The plan was to use Helsinki as both a military depot and a naval base. A commission was sent to survey the town's terrain in the summer of 1747: it came to the conclusion that the central fortification should be erected on the rocky island of Susisaari, since it was at that time beyond the range of fire from the coast. It would, of course, be necessary to construct defences on the mainland, too, in order to protect the town itself. The commission's recommendations were confirmed that autumn, and work got underway immediately. The project was so vast in scale that it would end up being the Swedish Crown's biggest infrastructure investment by some distance, only being surpassed in the 1820s by the construction of the Göta Canal.

Augustin Ehrensvärd, a 37-year-old fortification officer, was appointed head of the building project. As the chief architect behind the plans, he was well-acquainted with continental fortification designs, and he also had recent combat experience, having served as an artillery officer in the War of the Hats. His knowledge and practical expertise shone through in his draft drawings: the fortification's starlike form allowed its defenders to shoot in every direction, while simultaneously diminishing the threat posed by enemy fire. Besides the principal fortress on Susisaari, his plans also included two large bastions on the mainland.

In fact, it was on the mainland that the initial construction work began. In February 1748, the first explosions rang out at Siltavuori, where the northern bastion was to be built. The next site to be blasted was Kasaberg (nowadays Tähtitorninvuori), just south of the town, which was renamed Ulrikasborg in honour of Ulrika Eleonora, Queen of Sweden between 1718–20. However, no sooner had the name been changed than the project's focus shifted, and all building work in 1749 was instead focused on the Susisaari island. The aim was to get the sea fortress and naval base ready as quickly as possible. On Ehrensvärd's initiative, it was christened "Sveaborg" in 1750, to draw parallels with Göteborg (Gothenburg): the latter was the empire's western outpost, while Helsinki's new island fortress was to serve as its eastern one. Sveaborg was soon Fennicised as "Viapori"; it would only acquire the name "Suomenlinna" (Finland's Fortress) in May 1918, when it was officially rechristened following Finland's independence.

There is another interesting parallel to be drawn here, between the life's work of Ehrensvärd and Fort George in Inverness, Scotland. As it happens, ground was broken on this coastal fortification in the exact same year as it was on Suomenlinna. Fort George's starlike construction at the entrance to the Moray Firth bears close resemblance to Kustaanmiekka on the southernmost point of Suomenlinna. Both controlled the seaborne approach to their respective towns. And, what is more, both fortresses owed their existence to France's increasingly expansionist role as a European Great Power at that time. The British built Fort George to exercise more control over the Scottish Highlands after the French had incited the Scots into the Jacobite uprising of 1745. Suomenlinna, as has been noted, was largely financed by the French to help Sweden better stand its ground against the Russians.

Unlike Fort George, however, Suomenlinna was never fully completed. Its planned bastions on mainland Helsinki were abandoned, which would later prove to be a fatal mistake. Still, even with these cutbacks, the sea fortress developed into an enormous building project. During the most frenetic period of construction, there were close to 3,500 soldiers working on the island each year. At the project's peak in 1751, the manpower was reportedly close to double that, with 6,700 soldiers employed. Arranging accommodation and provisions for such a mass of people was a logistical challenge in and of itself. The scale greatly exceeded what the town could handle at this time, for it only had circa 1,500 permanent residents. Skilled artisans and master builders were in such short supply that Ehrensvärd was periodically forced to recruit them from Sweden. The procurement of the principal building materials—stone, brick, limestone and timber—was another perpetual challenge with which he had to contend.

Nearly half of all the materials were supplied by Helsinki's merchants and citizens. They, however, colluded to fix their prices, which pushed Ehrensvärd to look further afield and make significant purchases from other regions on the south coast of Finland. Gradually, too, the officers and officials employed in the fortification project involved themselves in the supply chain, becoming subcontractors. This proved a lucrative business, to the extent that many had the money to buy—or have built—mansions in the vicinity of Helsinki. Ehrensvärd himself constructed Kulosaari Manor, which today can be admired in its leafy environs next to a strait of Vanhankaupunginlahti (Old Town's Bay). A little further to the east, in Herttoniemi, he also had a brickworks built. Nevertheless, it was a handful of merchants in Helsinki who made the biggest profits, for they controlled the local production of sawn timber and bricks.

Sweden's alliance with France might have made Suomenlinna financially viable, but, in 1756, it also dragged the Nordic country into the Seven Years' War (1756–63) on the Continent. This drastically reduced the amount of resources and manpower that the Crown was able to devote to the construction of the sea fortress. Helsinki's merchants and artisans suffered a sharp economic downturn as a result, and it took until the late 1760s before conditions started to improve. After this time, construction work continued at a slower pace. Besides the lack of resources, many in Stockholm had started to call the whole project into question, and, when Ehrensvärd passed away in the autumn of 1772, the fortress lost its driving force.

Still, the most concerted building phase on Susisaari had undeniably produced impressive results. Between 1748 and 1756, three strong bastions were erected, along with their ramparts, barracks and accommodation for civilians. These eight years had also seen the construction of a large dock, as well as administrative buildings bordering an artfully designed courtyard on the fortress's main island. Since the intensity of construction fluctuated so much over the years, so, too, did the number of people registered as living on the islands. Slowly but surely, however, the fortress's population began to stabilise at around 4,500 inhabitants, of whom over forty per cent were civilians, that is the family members and servants of those in military service, plus officials and artisans with their own households.

The majority of the fortress's artillery units were based on the mainland, which meant that, around the turn of the nineteenth century, the combined military force on Suomenlinna and in Helsinki came to circa 5,700 troops.

It goes without saying that the construction and maintenance of such a large naval and military base had a momentous influence on the development of the town itself. If the previous turning points in the town's history had been arduous and sometimes outright catastrophic, Suomenlinna would end up being Helsinki's lucky break. The sea fortress was an important factor in the town being appointed Finland's administrative centre in 1812. A little over a century later, the capital city of the Grand Duchy would, ultimately, become the capital city of the newly independent Republic of Finland.

In the short term, the garrison had a markedly positive impact on the hitherto languishing harbour town. The most obvious evidence of this was that Helsinki's resident population doubled during the second half of the eighteenth century, reaching 3,200 people in the early 1800s. If soldiers and officers are included, then the total population was closer to 9,000, or a sixfold increase in fifty years. And the military presence absolutely should be considered, for Helsinki's economy and everyday activity were so closely entwined with the fortress that there is ample reason to assert that it actually constituted a garrison town. Helsinki had thereby swelled to almost the same size as Turku, which had a population of 11,000 in the early 1800s and which had been, for centuries, the biggest city in the land by some margin.

The growth of Helsinki was not solely down to the construction of Suomenlinna and the subsequent economic boost the fortress brought to the town. It was part of a wider trend across the entire Kingdom of Sweden, which saw a steep increase in the size of its population during the second half of the eighteenth century. The rise was particularly rapid in

Finland, where the number of inhabitants nearly doubled, from 421,000 in 1750 to 835,000 in 1800. Nonetheless, even in this context Helsinki's growth was remarkable. During the same half-century, its erstwhile competitors for export markets and supply chains—the neighbouring towns of Porvoo and Loviisa—barely registered any population increase at all.

Fair Winds and Following Seas

While the symbiosis with Suomenlinna largely explains Helsinki's exceptional growth in the mid-to-late eighteenth century, there was another significant factor behind its economic development: a shift in the focus of global trade. The North Sea and the Baltic Sea became increasingly important shipping routes, which benefitted the British most of all, but which also worked to Sweden's advantage. The Swedish Crown's sea trade was mainly centred around the harbour towns with expedient locations: Stockholm, Gothenburg, Gävle and Helsinki.

The Finnish town held a number of trump cards in this regard. It shipped a continual stream of timber and fish to the old Hanseatic town of Reval. As the Crown's strict trade policies started to yield results, a growing proportion of Helsinki's excise revenue came from exporting lumber directly to the Continent. Although trade with St Petersburg remained small-scale until the 1830s, Helsinki's inhabitants indirectly prospered from the booming Russian capital's surge in consumption, as it stimulated shipping right across the Gulf of Finland.

They also indirectly benefitted from Russia annexing part of southeast Finland in 1743, for a number of merchants moved to Helsinki from Hamina, which was now on the Russian side of the border. They brought with them established connections to ports in the Atlantic and Mediterranean. To make the most of this network, the merchants needed to invest in a trade fleet, one that could direct goods to Helsinki and help maximise their profits. Shipwrecks and robberies were such frequent occurrences, however, that none of the merchants were initially willing to take such a financial risk alone. As such, they founded joint-stock shipping companies together, and built a shipyard for themselves just to the south of Ulrikasborg (henceforth referred to by its Finnish name, Ullanlinna). In time, this would come to be the launch site for a wide variety of vessels.

The first of these "Spain farers" (*Spanienfarare* in Swedish, an old-fashioned term for merchant ships that typically took cargo to Spain) was called *Generalguvernören von Rosen* and had thirty-two joint owners when it set out to sea. It managed to make five trips to Cadiz and other Spanish ports before it sank off the coast of Saaremaa, Estonia's largest island, in 1756. Nevertheless, by then it was clearly regarded as a successful venture, for some years earlier the merchants had invested in a second ship, this time renovating a vessel that had run aground off the Porkkalanniemi Peninsula, not far west of Helsinki and Suomenlinna. As a consequence, the ship was christened *Augustin Ehrensvärd* and sent off on its way to Cadiz and the Mediterranean, where it sailed for a few years before ending up wrecked off the Danish island of Bornholm.

The frequent shipwrecks did not noticeably dampen the Helsinki merchants' enthusiasm for shipbuilding, which indicates that they were making a healthy profit. On a number of occasions, they had transatlantic sailing ships built, then sold them on a short while later. The wealthy merchant Johan Sederholm independently commissioned one such ship in 1780, christening it *Cron Printzen Gustaf Adolph* as a public reminder that he was one of the godfathers of the newly born heir to the throne. His status thus affirmed, Sederholm sold the vessel only two years later, undoubtedly getting a good return on his investment. By this time, his business portfolio had become so extensive that he had become the sole owner of the Ullanlinna shipyard, where he had two schooners built, the *Fredrik Posse* and the *Anders de Bruce*. Together with the *Konung Gustaf III*, which Sederholm had earlier part-financed, these would go down in history as the biggest boats in Helsinki's fleet during its time under Swedish rule.

Demand for imported goods steadily increased in this period, and the transatlantic ships brought a diverse range of products to Helsinki. Of these, the most important was salt, a staple needed in every household. The big salt suppliers were found far south of the Gulf of Finland on the Iberian Peninsula and in the Mediterranean. The ships departing Helsinki for these shores would typically put in at a number of different ports en route, perhaps to exchange some of their timber cargo for other goods. Towards the end of the eighteenth century, an increasing amount of salt imports came from Lisbon and Porto. The Portuguese trading hubs offered wine, fruit and sugar for sale, alongside colonial delicacies like coffee, cocoa and all sorts of exotic spices.

There was an insatiable demand for such luxuries among the officers on Suomenlinna, many of whom were, like Ehrensvärd, well-travelled noblemen with a penchant for indulgent dinners. Their taste rubbed off on the town's richest merchants, who also came to form a reliable market for such imports. The mercantile elite's purchasing power far exceeded that of the officers, who were not generally inclined towards financial prudence, with the result that their wages and wealth were often at odds with their wants. These leading merchant families had made their fortunes through the regular supply of goods to Suomenlinna, and this flow of trade was the catalyst behind them founding mills, sawmills and brickworks in the vicinity of Helsinki. They also endeavoured to control the supply of foodstuffs and timber that came into the town from the Uusimaa countryside.

The revenue from their domestic business activities was necessary for their aforementioned shipping trade. To build a ship and send it out onto the Atlantic with a cargo of expensive lumber presupposed a sufficient supply of risk capital, for the investment could, quite literally, disappear into the blue. By no means everyone emerged from this game a winner, and one person's misfortune could have wide-reaching consequences. The majority of Helsinki's merchants took credit from each other, so a ship dashed on the rocks, or a cargo gone up in flames, could lead to cash crises or even bankruptcies for the guarantors.

As might be expected, the merchants' primary exports were a variety of timber products, but particularly thick beams and long planks, which were becoming increasingly scarce commodities in the unforested regions of the Continent. In contrast, tar exports had completely lost their significance in southern Finland, for two main reasons: lumber was a more profitable product, and North American tar producers had started to take over the market. In early 1800, British naturalist Edward Daniel Clarke paid a short visit to Suomenlinna and Helsinki on his way to St Petersburg. He described the town's merchants as taking timber to Spain and bringing back salt in return, and detailed the high quality of their deal planks, "some of which we found to be twelve feet in length and two inches in thickness, perfectly fair, and very free from knots".

Clarke's impression of the "small but handsome town" was positive in other respects. It contained many stone houses, its inhabitants were said to live "in perfect harmony and good will among each other", and they had been extremely welcoming towards their British guests. These sights and sentiments were shaped by the rose-tinted gaze of the privileged foreign traveller, but they were also a reflection of how Helsinki was faring in the early nineteenth century. It was then one of the Swedish Crown's most important shipping towns, with the Swedish military's largest naval base on its doorstep. It had also just gone through a significant growth spurt, although its street plan had not kept pace, being largely identical to that from one hundred years ago.

The stone houses that Clarke observed stood in a row along Suurkatu and around the town square. The Burgman House from the 1690s had, by the 1750s, been expanded into a two-storey building. Imposing for its time, it served as the residence of the County Governor until 1776, at which point the post was transferred back to Hämeenlinna and the house repurposed as the official home of the Commander-in-Chief of the Finnish Army. In the 1760s, Helsinki's customs warehouse was constructed between the Burgman House and the old wharf. The other stone houses on Suurkatu were built in roughly the same period. The first of these, finished in 1758, was Johan Sederholm's grand three-storey townhouse at the Great Square. Both this and the customs warehouse are the oldest buildings in the city centre today, as they were two of the very few properties left standing after the raging fire of 1808.

The shipyards and shipping companies that developed around modern-day South Harbour attracted more and more of the town's seaborne trade, and the area became known as Kaupunginlahti, or Town Bay. Its south-western shore was dominated by the shipyard at Ullanlinna, around which were built warehouses and private dwellings. A similar collection of properties also sprang up in Katajanokka, on the bay's north-eastern side. At the northernmost end of Kaupunginlahti—where the Market Square lies today—another shipyard was built, as well as a quay, which became an increasingly popular spot for ships to unload their cargo.

Otherwise, the town's buildings were still clustered around its two main streets: Suurkatu, running east to west, and Hämeentie, running north to south. They crossed, in classic fashion, at the town square, but they diverged in their characters. Suurkatu was, in the main, lined with the stone houses of the rich merchants, the high-ranking officers and the town's senior officials. Hämeentie, on the other hand, was populated by a miscellany of traders and artisans as it wound its way north towards Siltasaari. People of a similar hodge-podge of professions lived in the buildings closest to Kluuvinlahti and in the quarter around Ullanlinna. The town's layout would keep much the same appearance until the end of the 1810s, when it would be subject to a colossal transformation.

In the summer of 1816, the Swedish artist Erik Wilhelm le Moine captured a last glimpse of this landscape in a picturesque oil painting. It gives a sweeping view over the whole of Helsinki from the hill at the south of the town, then called Ullanlinna but today known as Tähtitorninvuori (Observatory Hill). In the foreground stand the last remnants of Ullanlinna's half-finished bastion, below which lie the South Harbour, with its proud sailing ships, and the town centre, with its church and belfry discernible landmarks among the densely built blocks. Clear-felled hilltops rise in the background, while the inner archipelago of Vanhankaupunginlahti can be glimpsed even further in the distance.

Fateful Networks

Helsinki's social elite was made up of three distinct groups in the second half of the 1700s. They were the Crown's highest-ranking officials, the town's richest merchants and the officers on Suomenlinna. The latter were nominally at the very top of the pecking order in the garrison town, thanks to their military positions, their noble heritage and their direct contact with Stockholm's political decision-makers. The merchants' status was officially the lowest, but, in practice, all three elites were on fairly equal footing. The noblemen in military and administrative roles rarely had a sound head for business, unlike the leading merchants, who were shrewd, successful and far-sighted in their affairs. In consequence, these men of commerce had an abundance of economic power and influence. This can be seen by the fact that, in the 1700s already, a significant proportion of the noblemen's manor houses and estates in the countryside were sold to the foremost mercantile families. In the same period, these merchants secured dominant ownership of the water mills along the Vantaa River, which allowed them to effectively control the lucrative timber trade to the Continent.

The merchants' growing prosperity led to a number of convoluted power struggles with the town's officials. The latter had been appointed by the Crown and were therefore, in theory at least, not under any obligation to acquiesce to the demands of the former. The most notorious of these battles was waged over many decades between the town's mayor, Johan Kuhlberg, and its wealthiest merchants, Johan Sederholm and Carl Magnus Sunn. In the summer of 1767, smuggled goods were discovered hidden in a shed on Kuhlberg's property, which his opponents regarded as proof that he was involved in criminal activities. In the legal proceedings that followed, Kuhlberg escaped punishment for the contraband, but was forced to pay hefty fines for having, during the heated dispute, insulted the customs inspector who had investigated the offence. One year later, he was assaulted during a booze-sodden party at one of the merchant's homes. All the lights on the premises had suddenly been extinguished, and, in the tumult that followed, Kuhlberg was beaten and bitten to a bloody pulp. Due to the darkness and the chaos, the perpetrators managed to avoid being brought to justice for their attack, but it certainly fuelled the long-running feud between the mayor and the merchants.

Behind the scenes, their rivalry might also have been about the control of the illegal trade in spirits and other easily saleable consumer goods, although the historical details surrounding this are understandably hazy. It is clear, however, that their dispute became increasingly acrimonious after Kuhlberg got the town's lower-ranking burghers on his side. These residents thought, and not without justification, that the richest merchants had accrued too much power for themselves. In the town's 1771 election of its Riksdag representative, Kuhlberg emerged victorious over Sunn precisely because of these burghers' votes. Nonetheless, in the long run, the ultimate winner of this power struggle would be Johan Sederholm. He kept himself in the background for the most part, but he saw to it that Kuhlberg faced increasing difficulties during his time as mayor and fell deeply into debt in his final years.

Sederholm's life followed the exact opposite trajectory, for he rose from rags to riches. If Augustin Ehrensvärd is rightly seen as personifying the creation of Suomenlinna, then Sederholm, twelve years his junior, embodies Helsinki's phenomenal growth into one of the Swedish Crown's most successful trade and shipping towns. He was born into the impoverished family of a Helsinki customs officer in 1722, at a time when the town still lay in ruins after the Great Northern War. After a short stint at school and assorted odd jobs, he gradually began to establish himself in commerce. The real breakthrough in his mercantile career came in the early 1750s, when the construction of Suomenlinna was proceeding apace. Within a matter of years, he had become the wealthiest merchant in town, started a family and built a fine two-storey stone house, with a number of annexes, on Suurkatu. He fathered twelve children over two marriages, and employed close to thirty domestic servants.

Central to Sederholm's success was his ability to combine multiple long-term business interests while broadening his network of contacts to strengthen his social influence and reputation. His extended life (1722–1805) certainly helped him in this regard, as did his large gaggle of children, whom he used to tie his family to the town's high-ranking officers and officials, thereby bolstering his own and his trading house's prestige. His burgher friends and acquaintances were made godfathers of his eldest children, but, as his trading house grew in size and stature, he increasingly appointed godfathers from the leading military and administrative circles in Helsinki. When his daughter Hedvig Catharina was born and baptised in 1762, Augustin Ehrensvärd himself was made godfather, along with a number of his fellow officers.

Hedvig Catharina passed away soon after the ceremony, but most of her siblings survived to adulthood, and married exclusively into the families of officers and officials of the Swedish Crown. During the second half of the eighteenth century, comparable social climbing occurred in the realm's other large towns and cities. In Stockholm, for example, these *nouveau-riche* merchants came to be called "the quay nobility". A small fraction of the rich burghers formed familial and friendship ties with the old social elite, which helped distance them from the rest of the merchant class and, in many cases, resulted in entry into the nobility. Sederholm never received a title, but he was chosen as one of the crown prince's godfathers by Gustav III, in recognition of his political and economic services to the kingdom. And when the Swedish monarchs visited Helsinki, they made sure to give Sederholm special attention.

During Sederholm's lifetime, the relative size of the burghers in Helsinki shrank, and by the early 1800s they made up only fifteen per cent of the town's inhabitants. Despite the surge in commerce in the town, the number of merchants did not dramatically increase, but fluctuated between twenty and thirty-five people throughout the entire second half of the eighteenth century. There was a similar lack of growth in the lower stratum of the burghers, which indicates that the merchants, as was their wont, were lining their pockets at the expense of the other residents. The exception were the master artisans, whose number more than tripled from thirty to a hundred in the same period. This was a consequence of the steady rise in availability of various consumer products, which, in turn, increased the need for new specialised professions, such as coppersmiths, watchsmiths and gardeners.

Another notable category of resident was the burgher widow. This was a woman who inherited her late husband's burgher rights and could, therefore, continue to operate his business. These rights were originally granted by the local magistrates, and they were a prerequisite to engage in mercantile or artisanal activity in Helsinki. Such a widow was, consequently, highly sought after by suitors, since there was a good chance that the new spouse would get his hands on the burgher rights, assuming he took on the responsibility of providing for the family into which he was marrying. In these cases, the widow's independent business activity was, of course, short-lived, but she avoided her family becoming reliant on the burgher community for support. And for many outsiders, marriages of this sort were the only way they could acquire burgher rights in Helsinki. In the autumn of 1781, for example, the town's magistrates, after a degree of hesitation, granted them to farmer's son Fredrik Wikholm when it became clear that "he wishes to enter into marriage with a burgher widow."

If the widow was ready and willing to take up the mantle of her late husband's trade, then it may well not have been in her best interests to remarry. In many cases, she was significantly younger than her deceased partner, so she could inject fresh vigour into his operations. During the second half of the eighteenth century, there were between five and ten burgher widows carrying on commercial activities in Helsinki. A modest total, no doubt, but an important reminder of women's under-reported role in the town's economic life. Within lower burgher and artisan families, in particular, women were very involved in business activities, since their husbands could not afford to employ any additional workers.

The most renowned burgher widow in Helsinki during this period was, more than likely, Ingrid Maria Dammert, who took control of her late partner's inn at the west end of Suurkatu in 1763. In common with Anders Byström, who owned the more fashionable restaurant and billiards hall on the block opposite, she regularly complained over the wretched state of her finances. Competition could be razor sharp in the hospitality trade. On occasions, the garrison town was positively teeming with taverns selling beer and spirits to the thirsty labourers and soldiers that passed through its streets. There were, at their peak, over seventy establishments licensed to serve alcohol in Helsinki, and no doubt plenty of other illicit grog shops besides. All the same, the widow Dammert successfully kept her inn and lodging house in operation for close to thirty years, until she relinquished her burgher rights in the summer of 1791, citing her advancing years. Who would not be a little curious to know what she had seen and heard during her decades spent presiding over the rowdy basement inn?

It must be assumed that everyday life was a little more run-of-the-mill for Erik Röö, the master ropemaker who, according to the population registers, was the wealthiest craftsman in town during the 1790s. Upon his death in 1797, his son, in adherence with common practice, took over the business. However, he, too, passed away the very next year, which meant that the two widows had to shoulder responsibility for commercial operations until the family's next male heir received the master craftsman's and burgher rights in 1805. Such arrangements were by no means unusual. If the head of the household passed away, it was in the whole family's interest to keep his business activities alive.

It was also by no means unusual for family members to die in quick succession, although the mortality rate had, on the whole, steadily declined during the second half of the eighteenth century, thanks to better harvests and shorter wars. It was still higher, however, in Helsinki and other urban centres than it was in the countryside. People lived on top of each other in towns and cities, often in extremely unhygienic conditions, so the outbreak of an epidemic almost always had devastating consequences. Between 1788 and 1791, wave after wave of disease crashed through Helsinki's streets. The death toll reached its nadir in 1790, when a whole ten per cent of the town's population perished. The quantity of corpses necessitated new burial arrangements, and it was decided that, henceforth, all deceased persons would be interred in Old Church Park to the west of Helsinki. Until then, Plague Park had only been used as a temporary burial ground on the previous occasions that epidemics had struck the town.

Whether from virus, gun or malnutrition, the threat of death was never far away in the eighteenth century. The mortality rate was particularly high for babies and infants, so the Crown, in an effort to ensure population growth, began to train midwives, and encouraged communities to employ them. Since all childbirth happened at home during this period, it was an asset to have an educated professional who could come to offer help and guidance. The first qualified midwife in Helsinki was Anna Gustafva Ekman: she began in 1759, and spent seventeen years in the role until she handed in her notice after falling out with the town's officials. In the second half of the eighteenth century, there were a little over one hundred babies born in Helsinki each year, so the town's midwives were certainly kept on their feet.

Gustavian Influences

One of the children that Anna Ekman could well have helped into the world was Johan Albrecht Ehrenström, born in Helsinki on 28 August 1762, the son of an artillery officer from the lesser nobility who was stationed on Suomenlinna. Ehrenström went on to have an eventful life as an officer and official in Gustavian Sweden before he returned home to the Grand Duchy of Finland in the 1810s to direct the great rebuilding of his place of birth.

Through his father's influence, the young Ehrenström soon came into contact with the European culture of learning and edification that was nurtured by the fortification officers. He quickly taught himself to speak and write passable French, and ploughed through many of the major works of the Enlightenment in their original language. Alongside this, he educated himself in cartography and the fortification technology of the period. And through his active participation in Suomenlinna's Society of Freemasons, he was influenced by officer circles that were secretly opposed to Gustav III's autocratic rule. Ehrenström's learning and self-instruction was, in this respect, entirely in line with the advice offered in a speech by August Ehrensvärd, which he had given in 1743 as a member of the Swedish Royal Academy, entitled "Tal om ungdoms upfostran til krigsmän" ("Speech on raising the youth to be soldiers"). Ehrensvärd noted that, while an able officer needed to be brave, this quality alone was not enough: he also needed to have good theoretical knowledge and sound judgement that was built on practical experience.

In this epoch, novice officers usually earned their spurs by serving in a military unit on the Continent, where they would immerse themselves in cultures of learning and personal development, while also improving their theoretical knowledge. Upon returning to Suomenlinna, they would disseminate these ideas and concepts further. A significant number of them gained their first-hand initiation in warfare by taking part in one or more of the four conflicts that Sweden fought between 1741 and 1809. This was also the case with Ehrensvärd, which certainly gives credence to his assertion that combat readiness was a combination of learned know-how and lived experience.

When Sweden's officers departed Suomenlinna, they left behind their books. These abandoned libraries were sold off at auction, and the one hundred or so book lists that survive provide an interesting glimpse into the literature that the officers read or, at the very least, owned. The most famous of these is that cataloguing Major Fredrik Granatenhjelm's collection, of which Ehrenström could avail himself, as the officer was a family friend. Indeed, after the Major's passing in late 1784, Ehrenström lavished praise on the book collection in his eulogy, stating that it revealed just how well-read Granatenhjelm had been, and just how many languages he was well-versed in. It included French literature and social philosophy, German and Latin science, Italian art history and Swedish treatises on warfare and hygiene. Such a broad palette of European cultural and scientific works is not to be found in the other book lists from the officers' shelves on Suomenlinna, although the majority of them do still contain fiction and non-fiction from the Continent.

Alongside the fortifications themselves, the colossal building project on Suomenlinna produced a number of technological innovations. The most significant of these took place at the fortress's dry dock: the design and construction of more advanced ships that would form Sweden's new archipelago fleet. Tempted by the opportunities on offer, many of the Crown's leading engineers came to ply their trade on Suomenlinna, and their libraries reveal that they, too, were engaged in theoretical studies, including aesthetics. Ehrensvärd himself was an aesthete who took pleasure in sketching the landscape, and is also said to have tried his hand at oil painting during his time on the islands.

The fortress's most distinguished artist would be Elias Martin, who was hired in 1763 to assist in the decoration of the archipelago fleet's vessels, and to instruct the officers in drawing. Over his three years on Suomenlinna, he produced a number of etchings and paintings of the fortress and its environs which capture in fine detail the fervour and frenzy of the construction project. Ehrensvärd was quick to identify Martin's talent, and is reported to have advised him to make his reproductions of reality as simple and unadorned as possible. After Suomenlinna, Martin went on to develop his abilities further at French and British art academies, before returning to Sweden and establishing himself as one of the leading artists of the Gustavian epoch.

Another lasting reminder of the artistic and aesthetic attitudes prevalent on eighteenth-century Suomenlinna is its stock of civilian buildings. At the time of their construction, their most striking features were their mansard roofs and yellow-painted facades, which soon came to be replicated in manor houses across Finland. The buildings' ornamental parks and gardens, which were cultivated within the shelter of the fortress's walls, also proved influential. For example, the soft and asymmetric shapes found in Piper's Park, on the fortress's main island, set a new trend for English landscape gardens in other parts of the Swedish realm.

Of all the eighteenth-century manors in the capital region, including those of Ehrensvärd and his officer colleagues, the best-preserved is that built by wealthy official Johannes Weckström in Tuomarinkylä, which was then part of the Civil Parish of Helsinki. The stone house, with its four annexes, was constructed in the early 1790s, after Weckström had purchased the estate a decade earlier. Its design was based on the drawings of the famous Swedish architect Carl Wijnblad, whose plans for such properties were highly influential in the late 1700s.

The buildings at Tuomarinkylä were arranged in strict symmetry around a quadrant, with the elongated manor house taking up the whole of the southern end. Although only three out of the four annexes remain today, they were originally laid out two apiece on the east and west of the quadrant, framing the main building. The manor's upper floor lies under a mansard roof, and its central axis is marked on both sides by narrow cross gables. To the south of the main house lies a park, which, in the 1700s, had a rich flora of ornamental and edible plants. There is scant information about the manor's interior decoration, but it is highly likely that the style mirrored the Gustavian moderation and light colour schemes found in the country houses owned by the nobility. Weckström was probably directly influenced by this trend because, in the late eighteenth century, Helsinki's leading burghers and officials were increasingly moving in noble circles.

The aristocracy might have become less exclusive, but the Swedish royals were another matter entirely. If they were lucky, the town's residents might get to bask in the regal glow a handful of times in their lives. Helsinki's representatives at the Riksdag, the parliament in Stockholm, got to spend time in the monarch's presence whenever its assembly was convened, but Gustav III only called it infrequently. Indeed, after ascending to the throne in 1771, he had, with the support of officers on Suomenlinna, staged a coup against his own Riksdag in August 1772. This had the desired intention of reducing the influence of the estates and concentrating power back in the hands of the King again.

Three years later, in a more benign approach to cementing his control over the realm, Gustav III undertook a lengthy trip through Finland, during which, in early June 1775, he spent more than a week in Helsinki. This prestigious visit included numerous public functions, giving the townsfolk ample opportunity to see the King at close quarters. Gustav III and his large retinue approached Helsinki in a procession of wagons along Turuntie, and were greeted by the town's leaders and its burgher cavalry at Espoon tulli, the toll house located a stone's throw south from where Runeberg's statue stands today on Esplanadi. The cavalry was part of Helsinki's burgher guard, to which every citizen possessing burgher rights was obliged to belong, although, in practice, its only tasks were to arrange parades and fire salutes during festivities.

The burgher guard had carried out meticulous drills in preparation for the King's visit. After the welcome ceremony at the toll house, Gustav III mounted his horse and rode into the town along Suurkatu, which had been decorated with triumphal arches in his honour. A significant portion of Helsinki's inhabitants no doubt followed his progress to the Great Square, where the burgher guard fired a salvo in salute. The King then continued on to his place of accommodation, the County Governor's house, from where he had an uninterrupted view of the North Harbour and the town's shipping fleet. The vessels had been proudly anchored in a row for his arrival, their flags and pennants flying.

The King's schedule was packed with public engagements: an audience with the ladies of the town, military inspections on the mainland and a big ball for Helsinki's elite. Then came a three-day-long inspection of Suomenlinna and a farewell ceremony back in the town, before he embarked for Porvoo, the next stop on his journey. The King's time in Helsinki happened to coincide with his name day on 6 June, which gave the army a good excuse to fire countless royal salutes, and the burghers a good opportunity to organise a fireworks display.

While on his tour of Suomenlinna, Gustav III laid the foundation stone to a monument for Augustin Ehrensvärd in the middle of the fortress's large courtyard. Ehrensvärd had passed away three years previously, and was, at that time, interred at the Ulrika Eleonora Church in Helsinki. Eight years later, in the early summer of 1783, his remains were transferred to the fortress and buried in the monument in the presence of the King. The memorial itself was, however, far from finished. Gustav III was very conscious of symbolism, and actively involved himself in the design process, alongside the kingdom of Sweden's foremost sculptor, Johan Tobias Sergel. It was only in the late autumn of 1807, in the dying days of Sweden's rule over Finland, that the memorial was finally completed. Before the winter's snow had melted the following year, the Swedes had surrendered Suomenlinna to the Russians, having succumbed surprisingly quickly to a short siege. Ehrensvärd's monument stands today, therefore, not just in memory of Suomenlinna's creator, but also as a nostalgic punctuation mark at the end of the Swedish period of Finland's history.

This turn of events was obviously not what Gustav III had in mind in the 1780s. Quite the contrary, in fact: from the middle of the decade, he began making plans to recapture the territories that Sweden had previously been forced to hand over to Russia. When Sweden's long-term enemy became embroiled in a war with the Ottoman Empire in 1787, Gustav III judged the time to be ripe to begin his surprise offensive, in which the squadron of the Swedish Navy stationed at Suomenlinna would play a key part. As he envisioned it, Hamina and Vyborg would be captured by land, while the Swedish battle fleet would first take control of the Gulf of Finland, then help the ground troops disembark near St Petersburg. Although the Swedish King went to great lengths to instigate the war in 1788, his grand plan ultimately proved to be a damp squib, and two years later the conflict concluded in a peace treaty that left the countries' borders entirely unchanged. With good reason, the abortive offensive has gone down in Swedish history as "Gustav III's War".

While Helsinki did not become a scene of fighting or destruction on this occasion, its residents learned that life in a garrison town also had its downsides. After the first sea battles, which did not play out at all as the King or his foolhardy advisors had expected, the Russian Navy managed to initiate a blockade of the Gulf of Finland, immobilising Helsinki's merchant fleet in the process. The vessels were, therefore, transferred over to the Crown's use, with the merchants receiving compensation in return. This mitigated some of their financial losses, but it also served to remind the townsfolk how dependent their economy was on the dynamic between the competing national security interests in the Baltic Sea region. The town's burghers were also irritated by their obligation to carry out guard duty and quarter soldiers, while the enlistment of residents en masse as temporary soldiers for the army was making daily life more difficult for even the richest merchants in the town.

Nonetheless, the worst suffering caused by the war was the painful fever that wreaked havoc among the Navy's sailors on Suomenlinna during the first summer of the war in 1788. It quickly spread to the town, where it claimed the lives of untold Helsinki residents until it finally petered out in 1791. According to some sources, the disease arrived with the body lice on the crew of a captured Russian warship. Whatever its provenance, its transmission was undoubtedly caused by the cramped and unhygienic conditions brought on by the high concentration of troops in and off the coast of Helsinki.

Once peace had been agreed in 1790, many assumed that life would gradually return to its former patterns. The town's trade activity and its military routine did regain their former rhythms, but a nagging doubt had developed about the state of Sweden. The country's stumbles and struggles in the war had, namely, increased suspicions that it would not be capable of keeping hold of the eastern part of its realm in the long run. In the short term, the dramatic assassination of Gustav III in March 1792 meant that Sweden was ruled by a regency government until Gustav IV Adolf came of age and was crowned king in 1796. Helsinki's residents took notice of these power shifts, but the changes of ruler in Stockholm had little effect on their day-to-day existence on the southern Finnish coast. In all probability, the news of the French Revolution aroused greater curiosity and unease among the town's inhabitants. It certainly had increasingly bloody consequences for the whole Continent, which would go on to have repercussions for Russo-Swedish relations.

A Bitter Surrender

The violent twists and reformist turns of the French Revolution were only a short episode of a larger geopolitical upheaval. During the second half of the eighteenth century, Great Britain outmanoeuvred France in the two countries' struggle for supremacy in various parts of the world. These setbacks on the global stage stoked demands for comprehensive societal reform in France, which first burst forth as domestic revolution, then spilled over into a protracted war between Europe's Great Powers. Ultimately, they resulted in redrawn borders and the creation of new states in both Europe and South America. One of these border adjustments would directly affect Finland, and would have profound consequences for the path of Helsinki's development.

Until the autumn of 1805, the war on the Continent did not appear to be a particular threat to the peace that then prevailed in the Baltic Sea region. However, it was at this point that Napoleon's army secured a crushing victory in Central Europe over the Third Coalition, an anti-French alliance of multiple European powers, including Britain, Sweden, Russia and Austria. This subsequently broke apart, and Russia went on to make a secret defensive alliance with Prussia the very next year, in 1806. When this, too, was swiftly overcome by the French Army, both Russia and Prussia switched sides, signing a peace deal with Napoleon in the East Prussian town of Tilsit in July 1807. At that same meeting, Napoleon and Alexander I agreed to force Sweden, Denmark and Portugal to join the trade blockade (the so-called Continental System) that France had instigated against

Britain. If Sweden refused to comply, Russia would force its hand by occupying Finland. To cut a long story short, this is precisely what happened in 1808 and 1809.

Instead of taking part in the blockade, Gustav IV Adolf signed a deal with the British in early February 1808, whereby Britain pledged to pay a monthly sum for Sweden to use to strengthen its army and navy. The hope was that this would put a stop to Russia's brazen military build-up on the eastern border of the Swedish realm. On 17 February 1808, however, the Swedish ambassador in St Petersburg received a Russian ultimatum, and four days later, the Imperial Army marched into Finland at various points along the border. It took only a week before Russian forces were closing in on Helsinki, as the Swedish strategy largely consisted of withdrawing the bulk of its army northwards in order to save its forces for the spring, when reinforcements could be sent over for a counter-offensive.

Suomenlinna also had a role to play in this strategy, since the fortress had been constructed expressly as a base for counter-offensive operations. Until these could begin, it would serve the purpose of tying part of the enemy's forces to southern Finland. As the prospect of a Russian attack became increasingly likely, it was supplied with additional troops and provisions. When Russian forces took Helsinki in early March 1808, the fortress was, therefore, well-prepared to withstand a siege until the sea ice broke up and reinforcements arrived.

Helsinki was occupied without resistance. The residents obviously did not want their town to be destroyed, but nor did the Russian commanders, since it would only have made the quartering of their troops more of a challenge. The fact that the Russians did not lay waste to the town contributed to the decision of Suomenlinna's commander, Carl Olof Cronstedt, not to bomb it. More and more enemy troops gradually arrived in Helsinki, until they totalled 6,500 men. The Russians knew that

Suomenlinna's military capacity was roughly the same size (it had 6,750 men and 2,000 cannons), so attempting to storm the fortress would be extremely risky and entail a large human cost.

The Russian commanders opted instead for a strategy of attrition, which had been deployed to great effect in many other sieges during the Napoleonic Wars. It entailed breaking off the Swedes' lines of communication with Stockholm, while spreading false rumours among the Swedish officers' families residing in Helsinki. They then passed this disinformation on to the troops stationed on Suomenlinna, which helped sap the soldiers' spirits. At the same time, the Russians began manipulative negotiations with the pessimistic Cronstedt, who quickly lost all sense of perspective and signed a conditional agreement of surrender in early April. This stipulated that, if Swedish reinforcements had not arrived within the next month, the fortress would yield to the Russians. Such a deal totally contravened the orders that Cronstedt had received, and was almost guaranteed to lead to the submission of Suomenlinna, as the Gulf of Finland was covered in an unusually thick layer of ice that winter.

And so, when 3 May came around and there was still no sign of extra forces on the horizon, Suomenlinna surrendered. Over the following days, one disarmed Swedish regiment after another marched across the ice to the mainland. The spoils of war they left on the fortress for the Russians were staggering: great quantities of firearms, cannons and ammunition. They even allowed the entire Swedish archipelago fleet to pass over into Russian hands, and, in so doing, considerably hampered Swedish attempts to land fresh troops in southern Finland in the summer of 1808. While the loss of Suomenlinna did not, in and of itself, decide the outcome of the war, it did leave a gaping hole in the Swedes' defences that they were never able to repair.

Some researchers have asserted that the under-pressure Cronstedt exhibited a complete failure of judgement in agreeing so readily to such a soft surrender. Others have, in contrast, characterised his decision as an example of successful realpolitik. In their framing of events, Finland was inevitably going to be incorporated into Russia, so giving up Suomenlinna without a fight helped this happen with far less bloodshed than if Sweden had entered into a prolonged war. The judgement of contemporaries was not so charitable: in Sweden, Cronstedt was charged with treason and sentenced in absentia to death. He spent the remainder of his days living in isolation in Herttoniemi Manor, just east of Helsinki.

On 17 September 1809, Sweden was forced to accept a peace deal whereby it agreed to join the trade blockade against Britain and to cede all its provinces in Finland to Russia. Alexander I had not originally imagined that he would capture such a large swath of Sweden. However, his ambitions grew in line with the Imperial Army's rapid gains at the start of the war, and, even before Suomenlinna's surrender, he had decided to add the whole of Finland to his empire. His occupying forces were, as such, under strict orders to show mercy towards civilians. In the summer of 1808, the Emperor issued a manifesto to Finland's population, in which he promised that not only could they keep their Swedish laws and Lutheran religion, but also retain their Diet, that is their representative assembly. In addition, they could, the manifesto declared, count on Russia for economic support.

In return, the Finns were expected to swear loyalty to the Emperor. Some elite circles had, in fact, already done so, having given up on Sweden's ability to defend Finland. The next step of the Emperor's orderly and accommodating takeover of power took place when he ratified his promises at the Diet of Porvoo in the spring and early summer of 1809, while the war was still ongoing. Finland was thereby to be attached to the Russian Empire as a separate Grand Duchy with its own administration. Over time, this proved to be fundamental to the country's development into an increasingly autonomous state and, eventually, into an independent republic.

Not for the first time, the geopolitical whirlwind spinning through Finland would have a transformative impact on the fate of Helsinki. Of all the Russian successes during this war, it was the capture of Suomenlinna that meant the most to the Emperor, as is apparent from his correspondence with Napoleon and from the great parade organised in St Petersburg to celebrate the sea fortress's surrender. This is hardly surprising: Russia's gradual takeover of Finland between 1721 and 1809 was primarily driven by a desire to protect, at all costs, its new capital at the mouth of the Neva River. With Suomenlinna under Russian control, St Petersburg's defences were even more secure than before. The Russian Navy now had a well-equipped sea fortress at their disposal, the location of which was far better than that of Kronstadt, for it gave the Russians complete control over the entrance to the Gulf of Finland.

Helsinki's burghers were obviously very conscious of the economic benefits of Suomenlinna continuing to function as a large garrison, the upkeep and provision of which created a large demand for the town's products and services. As a result, the town's elite put on an effusive display of hospitality when the Emperor, in the region for the Diet of Porvoo, paid his first two visits to Suomenlinna and Helsinki in 1809. Their lavish welcome presumably also stemmed from their dire need of economic assistance, for a great fire had torn through the town in 1808, when the whole of southern Finland already stood under Russian control.

The inferno had started on the night of 17 November. The servant Gustav Lindqvist had taken his master's horse to a makeshift stable in the yard while a south-westerly autumn storm howled around him. Having fed and watered the animal,

Lindqvist put out his candle, pinching the wick with his fingers and tossing a bit of it to the ground. It landed, unnoticed by Lindqvist, on a pile of hay. The storm soon got the wick glowing again and set the hay ablaze, before helping the fire grow into a fierce conflagration that could not be kept in check, despite the townsfolk's concerted efforts. When, four days later, the clean-up could finally begin, the scale of the catastrophe became clear: sixty-one residential properties and many shop stalls and shoreline storehouses had gone up in smoke. These had occupied the area between the eastern half of the town's centre and the North Harbour, which also had its wharf turned to ashes. Lindqvist, the fire-starting servant, was sentenced to fourteen days' imprisonment on bread and water, and served his time without complaint. About a quarter of the town had been reduced to smouldering ruins: as residents picked their way through these, they could scarcely have imagined that the fire had literally levelled the ground for the growth of a whole new Helsinki.

Despite the Emperor's repeated promises that he would help finance the town's rebuilding, very little happened in that regard before the autumn of 1810. This was when the discussion began in earnest as to where the new administrative centre of the Grand Duchy ought to be located. The matter had been briefly touched on at the Diet of Porvoo the previous year, when some representatives of the Estate of the Nobility ventured to question whether it was wise for Turku to remain the seat of the country's governance as, with Russian rule, it had become a border town. They suggested Helsinki and Hämeenlinna as alternatives. In October 1810, the new County Governor of Uusimaa and Häme, Fredrik Stjernvall, submitted a written request to the imperial authorities that Helsinki be substantially rebuilt. In conjunction with this, he proposed that it could be made the capital city of the new Grand Duchy.

Stjernvall referenced Helsinki's splendid location for both foreign trade and the Russian military, with the town integral to the maintenance of the large garrison on Suomenlinna. Indeed, some of the fortress's troops were still quartered in the town itself. The Emperor acquiesced to part of Stjernvall's request, and set up a committee for a preliminary investigation into how the town's reconstruction could best be arranged. However, he did not, at this stage, take a stance on the capital city question. His caution can partly be attributed to the less-than-enthusiastic response of Turku's administrative elite to the idea, and partly to the growing friction between Russia and France, which made the immediate future for Finland and the rest of the Baltic Sea region increasingly uncertain.

In February 1811, Alexander I accepted the proposed town plan of the preliminary investigation, which was largely along the same lines as Stjernvall's suggestion. The County Governor was made chairman of the official rebuilding committee, which was tasked with directing and supervising the extensive construction work. The new plan contained a number of improvements and expansions, but its guiding principle was still, in the main, the restoration of the layout of the old town centre. Nor was there anything in the committee's assignment to indicate that the Emperor was willing to move the capital to Helsinki.

Although a few building projects commenced quickly, most had still not got underway by April 1811. The slow start turned out to be fortuitous, as this was when winds of change began to blow through Helsinki. It was then, namely, that Stjernvall met Gustav Mauritz Armfelt for the first time. Armfelt was moving back to Finland after decades working for (and sometimes against) a succession of Swedish monarchs. Many years previously, he had been one of Gustav III's closest counsellors, and now he was quickly to become one of Alexander I's most important advisors on Finnish affairs. In no time at all, Stjernvall had managed to persuade Armfelt of the benefits of making Helsinki the capital city. Deploying his well-honed diplomacy, Armfelt proceeded to broach the matter with the Emperor on a number of occasions and, little by little, the assignment of the rebuilding committee began to change. In November 1811, Armfelt wrote to Stjernvall that it looked as though the Emperor "well-understood everything", and, in January 1812, it was noted in the proceedings of the committee that they had reserved a "plot for the imperial residence".

A few months later, the committee also recorded receipt of the Emperor's official decision that Helsinki would, indeed, be appointed capital of the Grand Duchy. To the twenty-first-century reader, it can perhaps seem like Helsinki was the natural choice, but, to the nineteenth-century Finn, this outcome was anything other than preordained. Turku had been Finland's biggest city and administrative centre since the Middle Ages. Its civilian population was 11,000 in the early nineteenth century, or over three times that of Helsinki, which then had 3,200 civilian residents.

It was also home to Finland's only university—the Royal Academy of Turku—which had been founded back in 1640. On top of that, most of the members in the Grand Duchy's Governing Council (which would be rechristened as the Senate in 1816) owned estates in the fertile region around Turku in southwest Finland (*Varsinais-Suomi*). Unsurprisingly, they were completely opposed to the idea that some windswept peninsula far away in Uusimaa would usurp Turku's status as capital city.

3

THE CAPITAL CITY

St Petersburg in Miniature

What was it that ultimately persuaded the Emperor to agree to make Helsinki Finland's capital city? It had undoubtedly an ideal location, dynamic shipping trade and proximity to Suomenlinna. Yet these factors have their caveats. The sea fortress's new function as a Russian naval base did not automatically imply that the Grand Duchy's capital would be placed within its immediate vicinity. It was not even officially a part of Finland anymore, having been swiftly designated Russian territory. It would remain so for the entire 108-year period that Finland was a part of the empire. As for the vibrancy of Helsinki's shipping and trade, this hardly rested solely on the town's administrative status, even if making it the capital would naturally have boosted employment opportunities and consumption levels in the town.

The decisive factor in Helsinki's favour was, yet again, Great Power politics. In early 1812, the Franco-Russian alliance had started to come apart at the seams, to the extent that Russia was forced to prepare for the possibility of the French Army

7

launching an attack against it. A key part of its defence strategy was a secret friendship pact with Sweden, which Crown Prince Charles Johan, formerly known as Jean-Baptiste Bernadotte, had helped orchestrate. Only a few years earlier, he had been one of Napoleon's closest generals, but in the autumn of 1810, he had been appointed successor to the Swedish throne. Thereafter, he was largely able to dictate the country's foreign and national security policy. He had originally been chosen in the hope that he would, with Napoleon's support, recapture Finland from Russia. However, as an experienced officer, Charles Johan realised that Sweden had more to gain by capturing Norway instead, as doing so would create a united Scandinavian peninsula. With this goal in mind, he promised Russia that he would not start a war of revenge against it, and the two countries made an agreement that they would unite against France.

The deal was struck on 5 April 1812: only three days later, Alexander I decided to change Finland's capital from Turku to Helsinki. The Emperor had been gently nudged in this general direction for some time, not least by his Finnish advisor Armfelt, but it is evident that he was not prepared to take concrete action while war with Sweden was on the cards. He had endeavoured to win over the Turku elite with high-ranking appointments and awards of royal orders, but their sentiments could easily swing against Russia if the capital was moved to Helsinki while the threat of conflict hung over their heads. Now, however, he was free to push ahead with the decision regardless of how much it aggravated Turku's high society. Not long after, in August 1812, he met Charles Johan in Finland's former capital to formally enter into an alliance against Napoleon, who had launched his military campaign against Russia two months earlier.

If this great altercation between France and Russia had ended in the latter's defeat, then it goes without saying that European politics would have taken a very different path, and so too would have Helsinki's development. The war itself still had a tangible impact on the city, delaying the implementation of much of the new street plan that the Emperor had approved when he appointed it the capital. Behind the plan stood a native of Helsinki: Johan Albrecht Ehrenström. Born in the city in 1762, he received a well-rounded education at Suomenlinna's Swedish officer corps, going on to become a fortification officer and public official. In common with Armfelt, Ehrenström had acted as one of Gustav III's closest advisors, until his career was derailed by the assassination of the King. He ended up receiving a long prison sentence for his part in discussions about usurping the acting regent Gustaf Adolf Reuterholm.

Ehrenström was pardoned a couple of years after Gustav IV Adolf came of age and took control of the monarchy in 1796. He declined to take up any sort of official role again, and instead retired to his estate in Östergötland. However, once Finland had become part of the Russian Empire, his old friend Armfelt convinced him to move back to his homeland in the autumn of 1811. Not long after, he also persuaded Ehrenström to start drawing up a new city plan for Helsinki. Ehrenström's blueprint makes it clear that he was very aware of the effort to encourage the Emperor to make the town Finland's capital. In both style and scope, his plan was a massive departure from all the schemes to rebuild the city that had come before. It was nothing short of a proposal to completely reconstruct the city from the ground up.

Indeed, the most revolutionary part of Ehrenström's plan was not its strict north–south grid layout, rather just how monumental and comprehensive its ideas were. What is more, they received the imperial seal of approval, so, with the exception of a few minor adjustments, they would all be made reality. The city's new centre would be built around a square situated in roughly the same place as the old one, but it would be four times the size. This would be the symbolic heart of Finland,

and it would be called Senate Square. Ehrenström lined its sides with the capital's most important buildings, which were to be far higher and wider than anything previously seen in the city. To the east would be the Senate building; to the north, the Main Guard Post, behind which would be a large Lutheran place of worship, later to be christened St Nicholas's Church. After some thought, it was decided that the square's west side would be home to the university, which was then based in Turku. There was an ideological imperative behind this proposal: Turku was seen as being too sympathetic to Sweden, while moving the institution to Helsinki would also make it geographically closer to St Petersburg.

Ehrenström's plan also involved doubling the width of the streets, and making space for an elegant plaza at the South Harbour, which would be called Market Square. Moreover, it took into consideration the capital's future expansion needs, and extended its grid pattern far beyond the city's existing borders. It went north all the way to Töölönlahti, south down to Ullanlinna and west through the swamp-like Kluuvinlahti, which was to be drained. A few years later, Ehrenström produced a revised plan— more detailed and broader in scope—which also included a city expansion to the south-west: *Uudenmaan Esikaupunki* (Uusimaa Suburb). Its main street was to be Bulevardi, one of the city's longest avenues. In the very centre of the city, the two principal thoroughfares were Esplanadi, a narrow park sandwiched by two roads running east-to-west from the Market Square to Erottaja, and Unioninkatu, which stretched all the way from Ullanlinna in the south to Pitkäsilta Bridge in the north.

The vistas we see and the spaces we experience when we stroll through Helsinki's centre today are still principally the product of Ehrenström's vision, drawings and work as chairman of the new building committee, as the rebuilding committee had, for good reason, been rechristened. The design of the individual buildings and the technical supervision of their construction was, of course, something that had to be delegated to the architect, but Ehrenström also had the final say in this appointment. As a result, his appreciation of the Gustavian style, with its emphasis on symmetry and correct proportions, would be indirectly imprinted on the exteriors and interiors that started to take shape in the city during the late 1810s.

German architect Carl Ludwig Engel was Ehrenström's choice for the project. He arrived in Helsinki in early 1816, and, together with Ehrenström, he came to lead the new building committee's activities with vim and vigour. Engel had been educated at Berlin's Bauakademie (Building Academy) and had worked in both Reval and St Petersburg prior to his post in Helsinki. While in Russia, his talent had been noted by officials responsible for Finnish affairs, but he faced stiff competition in the empire's capital. This was not the case in Helsinki: once there, the 37-year-old Engel sent a letter to a German colleague contentedly declaring that few were lucky enough to be able to "build whole cities".

This was no exaggeration. Almost all of the public buildings erected in Helsinki during Engel's tenure were his handiwork. They were built in an Empire style similar to that which was prevalent in St Petersburg at the time, although art historians have pointed out that Engel's work contains certain features that are more stripped back by design. The new building committee's mandate came to an end in 1825, but Engel's reputation was such that he was appointed Director of Public Construction in 1824. This made him responsible for the supervision of public buildings throughout the whole country, which meant that, all the way up to his death in 1840, he also designed plenty of new properties beyond Helsinki's boundaries. In addition to his public work, as the years went by, he undertook a large number of private commissions from all corners of Finland.

By a stroke of good fortune, Engel's appointment in the spring of 1816 coincided with a turning point for Helsinki and its rebuilding process. Until this point, the project had lacked both resources and sufficient support from Alexander I, since he had been preoccupied with quashing Napoleon's regime once and for all. However, in February that same year, the Emperor fulfilled the promise he had made at the Diet of Porvoo in 1809 and issued a decree renaming the Grand Duchy's Government Council as Senate. Immediately thereafter, he issued a second, ordering the Senate and the agencies of government to move to Helsinki within two years. This set the ball rolling in earnest, since Finland's body of public officials naturally wanted premises that befitted both their and the Grand Duchy's new status.

The project's progress was certainly not hindered by any penny-pinching. Over the time of Helsinki's reconstruction, 1816–25, the total cost to the Finnish state swelled to more than it took in revenue in a single budget year. Such a substantial investment would likely never have happened if the new building committee had not received an allowance directly from St Petersburg, as the size and the salaries of the Finnish administration expanded rapidly in this period. The Russian state also provided another form of economic support for the project by financing the construction of all military buildings in the city.

The biggest and most prominent of the military complexes were the Naval Barracks (*Merikasarmi*) in Katajanokka, the Guards' Barracks (*Kaartin kasarmi*) just south-west of the Market Square, and Turku Barracks (*Turun kasarmi*) at the western entrance to the city. The latter was burnt down during the Finnish Civil War in 1918, but the two other barracks remain imposing sights in the city centre to this day. They are reminders of just how strong the Russian military's presence was in Helsinki at the start of Finland's time as a Grand Duchy. During the first half of the nineteenth century, a sizeable portion of the city's building stock was contained within the area between these barracks, a triangle of both protection and surveillance. The effect was heightened by the fact that they were far bigger and grander edifices than the low wooden buildings that were located in their vicinity on the edges of the city.

During the intensive construction of the project's early years, explosions rang out regularly all over the city. Ehrenström's strict grid plan gave no quarter to the rocky heights or awkward dips that made up a large part of the landscape beyond the bounds of the old settlement. The greatest challenge in this regard was the northern half of Unioninkatu: this had to be levelled with both explosions and extensive filling. The street was christened by Alexander I during his visit to Helsinki in September 1819, after first rejecting the suggestion that it be called Aleksanterinkatu in his honour. He proposed instead that it be given a name that would be a permanent reminder of Finland's connection to—or union with—Russia.

The Emperor's choice of name complemented Ehrenström's city plan perfectly. The old Gustavian's overarching idea was that Unioninkatu would function as Helsinki's parade street, since it ran straight south from Pitkäsilta Bridge into the very heart of the city. Ehrenström consciously placed a significant number of the city's public buildings on this main thoroughfare, and, together with Engel, saw to it that a person walking south along it would be met with a growing sense of grandeur and splendour as they approached Senate Square. From the bridge, they would follow the slow, steady climb of the hill, on the brow of which was erected a small Russian Orthodox Church and, directly opposite, a school building for the sons of Russian soldiers, which was later converted into a military hospital. Beyond the crest of the hill, their gaze would be met, in turn, by the University Library, the main building of the Imperial Alexander University and then the Senate building. Nowadays, these last three edifices are known, respectively, as the National Library of Finland, the University of Helsinki's main building and the Government Palace.

The crowning glory was, of course, St Nicholas's Church, the Lutheran cathedral that stood tallest of all at the northern head of Senate Square, resplendent in its white facade and sky-blue dome. Its construction took much longer than the other buildings, and it was only fully finished in 1852. Contrary to what might be expected, this was not because it was by far the most complicated and towering structure of the project. It was rather because the church was to be placed above all the other buildings surrounding the square, on top of the hill. This meant its eastern half was erected on a sloping plane, requiring lengthy reinforcement of its foundations. Just as it was nearing completion, Nicholas I ordered four smaller domes be added to it, which undoubtedly went against Engel's original idea of a clean, classical silhouette in the Empire style.

In the late 1830s, when the new city was starting to take shape, many visitors were taken by how much it resembled the centre of the Russian Empire, playfully referring to Helsinki as St Petersburg in miniature. The comparison was flattering, and just what Alexander I and Ehrenström—with Engel's help—had strived to achieve. The new Helsinki was designed to reflect Finland's connection to the Russian Empire, its key buildings underlining its status as an autonomous Grand Duchy with its own administration and legislation. In line with this goal, the rebuilding project stripped any reminders of Swedish rule from the city. Ehrensvärd's grave, it is true, remained in place on Suomenlinna, but very few civilians were allowed to visit the sea fortress while it was Russian territory.

One of the visitors upon whom Helsinki left an impression was a Finnish expatriate, Bishop Frans Mikael Franzén. He had, at one time, been a famous professor at the Royal Academy of Turku but had lived and preached in Sweden for decades when he returned to Finland in 1840 for the university's bicentennial celebration in Helsinki. At this, he was granted the title of Jubilee Master, as it had been fifty years since he had received his master's degree. Once back home at his diocese in Sweden, Franzén wrote the poem "Resan till Jubelfesten" ("The Journey to the Jubilee Celebration"), in which he expressed, at length, his wonder at the total metamorphosis that the small harbour town had undergone in thirty years.

Franzén's enthusiasm for the redesigned city was shared by Russian officer Faddei Bulgarin, who reported on his reunion with Helsinki thirty years after Russia's siege of Suomenlinna. Although, in contrast to Franzén, Bulgarin had absolutely nothing good to say about its Swedish past, declaring that "poverty was characteristic of this wretched town." He offered an entirely different assessment of the city upon his return: after inspecting all the buildings around Senate Square, he wandered further along Unioninkatu, describing it as "Helsinki's Nevsky Prospect". He eventually made his way up to the Observatory, at the southernmost end of Unioninkatu, and also its highest point. This, too, had been designed by Engel, and erected on the same site where Ehrensvärd aspired to build Ulrikasborg all those years ago. Bulgarin expressed his admiration for the building's architecture, as well as the view out to the harbour and the sea, before noting pointedly that the position of astronomy professor at the university—that is, the head of the Observatory—was advertised as vacant.

Engel had carefully planned the Observatory around its technical requirements. These were dictated by the previous astronomy professor, Friedrich Argelander, who was uncompromising in his demands that the large telescopes be as stable as possible. Argelander was already an internationally renowned astronomer by this time, and the university had purchased the stargazing equipment to meet his research needs.

The Observatory was completed in 1834, but only two years later, Argelander left his post, tempted away by a more prestigious role at the University of Bonn. Before his departure, however, he used the Observatory's telescopes to calculate the direction of the solar system's movement more accurately than ever before, which provoked a great deal of interest in the scientific community.

City Districts and Linguistics

The Observatory's advanced apparatus was also used for a far more quotidian calculation. Namely, it enabled Helsinki residents to set their clocks: every day, at noon on the dot, a large, black cloth bag was dropped from the central tower. In misty weather, midday was announced with a cannon shot, which could even be heard beyond the city's limits, on account of the sparse vegetation and the low-rise buildings. For an indication of how prominent the Observatory was, consider artist Magnus von Wright's painting of the view over Helsinki on a clear morning in the summer of 1837. His perspective was from the northern side of Pitkäsilta Bridge, that is, from the opposite end of Unioninkatu, yet the central tower of the Observatory is still visible in the background, distant but distinct.

Unlike its modern incarnation, built of stone in 1912, the wooden Pitkäsilta Bridge in von Wright's painting lived up to its Finnish name, in that it was a long (*pitkä*) bridge (*silta*). From this viewpoint, von Wright captured the contrast between the city's Empire-style centre and the landscape immediately to its west, where wooden buildings peek out between the meadows, shrubbery and grazing cows. On the other side of this hill lay the reedy Kluuvilahti Bay, and further away, in the south-west, the low, single-storey timber houses that comprised the so-called Uusimaa Suburb. By the 1830s, this had already started to become a larger geographical area than Helsinki Proper

(*Varsinainen kaupunki*), which was the name Ehrenström's city plan had given to the Empire-style quarter and the buildings around it.

Many of the officials and university lecturers who had moved to Helsinki from Turku lived in Uusimaa Suburb, where they could have both a spacious home, various outhouses and their own vegetable garden. These uncrowded conditions were partly a consequence of the inexpensive plots of ground in the new city district, where the majority of the land was owned by the state. They were also a result of the prohibition on multi-storey wooden buildings, which the authorities deemed a fire hazard. The ordinance they issued further stated that houses should only be painted one of two colours: grey or light yellow. As time went by, this would bring a charming uniformity to the whole town.

The most famous resident of Uusimaa Suburb was Engel himself. By the 1820s, he was widely admired in Finland for his architectural achievements, and, when spotted out and about in Helsinki, he was always observed to be stylishly dressed and well-mannered. He acquired a large tract of land between Bulevardi and Uudenmaankatu, and, as might be expected, he drew up designs for all the buildings himself. In the autumn of 1828, he moved into the residential house on the property with his wife and three children. The house, which he would call home for the rest of his life, had ten rooms, two halls and a kitchen, which were separated into a public and a private sphere. The large drawing and dining rooms were intended for social intercourse between guests and the family, but the other rooms were private, such as Engel's own studio-cum-study, where he kept his drawing board and library.

In terms of the interior decoration, it was, naturally, the drawing room that stole the show. According to Engel's estate inventory from the 1840s, the furniture was all Biedermeier in style, with mahogany sofas, a table and a large number of chairs presumably complemented by tasteful wallpaper and pictures. In one of his letters, Engel excitedly relates how his whole family had helped make preparations for a large party in their home, to which over fifty people were invited. This must have seemed like an extravagant expense to the frugal architect, although the majority of the delicacies served to the guests most likely originated from the household's own domestic economy, including its vegetable garden, bakehouse, chickens and cows.

At this time, most households in the city would then have been principally reliant on their own food production. Such a facet of daily life is mentioned in the journalist August Schauman's vivid descriptions of his childhood in 1830s Helsinki. His parents' home was also located in Uusimaa Suburb, and their drawing-room windows provided a fine view of the city centre and Kluuvilahti, where Helsinki Central Station stands today. Long into the 1840s, this bay was, for the most part, "a stinking pool of water". Schauman was understandably proud that he had witnessed the rise of the new Empire-style city. He recalled how the stone town hall, built under Swedish rule in the early 1800s, was demolished in the late 1830s to make space for the north-eastern corner of Senate Square. From here, Nikolainkatu (today Snellmaninkatu) ran due north towards Pitkäsilta, having replaced the old and winding Hämeentie.

Many of the city's first Russian merchants set up shop on the stretch of Nikolainkatu that stood closest to Senate Square. As a result, these blocks started to be called "Narinkka", which comes from the Russian "na rynke", meaning "at the square". The first wave of Russian tradesmen had arrived in tandem with the military units that were billeted in the town and on Suomenlinna after the peace treaty of 1809. When the great building projects got underway, their number increased at such a rate that, by 1820, they accounted for twelve of the thirty-four merchants working in the city. They would continue to make up more or less a third of the city's total traders for the next thirty years.

The influx of Russians into the city's trading circles provoked, at the start, irritation among the established merchants in Helsinki. For one thing, the Russian soldiers and building contractors favoured their fellow countrymen, whose orders and profits were on such a scale that they could also invest in manufacturing and production, thus making significant headway as industrialists. For another, these Russian merchants, in common with other Russian immigrants, were often involved in the black market. On the plus side, however, the Russian mercantile elite brought a business-minded attitude to the city's economic life, as well as contacts with other parts of the empire, which would, over time, greatly improve the variety of products available in Helsinki. Until the 1870s, over fifty per cent of the city's colonial trade was in Russian hands, which is hardly a revelation considering the size of the market in St Petersburg for exotic goods from the furthest reaches of the empire. As the years passed, the leading Russian merchants and their families learned fluent Swedish, which was the dominant language in Helsinki until the 1870s.

The local traders' initial opposition to these foreign interlopers softened with time, perhaps because the Russian-speaking civilian population remained a small minority in Helsinki throughout the 1800s. Until the 1860s, the Russians' opportunities to compete were limited by the fact that a merchant had to obtain trading privileges before he could start operating in the city. Moreover, it was far from straightforward for Russians to gain Finnish citizenship, which meant that the number of Russian speakers never climbed above two per cent of Finland's population between 1809 and 1917. In Helsinki, this proportion was higher, reaching a peak in 1870, when a little over 3,900 Russian-speaking civilians belonged to the city's Orthodox

Church. Even so, they still only accounted for about twelve per cent of Helsinki's total population, which rose to 32,100 that same year.

This figure comes with a caveat, as it does not include the Russian garrison troops stationed in the city and on Suomenlinna. Their number ranged from 4,000 to 8,000 men, depending on the geopolitical situation in Europe and the Baltic Sea region. The Russian officer corps also resided on the island fortress and in Helsinki, but they did not have much to do with its civilian population at all, except when there were large ceremonies, such as military parades or an imperial visit. On these occasions, it quickly became very clear who had the final say about what happened in the city.

Helsinki experienced a population boom between 1810 and 1840, the very period when the city was transformed. It rose to new heights figuratively, as the new capital of the Grand Duchy, and it rose to them literally, as its rebuilt Empire-style centre took shape. During this time, the number of inhabitants nearly quadrupled, from 3,500 to 13,300. The rate of growth slowed somewhat over the next two decades, but the population still climbed to 22,200 in 1860, making Helsinki the biggest city in Finland and the same size as Reval, which had 20,700 inhabitants in 1858. While it had shot up in size, it was nevertheless an idyllic small town compared to the other nearby capitals in the early 1860s: Riga's population was then 72,200, Stockholm's 110,000 and St Petersburg's a colossal 660,000.

A significant share of Helsinki's residents had been Finnish speakers in the late seventeenth century, but the linguistic composition of the town shifted over the following hundred years. The construction of Suomenlinna in the second half of the eighteenth century played a key part in this shift: it attracted droves of migrants to the town, a sizeable proportion of whom were Swedish speakers. Some of them arrived from other parts of the Swedish realm, but the majority came from the Swedish-speaking coastal regions of Uusimaa. Indeed, as previously noted, Helsinki's growth at this time coincided with Finland's whole population doubling in size, so the town had a plentiful supply of workers from the surrounding countryside. The influx of regional labour continued throughout the first half of the nineteenth century, so that, by 1860, roughly eighty per cent of Helsinki's residents were Swedish-speaking and ten per cent Finnish-speaking. The remaining ten per cent had Russian, German or Yiddish as a mother tongue.

The supremacy of Swedish in Helsinki was, to a certain degree, down to geography. Besides the Uusimaa coast, parts of the province's interior were also Swedish-speaking or actively bilingual regions. This was in contrast to much of the rest of the country, for eighty-five per cent of Finland's population spoke Finnish. It had been the majority language ever since Finland had been separated from Sweden and had become an autonomous Grand Duchy of the Russian Empire in 1809. However, Swedish remained the language of higher education and the central administration all the way up to the 1870s, since it was the mother tongue of most of the country's social and political elite. This was, then, another factor behind its dominance in Helsinki, and in many of Finland's other coastal towns that this group inhabited. It led to some Finnish speakers switching over to Swedish, and even Swedifying their names when they reached a certain level in society, or when they moved to certain areas of the country.

If we were to walk the streets of Helsinki in the first half of the nineteenth century, what sort of Swedish and Finnish would we hear? The lion's share of the city's Swedish-speaking residents originated from the Uusimaa countryside, so we would encounter many of the region's Fenno-Swedish dialects. The pronunciation and everyday vocabulary would also be influenced by the migrants from different areas of Sweden who had settled in the city over the years. The bourgeoisie, for their part, adopted new patterns of speech following the arrival of the administrative and academic elite from Turku, which was clearly more influenced by the written and spoken Swedish in the former capital of Stockholm.

We have fewer clues as to the type of Finnish heard in Helsinki at this time. What we do know is that, until the 1860s, the majority of Finnish speakers hailed from Etelä-Häme and used Swedish regularly, so it is reasonable to assume they liberally peppered their everyday language with Swedish words and expressions. Take the city's international name today: "Helsinki" comes from the Finnish pronunciation of "Helsinge", which was a truncation of "Helsingfors" that was widely used in Swedish-speaking rural communities in Uusimaa. "Helsinge" was, of course, also the name of the ancient parish where the town first came into existence. In a similar vein, Sveaborg's Finnish name was, for centuries, simply its Fennicised pronunciation: "Viapori".

Linguistic borrowing and exchange in the city were not limited to these two languages. Russian words and concepts also took root in the quotidian Swedish and Finnish used by Helsinki residents. The majority of these popular expressions originated from their interactions with Russian merchants and the other Russian speakers in the city. And the more deeply the terms embedded themselves in the everyday language, the more tightly they weaved together to form a common slang, in which only the conjunctions and suffixes revealed whether the speaker was using Swedish or Finnish. Some of the words persist to this day: in both languages, a shop can still be referred to as a *lafka*, and a fool can still be branded a *daiju*.

In certain cases, it can be hard to determine the slang's exact origin. The classic example is the term for a good bloke: *kiva kaveri*. There is no doubt that the word *kiva*—nowadays meaning "nice" in Finnish—comes from Russian, but linguists have competing theories about how it arrived in the vernacular of Helsinki residents. Some assert that it stems from the Russian street sellers' shouts of *hiva* (from the Finnish *hyvä*, meaning "good"), others that it is derived from the Russian word for adulterated fortified wine (*sihúva*). A similar uncertainty exists around *kaveri* ("friend" in Finnish), although some researchers claim that it has snuck into Helsinki's slang from a European variant of Yiddish, in which *khaver* meant "companion" or "partner in crime".

Jews certainly numbered among the merchants who streamed into Helsinki from far and wide in the Russian Empire. At first, foreign traders had to get special dispensation to sell their wares, but, from 1858, all soldiers that had served in the Imperial Army for over twenty-five years gained the right to live in the location of their last garrison. In Helsinki, this gave rise to flourishing, if small, Jewish and Tatar communities. The former were involved in the colonial trade and the sale of used goods, while the latter, hailing from the Caucasus, quickly carved out a niche as rug dealers and tobacco vendors. This proved influential among Helsinki's bourgeoisie, to the extent that, in the second half of the nineteenth century, every aspiring gentleman's home had a cosily decorated smoking room, replete with Oriental mats.

In common with Helsinki's other ethnic minorities, the Jews and the Islamic Tatars kept up their religious traditions. For a long time, however, they had to be unobtrusive and modest in their observance of their beliefs, for many Lutherans in Finland were openly prejudiced against other religions, and particularly against the Jewish minority. In the 1880s, the Old Finn members of the Diet of Finland tried to force through legislation that would have further restricted their trade and residency rights. The motion was rejected by Alexander III, who saw no sensible reason to subject the handful of Jews in Finland to such a law.

In the 1870s, Helsinki's liberals, with Leo Mechelin at the helm, began to demand citizenship rights for Jews. However, it was not until Finland had declared its independence, in the late autumn of 1917, that such a law was first passed. This certainly did not mean that anti-Semitic prejudice had disappeared from the country, but it did, at least, improve the daily life of the Jewish community. By this time in Helsinki, the western end of Kamppi had become something of a Jewish quarter, particularly after a synagogue had been opened on Malminkatu in August 1906.

The city's German-speaking minority was mainly Protestant, and they founded their own Lutheran community in 1858. Six years later, they built the German Church at the very south of Unioninkatu. Their status in Helsinki was very different to that of the other minorities, which was a consequence of two key factors. The first was that, ever since its founding in 1550, Helsinki had been populated by German-speaking mercantile families. Thanks to their close ties with German trading houses in different parts of the Baltic Sea region, they often occupied a central position in the city's commercial and social life. The second, connected factor was one of language, for German persisted for centuries as the region's lingua franca. As a rule, the language bridged social divides in Helsinki, for residents from a variety of backgrounds had some knowledge of it, and intuitively identified themselves with the German-speaking cultural sphere in Northern Europe. This was also the case for the majority of the Russian governor-generals in Finland, especially those who were of Baltic German descent.

Innovations and Ideas

The governor-generals probably spoke just as much French as they did German with the Finnish senators, few of whom found cause to learn Russian during the 108 years Finland was part of the empire. French was also the language with which Helsinki's social elite typically welcomed the Russian emperors to their city. Their infrequent visits were huge events, recorded in minute detail by the daily newspapers that began to emerge in the 1830s. Nicholas I graced Helsinki with his presence on three occasions during his thirty-year rule: 1830, 1833 and 1854. Of these, it was the second visit, made by steamboat in June 1833, that left the biggest impression. Calm had just been restored to the Russian realm after the repression of the November Uprising in Poland, and Nicholas I could take the time to admire the rapid development of Finland's burgeoning Empire-style capital.

The Emperor and his consort, Empress Alexandra, visited many of the brand-new buildings, and had the opportunity to praise Engel for his work in person during a viewing of the recently inaugurated university building. Nicholas I introduced Engel to his Prussian wife with the words "Your countryman, our architect, who built this city". In memory of the visit, an obelisk was erected in the Market Square in 1835, at the very spot where the imperial couple stepped ashore from *Ischora*, their steam frigate. The monument's inscription, written in both Latin and Finnish, only references the Empress's arrival in the city, since the Emperor had already been immortalised in the name of Helsinki's new cathedral: St Nicholas's Church. The obelisk was crowned with the Russian double-headed eagle, on the breast of which was engraved the Finnish lion crest. The memorial soon gained the moniker "the Empress's stone", and gave a welcome aesthetic boost to the Market Square.

Nicholas I and Alexandra's arrival by steamboat was, in and of itself, a great spectacle for Helsinki's residents. The city had occasionally been visited by a paddle steamer that travelled between Stockholm and St Petersburg in the 1820s, but both the rarity and the rapid technological advancement of these nautical vessels were a cause for excitement. In 1834, a shipping company was founded in Turku, principally financed by capital from St Petersburg, which had two steam ships built: the *S/S Furst Menschikoff* and the *S/S Storfursten*. In June 1837, they began operating a regular line between Stockholm and Kronstadt, calling at Turku, Helsinki and Reval en route. In Helsinki, there was a real sense that this ferry was connecting the city to the wider world in a whole new way, since it was suddenly possible to travel to and from other Baltic Sea cities much faster and on a far more precise schedule than ever before.

One of the investors in Turku's new shipping company was Henrik Borgström, Helsinki's shrewdest businessman in this period. He knew an opportunity when he saw it, and hence he founded a spa company in 1834, one designed to profit from this new steamboat traffic. He set about building fashionable baths on the southernmost peninsula in Helsinki. This would target wealthy summertime pleasure-seekers from St Petersburg, who had begun to frequent various Baltic watering places after Nicholas I imposed stringent restrictions on foreign travel.

During his time studying in England, Borgström had developed a keen interest in flower growing and ornamental parks, which he was able to put to good use in this venture. Under his direction, the cold and desolate environment on the outskirts of the city was transformed into a leafy health resort, with a large bathhouse on the shore and a light and beautifully furnished restaurant in the middle of its park. This latter building was called Kaivohuone—the well house—as it also offered a range of health-giving mineral waters for the guests' consumption. The sweeping green space had well-maintained ponds and sand-packed pathways, its own skittles alley, deciduous trees and carefully arranged flower beds.

The baths welcomed their first guests early in the summer of 1838, and their popularity fast exceeded Borgström's expectations.

Throughout the 1840s, between 200 and 300 Russians per year came to sample their curative properties and, in so doing, spend at least a portion of their summer in Helsinki. This gave rise to an extremely lucrative market in villa and accommodation rental, although the richest aristocratic families could afford to construct their own holiday houses around Kaivopuisto. Princess Zinaida Yusupova was one such spa guest with the resources to do so, and her villa came to be frequented by some of the most talked-about personalities in St Petersburg's high society. The presence of the rich and famous led to a noticeable increase in the import of all sorts of luxury goods to the city, which, thanks to Finland's favourable customs regulations, were often much cheaper in Helsinki than St Petersburg.

The quality-conscious summer guests also breathed life into the city's fledgling restaurant and café culture, which soon took inspiration from Kaivohuone's exclusive menus and finely honed service. In fact, some of those who helped launch the venture at Kaivohuone, such as Louis Kleineh and Catharina "Cajsa" Wahllund, also ran their own inns and dining establishments within the city centre. The Russian visitors were undoubtedly big spenders, but the spa season was so short that these restaurateurs still earned most of their money by catering to the city's year-round residents.

The German-born Kleineh's primary source of income was from Seurahuone, his hotel, restaurant and entertainment venue on Pohjoisesplanadi. Designed, of course, by Engel, it was considered to offer the finest overnight accommodation in Helsinki until the early 1900s, when it was converted into the city hall, which it remains to this day. For her part, Cajsa Wahllund had made a name for herself with her dining establishments in Turku before moving to Helsinki in 1819. For the next couple of decades, she ran a number of the city's inns, until she got the opportunity to build her own restaurant on the southern shore of Töölönlahti in 1839. This area had been used for horticulture since the 1700s, and the city plan of 1812 earmarked some of it for a public park, which came to be called Allmänna Promenaden (Public Promenade).

The restaurant was constructed on the park's northern cape that extended into Töölönlahti, giving diners a fine view of the bay's waters. The warm and motherly Cajsa Wahllund had been hugely popular among young students ever since her time in Turku, so they immediately became a regular fixture at her new establishment. They even organised annual birthday tributes for her on 1 May, which have endured to our present era in the form of the Academic Male Voice Choir of Helsinki's popular concerts in the park on that same date each year. It was not long before the park itself was given the moniker of Kaisaniemi—that is, Cajsa's Cape—in the restaurateur's honour. This marked the first time that a place name in the city was coined in Finnish rather than Swedish, and it did not happen by chance, for there had been a surge of interest in the Finnish language among the academic elite at this time. This movement was termed Fennomania, and many of those caught up in it lent their support to a growing demand to establish Finland as its own nation with its own mother tongue.

The heyday of Kaivopuisto's spa and health resort came to an abrupt end with the outbreak of the Crimean War in the early 1850s. And, once a peace deal had been struck a few years later, the Russian authorities relaxed restrictions on foreign travel, which led to more and more Russians venturing to the Continent for both health and pleasure. As a result, Helsinki's summers lost much of the glitz and glamour that the St Petersburg set had provided, yet their absence was no great catastrophe for the city's economy. Over the 1840s, the social life and cultural world of Helsinki's residents had further expanded as their city had developed in status and influence as a centre of government and a home of university education.

From its base in the heart of the city, the Senate of Finland was able to pursue increasingly independent economic policies. It financed a number of big infrastructure projects, not least the Saimaa Canal that runs from Lappeenranta to Vyborg in the country's south-east, connecting the huge Lake Saimaa to the Gulf of Finland. It also used its resources to enlarge the country's public sector and broaden its educational remit. The university, standing directly opposite the Senate building on Senate Square, had grown in prestige as a dynamic setting for public debates and as a pipeline for new knowledge and expertise. It was in this milieu that, slowly but surely, a new conception of Finland began to take form, which saw the country as not merely a nation, but also as its own state.

Where Helsinki had once been important for trade and troops, it was now defined increasingly by government activities and academic affairs. It was a place where new ideas were formulated and foreign inventions were adopted before spreading to other parts of the land. The majority of its leading public figures and businessmen in the 1840s were not Helsinki natives, but had moved to the city precisely because of the opportunities it offered. That Helsinki became increasingly conscious of its heightened status in Finland and the Russian Empire more broadly can be seen from the street signs in two—and later three—languages that were gradually erected on every corner in the city. In 1833, the Senate ordered all property owners to include the Russian name in Cyrillic script alongside the existing Swedish one on their street signs. Three decades later, in 1864, it instructed that the Finnish street name should likewise be added.

The city was not just a distribution centre for the nation's ideas, but also for its products: during the first half of the nineteenth century, its trade networks became more focused on the import and production of goods that could be sold across the whole land. Sometimes new regulations were brought in to give an advantage to domestic industry, as was the case in the 1840s, when Henrik Borgström's tobacco factory became increasingly profitable due to a hike in the customs duties on all imports from Sweden. Located only a couple of blocks east of Senate Square in Helsinki, it remained Finland's biggest tobacco producer until the 1870s. Borgström's remarkable success in business allowed him to actively support and participate in the city's cultural events. As a consequence, he became personally acquainted with a number of the epoch's foremost musicians, scientists and authors. Many of those who grew up to shape public opinion in Finland received Borgström's backing at an early stage of their careers. He also struck up a close friendship with the country's leading conductor and composer, Fredrik Pacius, who migrated to Helsinki from Hamburg in 1834 and wrote the music for Finland's national anthem "Maamme" (known by its original Swedish title as "Vårt land" and in English as "Our Land") in 1848.

Strains of the growing nationalist sentiment in Finland started to emerge immediately after the university had moved from Turku to Helsinki in 1828. These were fostered within the confines of a small and closed circle of young academics and officials, which would come to be known as *Lauantaiseura* (The Saturday Club). The members often met in the home of the intellectual J. L. Runeberg in Kruununhaka, a short walk east from the university. Runeberg would go down in history as Finland's national poet, but, at this time in the early 1830s, he was only just beginning to get his verses published. The Saturday Club, alongside university gossip and discreet criticism of the Russian regime, gave birth to a number of initiatives that would prove to be important for both Helsinki and Finland as a whole. They founded both the city's first private upper-secondary school, Helsinki Lyceum, and the Finnish Literature Society in 1831, as well as the newspaper, *Helsingfors Morgonblad*, in 1832.

The Russian authorities' strict censorship prevented the publication of political opinion. In spite of this, *Helsingfors Morgonblad*'s writers managed to stir up interest in Western ideas of civility and freedom of speech, which had already taken root in neighbouring Sweden. They did this principally through their reviews and their politically-infused cultural contributions, although Fredrika Runeberg, the editor-in-chief's wife, was also a central—if invisible—part of the process. Her anonymously published short stories and translations of foreign newspaper articles highlighted issues and debates that were particularly relevant to women's position in society.

One popular member of the Saturday Club was the physician Elias Lönnrot, whose keen interest in the Finnish language and its folklore was a key inspiration behind the birth of the Finnish Literature Society. Its first-known text was the Finnish national epic *Kalevala* (1835), which was a product of the folk poetry that Lönnrot had collected on his travels round Karelia. The lack of a public sphere in Finland meant that the society, for the first two decades of its existence, functioned as an important platform for a debate about the nation's culture. As did, to a certain extent, the Finnish Society of Sciences and Letters (founded in 1838), since many of its members were public-spirited and culturally engaged professors and officials.

The university's magnificent main building in the very centre of the city was an unambiguous indication of its national importance. The academics also benefitted from the support of Alexander I himself, for he ensured that professors received a sizeable increase in salary. This elevated their status and gave them an entirely different lifestyle to that which they had experienced in Turku, where many had seized the opportunity to bolster their income by becoming clergymen to rich congregations. The scientific community further benefitted from the construction of more university buildings across the city, the most ostentatious and imposing of which were undoubtedly the Observatory and the University Library. The Faculty of Medicine was provided with two large building complexes, *Kliininen instituutti* (The Clinical Institute), on the northern end of Unioninkatu, and a psychiatric hospital in Lapinlahti, on Helsinki's west coast.

Both medical facilities were designed by Engel, but the latter was only completed seven years after his death, in 1847. Its slow construction notwithstanding, it was a strikingly modern psychiatric hospital for the period, with the layout of both the building and the expansive park taking careful consideration of the patients' various symptoms and care needs. The pride it inspired in Helsinki's residents can be seen in a map that was printed two years before the institution welcomed its first patients, on which is marked "Lunatic Asylum" in letters almost as large as the city's name.

The city's dazzling architectural metamorphosis gave the Finnish elite more than just esteem: together with the well-functioning central administration and the improved state finances, it strengthened their faith in the future of Finland. The country's annexation by Russia had certainly not been a catastrophe, since both its Swedish laws and its Lutheran beliefs had remained intact. Their growing interest in Finnish culture and the Finnish language most often stemmed from an earnest desire to "awaken a slumbering national sentiment" and make a cohesive identity for Finnish people. That said, the notion of a shared Finnish identity was by no means fully formed, and, in the back of many advocates' minds, there also lingered a disquiet about the country's long-term fate. The concern was that the Russian Empire, with its vast resources, would pull Finland ever more closely into its orbit, watering down the country's Western culture and values until they eventually disappeared entirely. The aim of improving the standing of the Finnish language was, in other words, also a pragmatic defence strategy. If the nation was to continue to exist, its elite must eventually be able to lead the country in the mother tongue of the majority.

The ulterior motive of this cultural movement was only divulged behind closed doors in late 1840s Helsinki. The Russian authorities had intensified their censorship of the press and their surveillance of students for fear that the calls for democratic reforms that were then spreading in Central Europe would find their way to Finland, too. When the students organised their traditional celebration of spring's arrival—*Kukanpäivä*, or Flower Day—on 13 May 1848, their professors were at pains to ensure that no revolutionary songs or speeches would occur during the boisterous event. It began with a march from the city out to Kumtähden kenttä, a meadow north-east of the centre, where the main festivities were held. As they walked, the students repeatedly sang Runeberg's new national anthem "Maamme" ("Vårt land"), in which the poet expressed his love of the Fatherland in a Romantic style, through fervent praise of its nature. The great orator, Professor Fredrik Cygnaeus, was one of those who addressed the students at the meadow. The title of his talk was "Finlands Namn" ("Finland's Name"), and the feeling afterwards was that it had been unforgettable, even if the level of intoxication was such that there was little clarity about what, exactly, he had said. Indeed, that the whole occasion passed without any political consequences might be partly down to just how freely the alcohol had flowed.

In their close readings of the lyrics, some scholars of literature have asserted that it is really about the Finnish people and their country's future. The pronoun "we" appears frequently, and the song's final verse begins with the lines: "Thy bloom, still to its bud confined/Shall blossom from sheer force." With the benefit of hindsight, these words have been readily interpreted as a veiled prophecy of Finland's future independence. However, neither Runeberg nor anyone else in the late 1840s could have conceived of the country's development taking such a monumental turn. The best they could have hoped for was that the Emperor would permit Finland to preserve its language and the institutions that were already in existence. The majority of the country's elite were, therefore, careful to display their consummate loyalty to the Russian Empire in all public contexts.

The Crimean War

During the first half of the 1850s, the Finns' allegiance to the Emperor was solidified as Russia became embroiled in a Great Power conflict, one that ultimately had repercussions for Finland, too. It began as an armed struggle with the Ottoman Empire over control of the Bosphorus, which was the only point of access for the Russian Black Sea Fleet to the Mediterranean. In the spring of 1854, however, Great Britain and France joined the war on the side of the Turks, in order to prevent Russia from getting a foothold in the Eastern Mediterranean that could allow them to challenge British control of the world's oceans. The war got its name from the key battles that were fought over the naval base of Sevastopol in Crimea. In support of this main offensive, the Western Powers also launched an attack on the Russian Empire via the Baltic Sea, with the aim of forcing the Emperor to devote resources to protecting St Petersburg. Between the spring and autumn of 1854, British and French fleets carried out a number of forays along the Finnish coast, which stirred up considerable ill-feeling towards the Western Powers among the local population, while also serving to bolster its defensive spirit. In August, the Western aggressors seized Bomarsund Fortress on the Åland Islands after a brief siege and bombardment. They then set about destroying it brick by brick, which caused the Russian military to hurriedly implement better defensive preparations at their other coastal fortifications around the Gulf of Finland.

Russia's most important naval base in the Baltic Sea region was Kronstadt, at the entrance of St Petersburg. Its coastal artillery was considered strong enough to fend off all but the most sustained maritime attacks on the city. However, the Russian Navy's firepower and technology was no longer on the same level as the seaborne forces of its Western rivals. Their ships, in contrast to Russia's Baltic Fleet, were also steam-powered, and their cannons had a far greater range than anything on the Russian side. These deficiencies made the coastal fortifications particularly significant, all the more so as Russian strategists asserted in the autumn of 1854 that the Western Powers would land in Finland with a large army the following summer.

It was a pressing concern, then, that Suomenlinna and Helsinki's other fortifications had been in want of strengthening and development for decades. The Russian military had to act fast to make up for lost time: they reinforced Suomenlinna's bastions and built new defences on Vallisaari, Kuninkaansaari and Santahamina, three hitherto unprotected islands east of the sea fortress. After the Battle of Bomarsund, when the enemy's attacks from the surrounding countryside proved instrumental in defeating the fortress, Russia was wise to the risk that the nearby terrain posed to Suomenlinna and Helsinki itself. For this same reason, Russian forces also constructed new artillery posts along the southern and western coasts of Helsinki, and strengthened the batteries that were already stationed at Ullanlinna. In so doing, Russia's military leadership tried to apply the lessons it had learned from the defence of its fortress in Sevastopol, where the war's main clashes were still ongoing. However, there was a distinct lack of both time and resources, so the bulk of the work ended up being half-finished.

There was, nevertheless, one aspect of Suomenlinna and Helsinki's fortification that turned out to be fairly effective: the sea mines. These had been developed in the 1840s by engineers working for the great naval powers of Europe, and they were taken into use by the Russian Navy at the start of the Crimean War. In the summer of 1854, four British vessels were blown up by mines while on a reconnaissance mission at Kronstadt, which helped deter the Western Powers from trying to capture the naval base. It also helped convince the Russian military leadership of the explosives' utility, and, the following spring, the decision was made to sink almost a thousand sea mines approximately one kilometre out from Suomenlinna. These curved in an arch from the coastline of Lauttasaari in the west to the islands east of Santahamina. The distance was dictated by the range of the Russian artillery, which was a little over a kilometre, for they wanted to prevent the enemy's minesweeping efforts with cannon fire from Suomenlinna and other island batteries.

The vast majority of the floating explosives were so-called contact mines, which had been developed by the Swedish inventor Immanuel Nobel, who had moved to Russia after falling into bankruptcy in his homeland. In St Petersburg, he devised a number of weapons for the Russian war machine, and he and his sons amassed a considerable fortune. The remainder of this was bequeathed by his grandson, Alfred, to a trust for the purpose of establishing the now world-famous Nobel prizes, including the Nobel Peace Prize.

Neither Alfred, who famously invented dynamite, nor his grandfather would have been fitting recipients for such an accolade. Immanuel's conical sea mines were a little over 60 centimetres in height. Anchored at a suitable depth under the water, the device detonated with a powerful blast the instant a vessel collided with it. The new contraption was a source of both consternation and curiosity on the decks of the Western Powers' ships, as evinced by the nickname it received: the Russian Infernal Machine.

In late May 1855, the first divisions of the enemy's large naval fleets were sighted in the Gulf of Finland. A month later, a brief exchange of fire broke out between the Russian coastal artillery on Santahamina and a British ship conducting reconnaissance. This vessel was one of many spotted operating in the archipelago, prompting concern that the Western Powers were planning a large attack on Suomenlinna. The fear was warranted: on 6 August, a sizeable enemy fleet was observed taking a position due south of Helsinki in the outer archipelago. Three days later, on the morning of 9 August, the 77-vessel armada launched an enormous bombardment of the sea fortress, the likes of which had never been seen in the Nordics. Suddenly, Suomenlinna's walls and ramparts, some of which had survived unscathed for over a hundred years, were thrown into serious jeopardy.

The barrage lasted for two days. It was a one-sided affair, for the Western Powers' cannons had a far greater range than those of the Russians, making it futile for Suomenlinna's defenders to expend gunpowder returning fire. The Russians' saving grace was the chain of sea mines around the sea fortress, Helsinki and the nearby archipelago, for it successfully prevented enemy troops from storming their position. The enemy bombs still caused substantial damage, however, including raging fires, the explosion of four gunpowder stores and the destruction of several ships. In spite of this, the Russian troops did not show any signs of surrendering and, after forty-six hours of bombardment, the French and British guns were abruptly silenced on the morning of Saturday 11 August. Only a few days later, both Russian troops and Helsinki residents looked on with relief as the enemy ships began sailing away from Finland's islets.

The commanders of the Western fleet reported that the operation had been terminated after Suomenlinna had been rendered defenceless. In reality, the assault was called off because the ships' ammunition was starting to run out, and because it quickly became clear that they could not take the fortress without landing forces, which they did not have at their disposal.

A month later, the Western Powers won a decisive victory on the war's main front in Crimea when they captured Sevastopol, the Russian naval base. In London, British military leaders immediately began to make plans to launch a similarly massive attack on the Kronstadt Fortress outside of St Petersburg the following summer.

In the end, this never came to pass, as defeat at Sevastopol extinguished Russia's fighting spirit and led to a peace agreement in March 1856. This forced the newly crowned Emperor, Alexander II, to return the land Russia had captured from the Ottomans in the Black Sea region, and to demilitarise Åland. The outcome of the war resulted in a great loss of prestige for Russia. It had been a dominant force on the European Continent ever since its defeat of Napoleon, but now its military capacity had been found to be severely lacking when set against that of the West. Consequently, Alexander II immediately undertook an extensive modernisation of the Russian Empire's army, infrastructure and economy, which, before long, would have a transformative impact on both Finland and Helsinki.

Although the bombardment of Suomenlinna was a peripheral skirmish in the Crimean War, it received a fair amount of coverage in the Western European and Scandinavian press. The journalists and artists embedded with the naval fleet did their best to portray its actions as a great success, for example, by vastly inflating the Russian losses and by characterising Suomenlinna as the "Gibraltar of the North". The most fanciful illustrations depicted the fortress islands as enormous cliffs rising out of the sea. Vividly coloured paintings of the barrage at night were disseminated in the aftermath of the battle: brimming with flying missiles and blazing fires, they give the impression that Suomenlinna was caught in the midst of a particularly elaborate firework display. It did not take long, though, before more critical accounts of events emerged, since it did not go unnoticed amidst all the jingoistic depictions of the battle that the fortress had not actually surrendered.

The Imperial Army's struggles in the Crimean War had been a cause for optimism in Stockholm. Some among the Swedish leadership had even discussed the idea that things might deteriorate for Russia to such an extent that Finland could be reunited with Sweden. There was little willingness, however, to join the conflict on the Western Powers' side, and the momentum behind the idea quickly fizzled out once peace had been struck. In Finland, public opinion followed an inverse trajectory. Most Finns had felt a strong loyalty towards the Russian cause for the duration of the war, and it was only once everyday life returned to normal and foreign connections were re-established that they began to desire change. There were growing hopes that the Emperor's modernisation programme would bring with it reforms that would strengthen Finland's autonomy and national ambitions.

Such hopes were heightened in Helsinki following its residents' rather atypical experience during the bombardment of Suomenlinna. The Western Powers had, namely, spared the city by directing their enormous cannonade almost exclusively towards the sea fortress. Once this became clear to the inhabitants in the aftermath of the assault, there was a swell of gratitude and pro-Western sentiment among them. Prior to the attack, the mood in the streets had been quite the opposite. The military preparations and rearmament caused the city and its environs to be inundated with Russian troops in the spring of 1854. They were either charged with defending Helsinki, in which case the larger households were duty-bound to quarter a certain number of them, or they were on their way to other positions in Finland, in which case they set up camp in a variety of locations on the outskirts of the city.

Even if scant few Helsinki residents had any idea of how deficient the Russian preparations were, many feared that their city was on the brink of complete destruction, not least because they had heard how Bomarsund had been levelled to the ground. So there was a profound sense of relief when the war's first summer and navigation season passed without an assault on Suomenlinna, although this did not stop some disgruntled murmurings about the impositions of wartime. When the sea ice began to break up in the spring of 1855, however, alarming reports circulated of the Western fleet's operations in the Gulf of Finland. Eventually, the terrible vision that had been haunting the city's residents for the past year became reality, as the enemy's naval forces assembled on Helsinki's horizon. As British and French fire began raining down on Suomenlinna that morning on 9 August, the civil populace in the city rushed to evacuate everything they could from their homes. Some took shelter in the urban green spaces and parks, others set off into Uusimaa's interior.

The panic was not without cause: a few stray shells had struck the southern and western outskirts of Helsinki, which strengthened the citizens' misgivings that the enemy would not spare the city. And, as it happens, they were right to be concerned, since it was by no means inevitable that Helsinki would be granted clemency. When the Russians showed no signs of surrender after twenty-four hours of constant bombardment, the Rear-Admiral of the French fleet, Charles Pénaud, suggested that they should turn their cannons on Helsinki, instead. The plan was to advance with gunboats through the waters north of Suomenlinna, since the fortress's defences were far weaker in that direction. It was only the British commander's unwillingness to risk his own vessels that put an end to the idea and, ultimately, saved Helsinki. As the hours passed and Suomenlinna continued to be the sole target of the bombing, the city's civilians grew emboldened and ventured to follow the fiery spectacle increasingly openly from Ullanlinna and other sites that afforded a good sea view.

August Schauman, the famous chronicler of Helsinki during Finland's Russian era, arrived in the city by horse-drawn carriage on the first night of the assault. Even from a great distance away, he saw "the whole fortress burning like a sea of fire, the bombs' explosions and the rockets' long streams of flames". Once back in the city itself, Schauman hurriedly climbed to the highest point of Ullanlinna and saw in surreal detail the great parabolas made by the bombs as they arched upwards from the enemy boats before curving down and bursting among the fortress's burning buildings.

A much more peaceful—if not picturesque—scene met Schauman and some of his friends the following night, when they strolled through the city's parks and found residents crashed out exhausted on their beds and sofas. As luck would have it, the weather was perfect for such al fresco slumbering. When the roar of the cannons ceased, the city and its surroundings were enveloped in a strange ambiance. The sea lay smooth as a mirror, while from the still-smouldering Suomenlinna could be heard the bells of the Orthodox church calling worshippers to evening prayer, and from the edge of the archipelago echoed sounds of jubilant celebration from some of the Western Powers' ships.

The National Arena

The social reforms implemented by Alexander II across the Russian Empire in the 1860s helped usher in a new era in Finland, too, and nowhere more so than in its main arena for public debate, Helsinki. The Emperor would have preferred to issue the reforms by decree in the Grand Duchy, as he had done in Russia, but they would have been difficult to carry out effectively without the approval of the Diet. And so, after some degree of hesitation, Alexander II agreed to let Finland's Diet of the Estates convene in the autumn of 1863. It had lain dormant since 1809, but, in his opening speech at its assembly in Helsinki, the Emperor promised to let the estates meet regularly henceforth.

Over the next forty-three years, between 1863 and 1906, the Diet passed almost 400 laws, effectively paving the way for a multi-layered civil society and a capitalist economy. This was quite the achievement, given the circumstances: only ten per cent of the adult population had the franchise in the Diet's elections, the four estates met and voted on legislation separately, and its ratification depended entirely on the Emperor's whim. On the other hand, the laws were drafted in committees made up of representatives from all four estates, which developed a political culture of negotiation and compromise that laid the foundation for the democratic parliamentary reform of 1906. A contributing factor was that the social structure and judicial system from Finland's time under Swedish rule had been preserved by the Grand Duchy's central administration during the Diet's fifty-four-year hiatus. This continuity had helped maintain people's belief that, in the words of the old Nordic legal rolls, "a country shall be built with law."

The raft of new legislation in Finland was also influenced by trends in other Nordic countries. Over the preceding decades, the social elite in Helsinki had closely followed how the demands for political rights and freedom of speech had borne fruit in these lands. Those of a liberal persuasion were hoping that Finland would go down a similar route to Sweden, which had replaced its estate system with a bicameral legislature in 1866. The Emperor's goodwill did not extend this far, but, in many other respects, there was a significant expansion of the public sphere and social debate during the 1860s and 1870s.

The first political discussions took place in the country's daily press in 1856, immediately after the Emperor had announced his specific programme of reforms for Finland. At this point, however, such papers were few and far between, and the real breakthrough for the bourgeois public sphere occurred some years later, before and in association with the recall of the Diet, when three new dailies began publication in Helsinki. The first was *Helsingin Uutiset* in 1862, which was set up by young academic Fennomans as a rival to *Suometar*, which had hitherto been the country's leading Fennophile daily paper. The founders of *Helsingin Uutiset* were frustrated by the *Suometar* editors' unwillingness to take a sufficiently pro-Finnish stance in the language debate of the period. Eighteen sixty-two also saw the inception of the liberal *Helsingfors Dagblad*, and, two years later, the prolific writer August Schauman established *Hufvudstadsbladet*. The paper's premise was to provide reader-friendly coverage of the city's cultural and entertainment life, and it proved a resounding success, becoming the biggest-selling daily publication in late-nineteenth-century Finland.

The newspapers were distributed across Finland, but the vast majority of their subscribers lived in Helsinki, which influenced their content from the very beginning. The Fennomans had achieved an important milestone just before the Diet was assembled in 1863, when the Emperor signed a language decree. This declared that Finnish and Swedish would, after a twenty-year transition period, have equal status as administrative languages. The Fennomans' next objective was to mobilise political support to help make Finnish the country's principal public language. To this end, they threw their collective weight behind a new paper, *Uusi Suometar*, in 1869, in which a sizeable number of column inches were given over to news and correspondence from the country's Finnish-speaking regions.

This strategy would ultimately prove effective, and, over four decades, one of its main proponents was the historian and Fennoman Georg Forsman. As with the majority of the other Finnish-language advocates of the era, he had grown up in a Swedish-speaking household. However, unlike the early leader of the Fennoman movement, J. V. Snellman, who never wrote in Finnish or spoke it in public, Forsman was methodical about using Finnish whenever the opportunity presented itself. He Fennicised his name to Yrjö-Koskinen and coined new concepts that were needed before any discussion of social questions could take place in Finnish. Nonetheless, until the 1880s, Swedish remained absolutely dominant as the language of political and economic debate in three of the Diet's four estates: the nobility, the clergy and the burghers. It was only in the peasants' estate that Finnish prevailed, as it was the sole language that many of the representatives knew. When they discussed matters with the other estates, they were, therefore, forced to rely on interpreters. As for the written proceedings of the Senate, these would continue to be recorded in Swedish all the way up to 1902.

The meetings of the estates at the first Diet since 1809 were held in the newly inaugurated House of the Nobility in 1863 and 1864. As the name implies, the building had been constructed by the Finnish nobles; it was neo-Gothic in style, and located in the quarter immediately east of Senate Square. The premises, however, quickly became too small for the other estates, who were given permission to assemble in other meeting places in the city until 1891, when the House of the Estates—a majestic neoclassical building two blocks north of the Senate—was opened for legislative business. In the preceding years, both the Bank of Finland (1883) and the National Archives (1890) had been constructed on the edges of the same small park. In time, it would also become home to statues of two of the most well-known statesmen from the Russian era: J. V. Snellman and Leo

Mechelin. A little over fifty years prior, these blocks of the city had been named "Narinkka Square" after the Russian merchants who set up shop there; now they had been transformed into an architectural expression of the Grand Duchy's growing autonomy.

Reinforcing this impression was the finishing touch applied to the House of the Estates in the early 1900s, namely its triangular gable frieze, "Alexander I and the Diet of Porvoo 1809". The political message was clear as day: the bronze tympanum depicts the Emperor confirming Finland's Swedish "constitutions", his right arm gesturing towards a large tome inscribed with "Lex" and two dates, 1734 and 1772. These denote, respectively, the introduction of Sweden's Civil Code and the passing of King Gustav III's Instrument of Government. The frieze's construction was a symbolic act at a time of fierce political disagreement between Russia and Finland. From the 1890s, the Russian central power wanted to tie the country—which was functioning increasingly as a state within a state—more tightly to the empire. At that point, however, it was already too late to dispel the idea of national identity from the collective consciousness. There are a multitude of opinions in Finland about when and how Finnish nationhood emerged, but, by the time the political reforms took place in the 1860s, the social elite had already reached the unanimous conclusion that the country was unequivocally its own state.

Senate Square continued to serve as the stage for the Russian military's parades and the Emperor's visits, which meant that the plaza was, first and foremost, associated with Finland's role in the Russian Empire. As a result, the statue of Alexander II in the middle of the square has often been interpreted as an expression of Finland's unwavering devotion to the imperial dynasty, but when it was unveiled in the spring of 1894, its message was rather seen as one of conditional loyalty. The date, 1863, is inscribed in the statue's granite base, as a pointed reminder of when the Emperor let the Diet commence its assemblies again. The Maiden of Finland, the female embodiment of the country, also stands at the base, in her guise as the Goddess of Justice. In his speech at the statue's inauguration, Leo Mechelin made her symbolism explicit: he stressed that the Emperor's confirmation of Finland's constitutions had made them inviolable. They could be dislodged by hostile forces "little more than the stormy sea can break the rocks of our shores".

Helsinki's centre, increasingly imbued with symbolism, was where Finland's elite came to work in the late nineteenth century, whether they were involved in civil service, higher education or politics. The vast majority of them had studied at the University of Helsinki, which meant that they were keenly aware of the great surge of national sentiment that the political and social reforms of the 1860s had brought into being. In many respects, the young students came to act as enthusiastic missionaries for this ideology, and even received support from the Finnish state, which approved the construction of Student House on the west end of Aleksanterinkatu. This was to be a dedicated building for the students' social and cultural activities. An essential part of its national fundraising effort came to be the concerts and cultural evenings organised all over the country, at which the students presented Finland's folk poetry and songs to regional audiences. Such events helped strengthen both the idea of a shared Finnish culture and the idea that the students were the great hope of the Fatherland. However, the inauguration of Student House in November 1870 ended up being overshadowed by the language war that had emerged in the wake of the previous years' political reforms.

The conflict would also come to colour the city's theatrical life, which, until the 1860s, had been based in a playhouse on the west end of Esplanadin Puisto. Designed by Engel, it was a beautiful building, but bitterly cold in the Nordic winters. A lack of resources and small audiences hindered the development of a domestic drama scene, so the theatre's programme consisted of troupes of foreign performers and upper-class Finnish amateurs. This continued to be the case even after a much bigger and better-equipped venue opened its doors in the autumn of 1860, at the very spot where Svenska Teatern (The Swedish Theatre) now stands.

This new playhouse lasted barely two years before it was burned to the ground. The city's theatregoers had no choice but to return to Engel's old building, which, in the meantime, had been moved from its former site to the north of Turku Barracks, where the south-eastern end of Arkadiankatu is today. However, the clamour for more fitting premises was so great that, only three years later, a new and equally impressive playhouse—Nya Teatern (The New Theatre)—was constructed on the plot where its predecessor had gone up in smoke. Slowly but surely, the Swedish touring ensembles extended their contracts with the theatre, which gave more opportunities for the performance of Swedish-language scripts produced by domestic playwrights, including the multi-talented wordsmith, Zacharias Topelius. Still, since almost all the actors engaged at the Nya Teatern before the 1900s came from Sweden, their Standard Swedish pronunciation could not always do justice to the domestic plays' Finland Swedish dialogue.

In terms of establishing a national dramatic arts scene, a far more seismic event was the founding of the first Finnish-language theatre in the spring of 1872. Known, fittingly, as the Finnish Theatre, it put on its productions in Engel's old playhouse on Arkadiankatu until the early 1900s. A pair of siblings stood behind the initiative: Kaarlo (formerly Karl) and Emilie Bergbom, who had already made a sizeable splash a few years earlier by putting on the country's first-ever Finnish-language play. This was *Lea*, by Aleksis Kivi, the then-unknown writer who would go on to be a pioneer of Finnish fiction. Today, he is celebrated as Finland's national writer, and Finnish Literature Day is organised every year on 10 October, the date of his birthday. The premiere of his play, on 10 May 1869 at the Nya Teatern, has also gone down in history, for it is considered the birthday of Finnish theatre. It was largely off the back of the production's success that the Suomalainen Seura (The Finnish Society) was set up only a few months later, with the aim of supporting the use of Finnish across the arts.

As with the majority of Fennophile cultural figures in 1870s Helsinki, the Bergbom siblings had only learned Finnish in adulthood, which meant that, at first, their theatre company usually communicated in Swedish behind the scenes. Indeed, a notable number of the Finnish Theatre's personnel spoke Finnish just as haltingly as the managing duo. On stage, however, it was a different story: the actors uttered each line with such grammatically flawless and carefully articulated Finnish that they played an active role in shaping a "correct" version of the language in the public consciousness. The Swedish actress Charlotta Raa-Winterhjelm, who was then held in high regard in Helsinki's theatre scene, was a pioneer in this regard: in spite of not understanding a word of Finnish, she was sensational in the lead role in *Lea*, having learned every line off by heart.

Until this time, there had been a number of different ways of enunciating and intonating Finnish that had competed with each other for prominence in Helsinki's public life. It took the emergence of an intelligentsia that was ideologically motivated to speak Finnish before a linguistic norm gradually started to establish itself. Over the coming decades, it spread across the land through the steadily growing number of Finnish-speaking grammar schools, since all their teachers were educated at the University of Helsinki. There is surprisingly little information in the historical record about how this Finnish actually sounded.

What can be stated is that, in spite of its proponents' goal to establish the status of Finnish as a "genuine" language, it was heavily influenced by the pronunciation, diction and sentence construction of Swedish until well into the twentieth century. It has been claimed that this version of the language lasted longest of all among the University of Helsinki's Finnish-speaking professors. Even after the Second World War, some of them still sounded distinctly like they were Swedish-speaking Finns.

In the late nineteenth century, it was certainly not pre-ordained that Finnish would reach a dominant position in society in just a few decades' time. Many remained openly sceptical about the idea that Finnish could ever be the language of administrative governance. Moreover, in the 1870s, the Svecoman movement emerged among a faction of the city's Swedish-speaking students as a rival to the Fennomans. It asserted that Finland's Swedish-speaking population ought to form its own nationality. A similarly reserved attitude towards Finnish also prevailed among Russia's political elite, whose support for the Finnish language was principally born out of the cynical assumption that it would weaken the status of Swedish and thereby facilitate Finland's transition to a Russian-speaking public sphere.

A physical manifestation of their conviction that Finland would have a Russian future came in the form of the Uspenski Cathedral, which was inaugurated in 1868 on the highest rock in Katajanokka, due east of the city centre. Helsinki's Russian Orthodox community had, since 1827, held its services at the Holy Trinity Church on Unioninkatu, while out on Suomenlinna the military received their pastoral care in the fortress's Alexander Nevsky Church. These were, however, judged insufficient to serve the city's growing Russian-speaking populace, and so Uspenski Cathedral was born. When it was opened for the congregation's use, it was the biggest Orthodox place of worship outside of the denomination's heartland. The cathedral was built partly out of the bricks taken from the Bomarsund Fortress on Åland that had been destroyed so comprehensively during the Crimean War. It quickly came to be regarded as the architectural companion to the Lutheran St Nicholas's Church in Senate Square.

The same repurposed building material was used in the construction of the Alexander Theatre on Bulevardi, which held its opening performance in early 1880. It had been designed for the use of the city's Russian officials and garrison troops, but, because it did not have its own ensemble, they had to rely on touring troupes to put on shows, particularly those from St Petersburg. In the winter of 1917–18, prior to the Germans taking control of Helsinki in April, the theatre was used as a meeting place by the Red revolutionaries, and even played host to some performances by their amateur dramatic societies. The productions they put on, however, would pale in comparison to the drama that their actions would bring to the capital's streets, and to towns and cities across the country.

4

INDUSTRY AND INDEPENDENCE

Technology, Economy, Demography

On 11 September 1870, the railway line between Helsinki and St Petersburg opened, to great excitement in the press. Amidst the pomp and fanfare were voices of caution, like the influential writer Zacharias Topelius, who worried that this high-speed connection would lead to Finland's trade and industry being increasingly dominated by the Russian capital. It did not take long, however, for Topelius to change his tune and instead characterise the new railway as the greatest geographical transformation in Finnish history since the first settlement was established in the country.

This reassessment proved prescient. Over the next four decades, Finland's economy would see plenty of benefit from these direct railway connections. As time went by, they became faster and further reaching, establishing links with both Russian and Continental markets. The railway network from St Petersburg and Moscow stretched its tentacles all across Europe, and, by the early 1900s, a traveller could take the train from Helsinki all the way to Vladivostok on the Pacific Ocean. Indeed, it was Finland's capital and best-connected city that derived the most benefit of all from the railway. If the city's proximity to St Petersburg had been a dilemma under Swedish rule, it was now quite the reverse, for its location contributed considerably to the whole country's prosperity. In addition to its improved rail connections, Helsinki was also Finland's principal import harbour, which meant it was well-placed to profit from the increased steamboat traffic in this period. This arrived first from other harbours in the Baltic Sea region, then gradually from ports all across the world's oceans.

At the outset of the 1870s, Finland was still one of the poorest countries in Europe. Only a few years earlier, a prolonged cold snap had wrought a catastrophic famine on it, killing an estimated 150,000 of its populace. The railway brought with it access to the grain crop in southern Russia and Ukraine, which was so large that, until the First World War, a significant portion of the harvest was exported to different corners of Europe. With the grain supply outsourced, agriculture in southern Finland became more focused on the production of meat and dairy to be sold to St Petersburg. This resulted in increased market orientation, bringing into being a network of mechanised dairies in close proximity to the rail stations. At the same time, a new industry emerged in Finland: domestic cellulose and paper manufacturing, which benefitted just as greatly from the railway and the steadily growing demand from the Russian market.

The driving force behind all these changes was the increasing economic integration between countries across the world. This was the so-called first wave of globalisation, which started in the late nineteenth century and ended with the outbreak of the First World War. It was set in motion by the combined influence of a number of technological innovations (not least steam power, railways and electricity), which led to seismic transformations in societies that were best able to take them into use. The Nordic countries were undoubtedly in a position to benefit: they were law-abiding civil societies underpinned by well-functioning communications networks and Protestant values. In Finland, it was Helsinki that prospered the most from this global shift: its population quadrupled between 1870 and 1910, from 32,100 to 136,500. This was largely due to the city's improved communications, its fast-expanding industrial and service sectors and its increasingly modern infrastructure.

In fact, Helsinki's population had been just 22,000 at the start of the 1860s, but a series of economic reforms coupled with the opening of the railway line to Häme in 1862 had caused it to shoot up almost fifty per cent by 1870. At this stage, a significant chunk of the new arrivals still came from Uusimaa and Häme. However, as the rail network started to expand across Finland, an increasing amount of migrants descended on Helsinki from other parts of the country. As a result, by the start of the 1910s, over a quarter of the city's migrant population hailed from the eastern half of Finland.

As might be expected, two-thirds of the migrants were young, unmarried and from the countryside, the sort of workforce that was much sought after in the manufacturing and service sectors. A substantial proportion of them were also women, which was partly a response to the demand of the middle and upper classes for diligent servants. As the decades progressed, an increasing share of people moved to Helsinki with their families. There was a growing need for skilled labour that such older workers could provide, and there were also improved housing options for this demographic due to the emergence of a commercial building industry. By the outset of the 1910s, families made up forty per cent of the city's migrants.

This influx of newcomers caused a comprehensive shift in Helsinki's linguistic composition. In the early 1870s, well over half of the city's population spoke Swedish as their first language, while a quarter spoke Finnish and a little over a tenth spoke

Russian. Over the next decades, Helsinki's Finnish-speaking population swelled dramatically. In 1890, those registered as Finnish speakers accounted for nearly half of the total inhabitants, and two decades later they already constituted sixty per cent of its population—which is certainly not to suggest that the Swedish-speaking total had decreased. On the contrary, it had grown by 18,000 people between 1890 and 1910.

Helsinki, then, reached its peak as a multilingual city during this time. Before the upsurge in migration, Swedish had been the dominant everyday language of the city, and after the First World War, a growing proportion of the populace could only communicate in Finnish. In the decades around the turn of the century, however, the majority of Helsinki's inhabitants could at least get by in both languages. It is worth keeping this in mind when looking at the language registration statistics, recorded from the 1880s onwards, since they do not give a nuanced picture of the words and expressions that residents used to socialise and shape their days.

In the city's commercial, administrative and academic circles, Russian and German were also commonly used. It paid to be proficient in Russian if you had to interact with the sizeable military presence in the city, even more so if you wanted to profit from the steadily growing movement of goods and manpower across Russia's vast realm. As such, many Finnish officers, businessmen, engineers and sea captains learned fluent Russian during their careers in the ever-expanding empire. So, too, did the numerous artisans and railway employees that regularly commuted between Helsinki and St Petersburg. Moreover, Russian was a compulsory subject in all public grammar schools. In the early 1900s, Russian authorities ordered, in connection with their Russification strives, a sharp increase in the amount of teaching hours to be devoted to it, which naturally did not do much for the subject's popularity among pupils.

Among scholars, on the other hand, German was the dominant language internationally. As such, it was, like Russian, compulsory for grammar school students. A grounding in German was also important for anyone working in technical professions, as it was for anyone engaged in commerce around the Gulf of Finland, and not just in the Estonian port towns, but also, to a very great extent, in St Petersburg, too. The imperial capital's biggest and most prominent minority was German-speaking. The language also assumed more significance over the late nineteenth century, as Finland's foreign trade with Germany increased at a steady rate. By 1910, it was, in fact, almost the same size as foreign trade with Russia, which had fallen by over a third as a proportion of the total since the early 1870s, from forty-six to twenty-nine per cent.

The increasing imports from Germany created a trade imbalance that was countered by exporting more goods to Russia. From the former, Finland principally received shipments of grain, metallic and mechanical components, colonial products and textiles, while it sent comestibles and paper to the latter, mainly by train. The forest industry remained far and away Finland's biggest export sector, although Helsinki did not see any of its shipments to Western markets, as these were dispatched from other ports. Indeed, the city's share of Finland's total exports steadily shrank to around six per cent in the early 1900s; in contrast, nearly a third of the country's imported goods passed through Helsinki's harbours at this time.

Until the First World War, the beating heart of Helsinki's economy was the production of industrial goods for both the capital region and the domestic market more broadly. Machine shops and metal manufacturers played a central role here: already in the 1870s, they employed the majority of the city's factory workers, and they accounted for a third of the Finnish industry's total turnover. Long into the twentieth century, they would continue to be Helsinki's biggest employers and the most profitable operators in the industrial sector, even as new products were developed and new consumption trends emerged. Tobacco and sweets were two other lucrative lines of production, which together made up a third of the city's industrial output.

In 1914, the machine shops and metal manufacturers still employed thirty per cent of Helsinki's industrial workforce and accounted for a little over twenty per cent of the city's turnover. The most important products were unquestionably engines, iron bridges and ships for the burgeoning capital and its environs, as well as the growing towns, cities and sites of industry across the country. Smaller and less elaborate metalware, like milk churns and a miscellany of cans and boxes, were always in demand, too. They were extremely useful in large-scale distribution, which was becoming standard practice in a society where all the more products were manufactured industrially.

Other noteworthy metal products were water mains, sewage pipes and radiators, which were first introduced in Finnish cities in the 1870s. The need for better quality water became acute in Helsinki in the 1860s, leading to the installation of city pipes that were finally ready for use in 1878. However, the water mains originally only ran through the centre, which meant that many residents still had to content themselves with water from the city's district wells. These were considerable in number, but often also a considerable threat to public health. By the early 1890s, the western and northern suburbs of the city had been connected to the mains supply, too.

All the way up to the 1980s, the city sourced its water from the Vantaa River. It was pumped up to a water tower in Alppila, on the northern fringe of the city, in the late 1800s, and distributed from there to all the buildings on the mains network. It did not take long, however, for concern to grow that the water could be contaminated by bacteria from the populated areas along the

Vantaa River. Different filtration systems were trialled, but it was only with the use of chemical purification in 1909 that the water flowing out of Helsinki's taps was guaranteed to be safe to drink. In parallel with the water supply, the city also installed a sewage system that significantly improved hygiene in its centre. Unfortunately, it had the opposite effect on the city's shoreline, for the effluvia flowed straight into the sea, contaminating the water and creating a horrible stench around the mouths of the sewers. Over time, these were moved to more remote locations in the city. In the 1910s, the mere thought of taking a dip off the coast of Sörnäinen, where one of the city's large sewers discharged its contents, must have been enough to induce nausea.

It is clear that the fast-expanding city experienced a fair few growing pains. Still, as the years passed, the municipal decision-makers developed a better understanding of how to plan and manage urban infrastructure. Gas lighting had been introduced in many European capitals in the 1820s, but it took another four decades before the first streetlamps were set aglow in the centre of Helsinki, on 1 September 1862. Prior to this point, the city simply did not have a large enough market to make commercial gas production viable. A privately owned gasworks was finally established in 1860, located right opposite Turku Barracks, on the same plot where Postitalo (the Post Office's landmark main building) would later be constructed. The company was granted a forty-year concession from the city for its activities, and soon began to supply gas to private households, too. Little by little, however, it began to lose these individual subscribers after a private electric company began operating in the city in the late autumn of 1884. The city council acquired the gas company just before the turn of the century, and, after a prolonged public debate, it also purchased the electric utility in 1906.

Helsinki's adoption of electricity is a good example of how it started to modernise at a faster pace than the majority of cities on the Continent in the 1880s. The new technology was taken into use in London, Paris and Strasbourg in 1882, or two years ahead of the Finnish capital. In most other European cities, however, it was well into the 1890s before commercial electric companies sparked into life. In Berlin, an electric power plant was set up in the same year as in Helsinki, but since the German capital already had an established distribution network for gas, its transition to electricity was nowhere near as quick.

Berlin dwarfed Helsinki, having over a million inhabitants in the early 1880s, but the latter's small scale worked to its advantage in this context. In fact, it was the exceptionally rapid expansion of Helsinki's building stock at this time that, in essence, made the city's quick electrification possible. Electric lighting was easy to install in new industrial premises and residential buildings, which enticed foreign businesses to enter the market and which, in turn, quickly made the installation costs considerably lower for electricity than for gas. This maelstrom of activity resulted in a burgeoning domestic expertise in electrotechnical engineering, with Helsinki's Polytechnic Institute offering the subject from 1885. In 1908, this institute was turned into a university, and today it is a part of Aalto University in Espoo.

The introduction of the telephone in Helsinki followed a similar pattern. Alexander Graham Bell was granted a patent for his new method of communication in the United States in March 1876, and that very same year it was tested in Helsinki by the city's curious technology students. In 1882, with the Senate having agreed to finance the construction of local telephone networks, private telephone companies were founded in four Finnish cities, including Helsinki. The country's businessmen had clearly found a lucrative market, for only three years later there were nineteen telephone companies operating in Finland. By and large, it was the denizens of Helsinki who were at the forefront of this development: by the early 1910s, there were nearly 9,000 telephone subscriptions in the city, which equated to sixty per 1,000 inhabitants. This ratio might seem trifling in a world where the mobile phone is a cornerstone of our quotidian existence, but it was many times higher than almost anywhere else in the Russian Empire, which in 1917 had an average of 1.3 telephones per 1,000 people.

What caused such a craze for telephones in Helsinki? One clear catalyst was the decision of Finland's legislative body in the late nineteenth century to introduce regulations under which private telephone and electric companies could effectively operate. This stimulated investment and competition in the market, which quickly made it possible for the urban middle class to acquire home telephones. The Swedish government adopted a similar approach, but things did not develop quite so quickly in Russia, where the spread of the new technology was hampered by the political and the military authorities' concerns about letting the populace communicate too freely. In contrast, the Finnish Senate's supportive attitude enabled the development of a nationwide telephone network.

Many visitors to the city were struck by how quickly Helsinki's inhabitants had become accustomed to their telephones, noting that they were barely aware of how often they used them on a daily basis. In an essay collection about his time as Spanish consul in Helsinki in the late 1890s, Ángel Ganivet asserted that the telephone had become almost as common in the bourgeois household as kitchen appliances, and often functioned as an extra human presence. If a state of uncertainty prevailed about anything, a person could ring up an absent other to make an enquiry and receive a response "quite as if someone in company had given an answer".

North of Pitkäsilta

Another enlightening perspective on Helsinki around the turn of the century comes from the panorama taken by photographer Signe Brander in 1909. It shows the city on a beautiful summer's day from the vantage point of the tower of St Nicholas's Church, the same spot from which the Finnish photographer Eugen Hoffers had captured his shot of the city forty-three years earlier, in 1866. A comparison of the two reveals the sheer extent to which Helsinki had grown in height and breadth in less than half a century. In Hoffers's panorama, the Guards' Barracks stand tall in the south amidst the low wooden houses, with Ullanlinna's barren rocks and the Observatory rising highest behind them. In Brander's picture, these earlier landmarks are obscured by taller houses and the Observatory Hill's leafy park. Instead, it is the twin spires of St John's Church that catch the eye, along with the Erottaja fire station tower, with its appearance of a red-brick battlement. Both buildings were completed in 1891, the former in a neo-Gothic style, the latter with more of a neo-Renaissance air.

The biggest difference between the two 360° panoramas is, nonetheless, the city's landscape to the north, across Pitkäsilta Bridge. In Hoffers's photo from the 1860s, Kallio, Hakaniemi and Sörnäinen consist of a thin scattering of wooden houses, workshops and storehouses that lie mainly in the west near Töölönlahti or sit perched on the bare rocky hills. In contrast, Brander's picture from the late 1900s shows the districts filled with tightly packed working-class neighbourhoods, factories and high chimney stacks that disappear into the smoky haze of the horizon. She shot her panorama as part of a wider project: a commission to document the old sights and scenes of the city that were fast being erased by the frenzied building activity of the time. The result is a collection of pictures that provides a hugely informative and ethnographically detailed overview of the building stock and street life in early-twentieth-century Helsinki.

Of the nearly one thousand photos snapped by Brander, it is those from Helsinki's northern working-class quarter that contain the most dramatic contrasts and the most edifices from bygone eras. By this time, the neighbourhood extended from Pitkäsilta Bridge to the southern slopes of Kallio, and from there north-east along Hämeentie towards Vanhakaupunki and the Vantaa River. The catalyst for its growth was the opening of the railway line between Pasila and Sörnäinen Harbour in 1863. Over time, this connection helped create a cohesive logistical network of ports, factories, workshops and labourers' homes all located in close proximity. Worker accommodation was concentrated on Kallio's hills and in the districts of Sörnäinen and Hermanni, while manufacturing and production took place closer to the ports and the railway. Another important milestone in the area's development was the reclamation of the strait between Siltasaari and Kallio that took place in the 1890s and resulted in the construction of Hakaniemi Market Square, which has remained a bustling retail locale to this day.

The sociologist Heikki Waris published his doctoral dissertation on the birth of this working-class neighbourhood in 1932. Now a classic in the field of social history, it records how the community started to rapidly expand in the late nineteenth century, with its population more than doubling from 4,000 in 1880 to 9,400 in 1890. It maintained almost the same pace of growth over the next two decades to total 39,200 people in 1910, and by the First World War nearly a third of all Helsinki's residents lived north of Pitkäsilta. This seismic increase was largely down to the influx of Finns from other areas of the country: at the turn of the century, for example, two thirds of the neighbourhood's population had not been born in Helsinki. The fact that most of the migrants were young also meant that these northern districts experienced a faster natural growth (birth rate minus death rate) than other regions of the city.

It is no coincidence that children and adolescents feature prominently in Signe Brander's photographs of this working-class neighbourhood: long into the 1900s, they made up over forty per cent of its inhabitants. Although her primary concern was the city's buildings, the scenes she captured along Hämeentie and in some of the nearby city districts are teeming with young folk. Some of these shots, it is true, make it look as though the children are in a rural idyll rather than a grimy and noisy centre of industry, but Brander also trained her lens on some of the large blast sites and construction projects that were then ongoing in Kallio. The contrasting environs of these pictures underline the scale of the transition that the city was experiencing.

Manual labourers, of course, did not live exclusively on the northern side of Pitkäsilta, and could also be found in other parts of the city. However, half of all such workers did reside there in the early 1910s: they did not want to live too far from their place of employment, and Helsinki's factories and workshops were, largely for logistical reasons, concentrated to the north of the city centre. This was an unabashedly proletarian neighbourhood, with seventy-five per cent of the families registered as working class, considerably higher than the average of fifty-five to sixty per cent for Helsinki as a whole. The most common professions were listed as general labourer and factory labourer, while only a tenth of the inhabitants stated that they were merchants or in the civil service.

The great stream of new workers into Helsinki led to a chronic housing shortage. When this was combined with meagre incomes, unhygienic conditions and a baby boom, it created social suffering and an understandable resentment towards the better-off residents in the inner city. Even large families had to make do with one-room accommodation, which typically contained a sofa bed, a stove and some chairs. There might also have been space for a rocking chair, a pull-out bed, a cradle and a cupboard with a fold-out counter, on which food could be prepared for cooking. Raising a family in such conditions demanded an industrious and well-organised mother, one who would most likely have to juggle her domestic duties with paid employment outside the home. Not infrequently, she would also have to contend with the tribulations wrought by an inebriated husband.

The arduous daily life in the northern region of the city naturally came to shape the political sympathies of its populace, who, even before Finland's voting reform act in 1906, leaned sharply to the left. The country's Workers' Party had been founded in 1899; it changed its name to the Social Democratic Party four years later and adopted a socialist manifesto. During the general strike that spread to Finland from Russia in the autumn of 1905, the party's radical element had even been prepared to initiate a revolution. Its leadership, however, were more interested in reforming than overthrowing the system: they believed that universal and equal suffrage would pave the way for a more egalitarian society. Their approach certainly resonated with the nation at large, for the Social Democrats emerged as clear winners in the first democratic parliamentary elections in 1907, gaining forty per cent of the vote, or 80 out of the 200 seats available.

Their popularity continued to increase in the years that followed, and in the next parliamentary elections in 1911 they claimed 86 seats. Their share of the vote in northern Helsinki's most working-class neighbourhoods was over sixty per cent, which indicates why the area had a reputation among both labourers and the bourgeoisie as a hotbed of socialism. Another contributing factor to this perception was the construction of Workers' House (today officially known as *Paasitorni*), a stately Jugend building a couple of blocks to the west of Hakaniemi

133

Market Square. Completed in 1908, it became a meeting place for all strands of the political labour movement. So, too, did the square itself, which developed into an increasingly symbolic location in Finnish politics. As the years went by, a number of the country's trade unions built properties and opened their offices around its perimeter and in the neighbouring streets.

The demand for manual labour was not confined to the northern districts of Helsinki, of course, and vibrant working-class communities developed around Ruoholahti and Punavuori, close to the city's coast in the west and south-west. In common with their northern counterparts, they grew up around a new railway connection, this one to the city's western harbours. As a rule, their living quarters were larger than those north of Pitkäsilta, since skilled labourers, employed in professions like brewing and shipbuilding, made up a large proportion of the districts' working population. This gave the communities the financial clout to found their own housing companies to help collectively own and manage their buildings, resulting in quarters full of well-maintained wooden houses and courtyards.

The future Social Democrat leader and Minister Väinö Tanner was raised in one of these blocks in Ruoholahti, and his childhood memories provide a vivid depiction of everyday life in Helsinki during the 1880s and 1890s. His father, a railwayman, had joined forces with a number of other skilled labourers to found Finland's first worker-owned housing company, Alku, in 1886. Together, they moved into a new block of wooden buildings on the corner of Eerikinkatu and Hietalahdenkatu. While the owners of this company were all diligent and enterprising individuals, their families' living conditions were only a shade better than the most cramped quarters north of Pitkäsilta, for each of Alku's homes comprised a kitchen and a small room. Tanner's father could afford to send both his children to grammar school and thereby help them climb the social ladder, but in order to facilitate this, the family had to rent out their extra room over the winter season, so they spent much of each year living exclusively in the kitchen.

Tanner belonged to one of the first intakes at Helsinki Finnish Real Lyceum, an upper-secondary school specialising in modern languages and natural sciences that was founded in 1891. The majority of its pupils were from middle-class homes, so Tanner, during his school years, picked up bourgeois social etiquette that later served him well as a parliamentarian and as chief executive officer of the cooperative trading company Elanto. He also became conscious of the class conflicts engulfing Helsinki in the late 1800s. These were often seen by contemporaries as synonymous with language debates, since a large part of the city's public and commercial life was still held in the clutches of the Swedish-speaking upper and middle class.

The municipal reform of the 1860s had got rid of ruling magistrates in towns and cities, replacing them with a representative assembly. A person's right to vote for candidates was determined by how much municipal tax they paid. This meant that Helsinki's affairs were, in practice, governed by a handful of wealthy and, typically, Swedish-speaking residents until the democratisation of municipal elections in the autumn of 1918. They consciously developed their city into a modern and well-functioning society, but rarely prioritised measures to directly improve the living conditions of its poorest citizens.

Nonetheless, these clashes across the class divide were not solely, nor even principally, about language, and it would be a mischaracterisation to cast them in this light. A significant portion of Helsinki's migrant labourers came from Swedish-speaking coastal regions in Uusimaa and Ostrobothnia. Even in the early 1900s, a third of those living north of the Pitkäsilta registered their mother tongue as Swedish. Moreover, almost a third of the neighbourhood's residents considered themselves bilingual, a reflection of the fact that an increasing number of them had grown up in environments where both Finnish and Swedish were actively used.

Marriages across the language divide were common, and the offspring of such unions typically grew up bilingual. Such was the case with Väinö Tanner: his father, Gustaf Thomasson, hailed from a rural Swedish-speaking district; his mother, Maria Räsänen, grew up speaking Finnish, and only learned Swedish when she was employed as a domestic servant at the family home of a wealthy factory owner. Tanner's family spoke Finnish at home, but, as he himself noted, Swedish was so prevalent in his everyday surroundings that he already spoke it fluently as a child. Even if his memoirs cast a critical eye over the dominance of the Swedish-speaking upper and middle classes in late-nineteenth-century Helsinki, he freely admitted that his knowledge of the language had proved a real asset throughout his life.

Far into the twentieth century, being bilingual was a clear advantage in the Helsinki labour market. Working-class youths who knew both Finnish and Swedish found it easier to get a position in the commercial world, and they could quickly rise through the industrial ranks, too. Not least because foremen were typically expected to know both languages, since they were the principal line of communication between the workers and the company management. In some highly skilled sectors, such as metalworking, metal casting and carpentry, Swedish-speaking workers were, for a long time, over-represented. This was largely down to established tradition, which also gave them access to the networks that were necessary to prosper in such professions. Even so, language was not considered a controversial issue in quotidian settings: when gangs of working-class boys came to blows with each other, it was not their Finnish or Swedish tongue that they were defending, rather their quarter of the neighbourhood.

In the late nineteenth century, comparable bilingual working-class communities grew up around the industries and workshops that were established near railway stations in the rural municipalities bordering Helsinki. Although officially beyond the boundaries of the growing industrial city, their ties to it determined the pace of their work and the patterns of their existence. And the bigger the built-up areas on the outskirts of Helsinki became, the more intensely the capital was involved in another integration project enabled by the railway: that of tying Finland ever more tightly to the Russian Empire.

The Young Finns' Golden Age

The shift from a Swedish to a Finnish public sphere over this period caused greater strife among the city's bourgeoisie. The language question increasingly came to encompass a fight over government posts and other public positions in society. In the city administration, Swedish maintained its dominant status until the democratic municipal reform of 1918, but in other contexts Finnish usurped it as the language of choice. It was a landmark epoch for the Finnish language, which historian Bernhard Estlander would later describe as "a spring flood, sudden and furious, but also invigorating and life-giving".

Similar linguistic battles took place in many other regions of Europe, but Finland's was exceptional in both intensity and pace of change. Indeed, it is reasonable to doubt whether any other language on the Continent broke through as successfully as Finnish did. A key factor on its march to national dominance was the founding of Finnish-language grammar schools in all the larger provincial towns in the early 1870s. A decade later, a growing band of Finnish-educated students started their studies at the University of Helsinki, and set about shaking up public life in the capital. By the 1890s, as both their careers and Finland's civil society developed apace, they were able to harness the power of new technologies to heighten their demands for political and national rights.

These educated upstarts branded themselves "the Young Finns", and their advance took place on a number of political, social and cultural fronts. In the Diet, they increasingly positioned themselves in contrast to the Old Finns' policy of appeasement towards Russia, and ultimately allied with the law and order movement, which until then had been chiefly Suecophile in character. In so doing, they assumed an ever more central role in the fight against Russification measures in Finland during the late nineteenth and early twentieth centuries. This established the reputations of the leading Young Finns, and gave them a great deal of political influence when Finland gained independence in December 1917. Unlike the Old Finns, who saw Finnishness as principally a cultural matter, the Young Finns considered the battle over language to be primarily about equality, which, in essence, put them on the same page as the liberal movements elsewhere in the Nordics.

Little by little, the Young Finns captured the ground that had previously been occupied by the liberal circle behind the *Helsingfors Dagblad* newspaper. Although the latter group viewed the demands for more Finnish-language representation with reservation, they were, nonetheless, staunch advocates of political and social reform. *Helsingfors Dagblad* ceased publication in 1889, but a group of Young Finn journalists started their own daily paper—*Päivälehti*—in autumn that same year. This took up the reformist mantle, and quickly became more influential than its Swedish predecessor had ever been. It was not long before the new title provoked the ire of the Russian authorities: they shut it down in 1904, but almost immediately it was revived as *Helsingin Sanomat*, which later developed into one of the most prominent liberal mouthpieces in the Nordics. It remains the bestselling newspaper in Finland to this day.

Few at the turn of the twentieth century would have considered *Päivälehti* to be the direct descendant of *Helsingfors Dagblad*. It was not only their languages that were dissimilar, but also their social networks. The editors of *Helsingfors Dagblad* were long in the tooth and deep-rooted in Helsinki's Swedish-speaking high society, while the Young Finns at *Päivälehti* were barely thirty, and many of them painted themselves as irascible Fennophile authors and debaters. One of these firebrands was Juhani Aho, the son of a pastor from North Savo, whose varied and extensive oeuvre has come to have a significant influence on the development of modern written Finnish.

That the Young Finns' language was more vibrant and more direct than the stiff Finnish of the previous Fennophile generation was partly a consequence of the linguistic shift in public life. In the 1880s, Finnish was simply used more frequently, and in more contexts, than ever before. But it was also down to the Young Finns themselves: they were talented linguists who drew inspiration from the cultural trends in Scandinavia and on the Continent. When they connected these influences to their own experiences of the upheaval that was then taking place in Finnish society, they imbued the language with a new spirit and flair, qualities that were markedly absent from the rigid formality of the Swedish-language literature of the period.

A good example of this rejuvenated Finnish is Juhani Aho's first novel *Helsinkiin* ("To Helsinki", 1889), in which the author's alter ego travels by steamboat and train down from his hometown in Kuopio to the nation's capital, where he is going to begin his university studies. The closer he gets to Helsinki, the more clearly he perceives the class and language distinctions among his fellow passengers, and starts to wonder where he himself really belongs. Fresh off the train in Helsinki, his friends encourage him to go boozing in a restaurant, before ending the night with a visit to a brothel.

Many reviewers were offended by the unadorned tone and candid observations of Aho's naturalism. On the other hand, they were obviously impressed by his ability to capture the sense of Helsinki's rapid growth and pulsating nature in a few well-chosen lines and snapshots. In Aho's next novel *Yksin* ("Alone", 1890), published only a year later, Aho's lovelorn alter ego heads off on a study trip to Paris. As the steamboat weighs anchor in the South Harbour, he lets his gaze sweep over Helsinki, radiant in summer's glow, and finds himself awestruck by its beauty and vitality.

Although technological advancements made it increasingly easy for Finns to venture out from their northern European periphery into the wider world, Finnish culture did not yet travel quite so readily. As such, Helsinki remained the gathering place for Finland's cultural elite of the period, for it was where they were in greatest demand. In the early twentieth century, one subset of the country's leading artists formed the Lake Tuusula Artistic Community (*Tuusulanjärven taiteilijayhteisö*) in Järvenpää, a small locality 40 kilometres north of the capital. Those who built villas there included Juhani Aho, composer Jean Sibelius and his wife Aino, who was one of the renowned Järnefelt family of artists that formed a key part of the Young Finn movement. Thanks to Järvenpää's excellent railway link with Helsinki, the artists' idyllic rural surroundings were no barrier to them keeping *au courant* with the city's thriving cultural scene.

In his youth, Sibelius had composed a number of his symphonies while living abroad in the great European cities of Berlin and Vienna. After returning to Finland in the early 1890s, he found himself, like so many other artists, overindulging in Helsinki's pubs and taverns. Although he had periods of sobriety, his taste for alcohol would come back to haunt him in later periods of his life. His fondness for the city's nightlife was so notorious that, when he wrote the music to a play about the sixteenth-century Danish King Christian II (Op. 27) in 1898, some Helsinki residents facetiously claimed to hear, in the notes of its dance movement, the words "I'm going back, back to Kämp." They were referencing Sibelius's frequent visits to the hotel and restaurant, which became a favourite haunt of the Young Finns after it opened in 1887, and which continues to operate on Pohjoisesplanadi to this day. The debauched life of Helsinki's late-nineteenth-century artists is also captured by Akseli Gallen-Kallela's symbolic painting *Symposion* (1894). This depicts himself and Sibelius, together with a couple of other famous musicians, gathered contemplatively around a restaurant table laden with drinks, all looking decidedly worse for wear.

Gallen-Kallela was part of perhaps the leading generation of Finnish painters. They took inspiration from what they found on their frequent trips to the Continent, and are today celebrated as some of Finland's most revered artists. Another of their number was Albert Edelfelt, who made a name for himself in the Parisian art world and as a court painter in St Petersburg. Even with all his travels abroad, Edelfelt also kept a studio in Helsinki for the majority of his career, where he put the finishing touches to some of the finest landscape paintings of the city ever produced.

His most acclaimed work is surely *Nyländska Jaktklubbens hamn* ("The Uusimaa Yacht Club's Harbour"), which he painted for Finland's pavilion at the world's fair held in Paris in 1900. Today found hanging in the Presidential Palace, the picture shows the sailing boats of the yacht club and a passing steamboat in the foreground, while the Empire-style city stands bright and tall in the distance. Rising from the centre is St Nicholas's Church, its white tones contrasting with the red brick of Uspenski Cathedral at the painting's edge. Nonetheless, perhaps the pick of Edelfelt's Helsinki scenes is one from the mid-1890s that he painted looking northwards from the window of his attic studio on Liisankatu in the northern end of the bourgeois quarters. In the foreground, the wintry view is dominated by the snow-covered descent to Pitkäsilta Bridge and the strait's dark water, which is just at the point of freezing over. Further back, the landscape opens up to reveal the bridge's northern abutments, the factories of Siltasaari and the snow-covered roofs of Kallio's jumbled stock of houses.

Aho, Sibelius, Gallen-Kallela and Edelfelt are just a few examples of the authors and artists who entered fecund periods in late-nineteenth-century Helsinki. It is for good reason that this era is still considered a cultural golden age in Finland, when the creative elite's technical ability was exceptionally high and their eye for international trends unusually sharp. It was also the first time that Finnish artists received attention abroad, which, given the ongoing constitutional conflict with Russia, was a particular source of pride for Finns of the period. Political campaigns actively highlighted this success, which was, without doubt, partly a result of the musical and artistic institutions established in Finland during the nineteenth century. Yet, above all, it was the dramatic upswing in the country's economy and the improved foreign connections that gave these talented artists the opportunity to absorb new ideas from the wider world and integrate them into their creative endeavours.

Indeed, this golden age was by no means unique to Finland. The whole of Europe saw a comparable upswing in the decades immediately before the First World War, an age that would go down in history as *La Belle Époque*. The art and architecture from this time is still writ large across the big cities on the Continent, a tangible reminder of the wealth and resources the European empires had at their disposal thanks to their colonies and their dominance in global politics. It was not only the heyday of the fine arts, but also the high point of European architecture and the applied arts in general. Most profoundly of all, this manifested itself in the multifaceted Jugend style, which left its impression on everything from architecture and interior decoration to poster art and street signs, like those at the metro stations in the centre of Paris.

In architecture, as in so many other cultural spheres during these decades, the leading Finns took a great deal of inspiration from their Swedish counterparts. A handful of Swedish architects even worked in Helsinki around the turn of the twentieth century, signing off on a row of fashionable Jugend houses on Etelä-Esplanadi and Bulevardi. At this time, there was also a crop of young Finnish talent that started to rise to prominence as the country's foremost names in Jugend-style designs, including Herman Gesellius, Armas Lindgren and Eliel Saarinen. Between them, they garnered a number of commissions for large building projects in Helsinki.

For a few years, the trio even had an architectural firm together, the eponymous Gesellius, Lindgren, Saarinen. In 1905, it won the competition to build what would become their most famous creation: Finland's National Museum, at the southern end of Läntinen Viertotie (today Mannerheimintie). The construction project was unusually expensive for the period, with a granite facade and a high tower that was symbolic of the museum's ideological message: Finland had its own history, and, therefore, it had its own future, too. As the building was slowly erected over the next eleven years, Etu-Töölö, the city district surrounding it, also came into being, having previously been almost uninhabited. The area's street plan combined Jugend architecture with an irregular layout that followed the terrain and accentuated the distinctive features of the individual buildings. A comparable Jugend-inspired street network was drawn up for the villa quarter in the western part of Eira, the new district right next to the city's southern coastline. The other housing that was constructed in this style between 1895 and 1915 was all incorporated into

Helsinki's existing grid plan, such as in Katajanokka's uniform Jugend quarter.

During this same period, Helsinki gained three other imposing public buildings that were Jugend in form: the Finnish National Theatre (1902) and Helsinki Central Station (1909–19), both built around the Railway Square, as well as Kallio Church (1912), at the northernmost point of the city's north–south axis. This was the 2.5-kilometre straight line formed by Siltasaarenkatu and Unioninkatu, connecting Kallio in the north with Ullanlinna and the observatory in the south. The railway station's opening was repeatedly delayed by the First World War, but when it was finally inaugurated in March 1919, the framing of Helsinki's biggest public square was complete. On the northern side stood the Finnish National Theatre, while opposite it in the south was the grand edifice of the Atheneum, the Renaissance-style art museum built in 1887. To the west rose the new station building with its imposing clock tower, and to the east the fashionable neo-Baroque Hotel Fennia, its facade embellished with Finland's red and gold coat of arms, along with the gilded names of European capitals above each of its uppermost windows.

The curious city trekker can also find beautiful examples of Jugend architecture north of Pitkäsilta Bridge, not least along the shore of Siltasaari where it meets Eläintarhanlahti Bay, and in the quarters immediately around Kallio Church. If they venture even further north-east, into Sörnäinen, they will find Ebeneserkoti on the corner of Helsinginkatu and Tenholantie, which was opened in 1908 as one of the country's first purpose-built kindergartens. It was designed by Wivi Lönn, who herself was one of Finland's first female architects. Her most famous buildings are the Uusi Ylioppilastalo (1910) on Mannerheimintie and Estonia Theatre in Tallinn (1913), both of which she worked on in collaboration with her colleague, Armas Lindgren. While perhaps not so renowned, Ebeneserkoti (1908) has its distinctive charm: early in her career, Lönn had specialised in schoolhouses, and the cosy interiors she developed for this building showcase the Jugend style at its best. A nursery still operates in Ebeneserkoti today, as does a museum devoted to the history of kindergartens.

If our intrepid urban explorer has not had their fill, they could also visit the former garden cities of Kauniainen and Kulosaari, established in close proximity to Helsinki in 1906 and 1907 respectively. Both places are still home to large Jugend villas from the period. These were built by the young architects who helped found the neighbourhoods and by the many wealthy families who followed their lead, tempted by the areas' improved transport links. Kauniainen was connected to Helsinki by train, while from 1910 to 1951 Kulosaari had a tram line that ran between its villas and the western side of the Market Square. Here, too, is another prominent reminder of Helsinki during its Jugend period: Ville Vallgren's Havis Amanda statue, which was unveiled in the autumn of 1908 and has since been repeatedly chosen as the city's finest work of art.

Friction and Freedom

Public reaction to the statue was, however, far more mixed in the beginning. Vallgren was working in Paris when he was commissioned to make a sculpture that would function as a visual metaphor for how Helsinki rises up out of the sea. Liberal circles praised the elegant fountain with its ample female figure and water-spouting sea lions for its European charm, but a subset of the suffragette movement saw its brazen nudity as obscene. The workers' press found it ironic that the city's small number of decision-makers would rather decorate their own districts with expensive artwork than do anything about the dreadful living conditions north of Pitkäsilta Bridge. Nonetheless, it was the Old Finns' daily paper—*Uusi Suometar*—that was most indignant, for it was unable to discern any expression of national character whatsoever in the statue: "Nothing out of Kalevala, nothing from Finnish mythology, nothing about Finnish nature".

The sullen tone testified to the metamorphosis that Finnish society had undergone in the preceding decade. In early 1899, the newly appointed Russian Governor-General Nikolay Bobrikov was ordered by Nicholas II to begin a sweeping programme of Russification, in an effort to bind the increasingly westernised Grand Duchy more tightly to the empire. Finland's constitutionalists initially responded to these measures with passive resistance, but they soon started to radicalise and undertake more direct acts of defiance. These proscribed activities were sometimes carried out in close collaboration with Russian revolutionaries, who were also fighting against the authoritarian imperial regime.

Bobrikov responded to their challenge with a heavy hand: suspected activists were met with dismissals, expulsions and deportations, and news publications came under strict censorship. This resulted in a burgeoning underground press and, more explosively, in the assassination of Bobrikov himself, who was shot by an activist on the staircase of the Senate building early in the summer of 1904. Far from making Finnish society more compliant, Russia's uncompromising approach had instead completely undermined the Finns' respect for the imperial authorities. The backlash, however, was not confined to Finland, and, when the Russo-Japanese War ended in defeat for the Russians in the autumn of 1905, strikes, demonstrations and acts of violence broke out in many parts of its empire, forcing Nicholas II to make a number of political concessions.

These had ramifications for Finland, too: the Diet that assembled in the late autumn realised that the time was ripe to extend the franchise. The next year, it pushed through a parliamentary reform that guaranteed universal and equal voting rights to all Finnish men and women. In so doing, Finland not only became the first European country to enable women's suffrage, but it also became an international pioneer by allowing female candidates to stand in parliamentary elections. And women saw immediate success at the ballot box, making up nearly ten per cent of the elected representatives in 1907. Their participation in public and political debate only became more active in the years that followed, such as in the heated discussion that arose over the Havis Amanda statue in 1908.

The parliamentary reform also fostered a more organised and dynamic style of party politics. In tandem with less stringent censorship, it gave rise to increasingly caustic political rhetoric, especially in the run-up to the parliamentary elections. These were held on an almost-annual basis prior to the First World War, since Nicholas II repeatedly dissolved the Finnish parliament for failing to be sufficiently compliant to Russian demands. In so doing, he limited its ability to enact further reforms, undermining the very system of democratic representation that his concessions had helped bring into being. Indeed, his attempt at appeasement was short-lived, and from 1908 a new period of Russification began in Finland, inciting derisive tirades against all things Russian, as well as biting critiques of domestic opponents and minorities.

On top of the obstacles posed by the Russian Emperor and his authorities, the new parliament was faced with a very concrete problem: finding a plenary room large enough to accommodate 200 democratically elected representatives. Numerous reports were commissioned and various architectural competitions were organised over the years, but it was not until 1931 that the country's parliament moved into its own home. The length of the decision-making process reflected the strength of feeling involved. While the debate dragged on, parliament was forced to assemble in various other buildings around Helsinki.

The simplest option would have been to meet in the House of Nobility's assembly room. This had long been too cramped to accommodate all four estates for the Diets, for together they had well over 300 members in the late nineteenth and early twentieth century, but it would have been comfortably big enough for the new parliament. The room was, however, prominently decorated with the Finnish noble families' coats of arms, so it seemed inappropriate, to put it mildly, for democratically elected representatives to meet there. Consequently, parliament's first plenary sessions, beginning in the autumn of 1907, were held in the Helsinki Voluntary Fire Brigade's building, which was located next to Ateneum, an art museum, in the centre of the city. It was also at the heart of Helsinki's cultural life, even organising some of Finland's first film screenings in its cellar movie theatre, which just so happened to be called The World of Wonders (*Undrens värld*). Finland's politicians only convened at the premises for four years before moving to a Jugend-style building at the northern end of Kluuvikatu. The building was called Heimola, which had fittingly nationalistic connotations for the Finnish parliament. *Heimola* derives from the Finnish word *heimo*, which means "tribe" or "clan". Heimola, originally constructed as a restaurant and cinema venue, would go on to host parliament for two decades, from 1911 to 1931.

In spite of all these practical challenges, the nascent parliament increased civic engagement among the Finnish populace and brought a new generation of driven politicians into the public consciousness. These leading figures would, in their own ways, play a part in the country's development into an independent republic. One of them was the Young Finn politician and PhD in History Tekla Hultin, who had already gained a considerable public profile by the time she was elected to parliament in 1908. She had been a journalist at *Päivälehti* and its successor, *Helsingin Sanomat*; in addition, she had taken part in the active resistance against Bobrikov's rule, while also acting as a vocal lobbyist for women's suffrage.

Together with Social Democrat Hilja Pärssinen, Hultin quickly established herself as one of parliament's most spirited female representatives. During her turns at the rostrum, she made numerous contributions to debates on taxes and the constitution, and even spoke in support of some left-wing reform proposals, such as the prohibition on night shifts for female workers that was passed in 1911. Hultin would, however, end up on the opposite side of the barricades to Pärssinen during the revolutionary years of 1917–18, which culminated in the Finnish Civil War between the communist Reds and the bourgeois Whites. Hultin was a Germanophile and a committed monarchist, and so she joined the conservative National Coalition Party, established in 1918 by monarchist-minded politicians within both the Old and Young Finns parties. Simultaneously, their republican-minded party fellows formed the Progress Party. Pärssinen, on the other hand, worked with the Finnish People's Delegation that had been set up by the Red Guards as a rival to the Finnish government during the civil war. After a failed escape attempt, she was sentenced to twelve years' house arrest for treason in 1920, but was granted clemency three years later.

When parliament's representatives gathered for their last peacetime sessions in Heimola's plenary room in the spring of 1914, all this turmoil lay hidden beyond the horizon. Likewise, Speaker K. J. Ståhlberg, Tekla Hultin's party colleague who chaired proceedings, could have had little inkling that, barely five years later, he would be chosen as the Republic's first president in the very same setting. Ståhlberg was known for his willingness to compromise, but Hultin did not number among his admirers. In early April, she made a bitter entry in her diary about a speech he gave at dinner with members of parliament in the restaurant of the newly built Stock Exchange Building (*Pörssitalo*). She observed that the only discernible message he imparted was "better a bird in the hand than two in the bush", before noting wryly that she had no idea as to which bird Ståhlberg was referencing.

Just four months later, the First World War broke out. In common with the majority of other Europeans, it struck Helsinki's residents like a bolt from the blue. Certainly, the political schism between Finland and the Russian central power was still unresolved, but the broad economic outlook had been promising. Business had been booming in the industrial belt around St Petersburg in the early 1910s, and southern Finland had been carried along in its slipstream. The region's economy had grown at a terrific pace, which had a positive impact on nearly all employment sectors in the Finnish capital. This had been fortuitous timing for Helsinki, as it was just then starting to suffer from growing pains.

While the Eastern Front lay far away in Prussia in the late summer of 1914, preparations for war began immediately in Finland. The Russian military leadership was wise to the possibility of the Germans trying to attack St Petersburg (renamed Petrograd in the autumn of 1914) via the Finnish coast. Suomenlinna was a key part of its defence plans in this regard. Since the 1880s, the sea fortress had functioned as a base for the Russian Baltic Sea Fleet's minelayers and torpedo boats, although these vessels had, from the 1890s, been anchored and maintained in the more suitable harbour environment on the northern shore of Katajanokka. This is, as a point of interest, the same place where the Finnish icebreaker fleet is moored today during the summer season.

In the early 1900s, Russia incorporated its coastal defences in the Gulf of Finland into a single entity called Peter the Great's Naval Fortress, and it selected Suomenlinna as the military network's command centre. The eighteenth-century construction was, by that time, well past its prime as a fortress, but its geographical importance as a naval base remained undiminished. The Russian leadership also had an obvious political motive for keeping its naval command at Helsinki. The constitutional conflict between Finland and Russia had markedly increased its distrust of the Finns, so the military presence was required to keep a close eye on the groundswell of anti-Russian feeling in Finland's capital.

Upon the outbreak of war, the Russian Navy's first step was to mine the Gulf of Finland. In parallel with this, it launched a comprehensive overhaul and rearmament of the greater Helsinki region's coastal artillery and inland fortifications. The scale of the project was so extensive that, over the years that followed, thousands of workers from all over the empire were employed on it, alongside the local population. The biggest and newest cannons, with a range of around 20 kilometres, were installed on batteries in the archipelago surrounding the city. Their purpose was to keep the enemy's battleships at bay and protect the minefield that had been laid between the archipelago and the open sea. Suomenlinna, Vallisaari and Santahamina formed the coastal artillery's inner ring, and were equipped with short-range guns to ward off forays by smaller enemy vessels. By the spring of 1916, all this firepower was finally in place. Vallisaari, the island directly east of Suomenlinna, had been made the new command centre, with one of the most modern coastal artilleries in the world at its disposal. It stood in stark contrast to the fortification work on the mainland, which ended up, more often than not, slipshod and half-finished.

All things considered, the unexpected onset of the First World War was not a great catastrophe for Helsinki, nor for the Finnish people in general. Which is not to say that they were entirely sheltered from the conflict's negative consequences: it did not take long before there was a shortage of consumer goods, such as butter and coffee, and the rising cost of wood became an acute issue during the bitterly cold winter of 1916–17. On the other hand, Finnish men were not conscripted en masse into the Russian Army, since the imperial authorities had abolished compulsory military service for Finns at the turn of the twentieth century, in order to quell protests against Russification. Instead, they had decreed that the Finnish state should pay a sizeable annual sum in compensation into the Russian war chest. As a consequence, it was only Finnish regular officers and Russian subjects residing in Finland who were called up for active frontline service. Among this latter category were Finland's Jewish and Tatar minorities, who were only made eligible for Finnish citizenship after the country had gained its independence.

Until the autumn of 1916, the Finnish economy greatly benefitted from the high demand in Russia for the goods and products required to fuel its war effort and sustain its home front. Although there was a drop in Western trade in Finland, the shortfall was largely filled by Eastern markets. The big winners in Helsinki's booming wartime economy were not only the metal and textile industries, but also a number of speculators on the city's stock exchange, who saw the price of their shares steadily increase until, in the autumn of 1916, it rocketed to an all-time high. Some of these investors sensed that a turning point was fast approaching and managed to secure their capital in property before the chaos of 1917 struck. The majority, however, were completely caught off-guard by the societal breakdown of the years ahead, and suffered large financial losses as a result.

In early 1917, then, the atmosphere in wartime Helsinki was a peculiar mixture of hope and despair. For as long as the Russian Army held its positions and the home front could put food on the table, Finnish society could function much as before, even if the prevailing state of war had interrupted parliament's operations and brought strict press censorship into force. In the capital city, it had also led to increased friction between the Russian police authorities and activist circles. Back in the autumn of 1914, just after war had broken out, a coterie of bourgeois activists began secretly recruiting volunteers to travel to Germany for military training. Their aim was to establish an armed militia that could, with German help, bring about Finland's independence from Russia. The initiative became known as the Jäger Movement, and, in spite of a concerted effort by the police to stamp it out through arrests and imprisonment, it resulted in 1,900 Finns going to Germany to acquire military experience. Many of these men would go on to join the bourgeois White Guards during the Finnish Civil War in 1918, using the martial skills they had developed to put down the Red Uprising.

The Jäger Movement was born among activists in the Uusimaa and Ostrobothnia student nations (organisations representing the different regions—and peoples—of Finland) at the University of Helsinki. As Finnish citizens, they avoided Russian mobilisation when the war began, and their sympathies lay firmly with Germany, even at this early stage. Consequently, these students were well-represented among the first batch of Finns who attended the military training camp in northern Germany, and many of them went on to have successful careers as officers in the Finnish Army after emerging victorious from the civil war. Indeed, the majority of the generals in the Finnish Headquarters during the Second World War were Jäger officers.

The recruitment of Jägers was not the only treasonous activity to take place in Helsinki that Germany was directly supporting. Since the turn of the twentieth century, the close contact between the Finnish Social Democrats and their left-wing counterparts in Russia had been a thorn in the side of the Russian police authorities. Both groups were working against the imperial regime, which meant that, during the First World War, the Social Democrats harboured many Russian revolutionaries in Helsinki. The most famous of these was none other than V. I. Lenin: following several years' exile in Switzerland, he had returned to Russia amidst the turbulence of the spring of 1917 to start a revolution, but had fled to the Finnish capital after the Bolsheviks' attempted coup failed in July. He hid in Helsinki waiting for the heat to die down, before returning to Petrograd in the autumn to help instigate the October Revolution.

The Provisional Government in Petrograd had issued arrest warrants for Lenin and the other Bolshevik leaders, but not solely on account of their failed coup. It had also found out that the German government had arranged Lenin's return to Russia via Sweden and Finland, and that the Bolsheviks were receiving a substantial amount of financial support from Germany. This detail was of little concern to the Finnish Social Democrats, especially as Lenin had promised them that the Bolsheviks would wholeheartedly support the demands for sovereignty from minority nationalities in the empire. After undergoing various hardships, Lenin arrived at Helsinki Central Station on 10 August 1917, where he made for an address on the north-eastern corner of Hakaniemi Square: 1 B Sörnäisten rantatie, to be precise. Here he was quartered by the socialist Kustaa Rovio, who was then both the acting police chief of Helsinki and the head of the labour movement's militia in the city.

The Bolshevik leader lay low at this address for two weeks, then spent a few nights in a flat in the centre of the city before lodging in Taka-Töölö with train driver Arthur Blomqvist and his wife Emilia. Ever since 1905, the couple had regularly shared their home with Russian revolutionaries. Their house at 46 Töölönkatu, destroyed in the Soviet bombing of Helsinki in February 1944, was the setting in which Lenin wrote the majority of his call to arms, *The State and Revolution*. In this, he asserted that power must be seized by force. When the dictatorship of the proletariat had been achieved, then the end result would be communism, that is a society in which everyone's character and needs would be accommodated. At the Lenin Museum in

Moscow, one could, at least in the days of the Cold War, view the book's original manuscript: a black wax booklet bearing the emblem of Helsinki's well-known stationer's, Wulff.

The Red Uprising

Helsinki's contribution to the global revolution envisaged by Lenin was not confined to hideaways and writing materials. Over the six months of winter between 1917 and 1918, the city took on a key role in the escalation of the violent civil war that tore through so many regions of the crumbling empire in the aftermath of the Bolsheviks' October Revolution in 1917. The immediate cause of the chaos was, naturally, the ongoing world war, for its destructive effects broke apart the empire bit by bit. It dealt the first blow in March 1917, when the war-worn and half-starved citizens of Petrograd took to the streets to protest food shortages in such great numbers that they forced Nicholas II to abdicate. As societal order began to fall apart, a series of provisional governments assumed power and made the fateful decision to continue the war against Germany on the side of the Western Powers. This only served to further deepen public discontent across the empire, paving the way for the bloody Bolshevik Revolution.

Few in Finland mourned the fall of the imperial regime. The Provisional Government that replaced the Emperor issued a manifesto on 20 March 1917 that rescinded, with immediate effect, most of the restrictions imposed on Finland during the years of Russification and war. A largely free press emerged from the shackles of wartime censorship and, in the surge of euphoria that followed, national sovereignty began to be openly discussed in the public sphere for the first time. A central forum for this debate was, for obvious reasons, the Finnish parliament, where the Social Democrats held a majority after elections in the summer of 1916. With a sizeable amount of Finland's autonomy restored by the new manifesto, the Social Democrats were able to appoint a Senate in late March 1917, which was split equally between a socialist and a non-socialist block.

The Chairman of the Senate remained, however, the Russian Governor-General, who opposed every attempt to detach Finland from the empire. In July 1917, a majority of elected representatives stood behind a bill that would have made parliament the highest power in the land, but at this point the Russian Provisional Government intervened. To prevent the law from coming into effect, it declared that new parliamentary elections would take place in September. In these, the bourgeois parties won a majority, which deepened the rift between the two political blocks, as the Social Democrats accused their rivals of having actively supported the dissolution of parliament. The parties had, until this time, cooperated in the organisation of regional militias, but the growing animosity between them caused their forces to split into two increasingly hostile factions: the Red Guards and the White Guards.

Above all else, it was the power vacuum at the heart of the Russian Empire that created such a polarised atmosphere in Finnish society, since it gradually eroded the citizens' trust in each other. Helsinki got its first taste of the emerging chaos in tandem with the Emperor's downfall in March 1917, when the Russian soldiers stationed in the city went on a killing and looting spree. The most grievous of their crimes took place on board a warship moored north of Katajanokka, where the revolting seamen slaughtered more than fifty officers and military personnel. They then formed a soldier and sailor soviet—that is, a collectively elected council—which took Finland's Governor-General prisoner and sent him to Petrograd, before seizing control of the former imperial palace on the north side of the Market Square.

Similar soldier, sailor and worker soviets were being established right across the empire at this time. In early May 1917, the Russian garrison soldiers and seamen in Finland founded their own regional committee in order to both strengthen their influence and to lessen the illegal status of their troops. In spite of the Emperor's abdication and the growing unrest, the Russian Army had not yet descended into total chaos. It continued to wage its war against Germany, and many of its old commanders were permitted to keep their posts if they accepted the soviets' influence. The soviets were not dominated by the Bolsheviks in the spring of 1917, but as war fatigue, food scarcity and general disorder all increased, the more the vacillating soldiers and workers were drawn to Lenin's promises of peace, land and bread.

On 7 November 1917, with the Russian capital in a state of paralysis, the Bolsheviks carried out their bloodless coup. Across the border in Finland, parliament seized its chance and immediately cut all ties with Russia, proclaiming itself to be the country's highest power. At the same time, it passed the laws that the Social Democrats had been demanding, namely for an eight-hour workday and for democratic municipal elections. This, however, did little to help restore peace to the country, for the leaders of the Social Democrats had instigated widespread demonstrations and a general strike to force through their political objectives. These had resulted in heightened tensions among the populace, not least because Russian soldiers and some domestic Red Guards had, amidst the unrest, committed a number of robberies and murders.

Even when the strike was called off, many of these armed gangs continued to terrorise Helsinki and other Finnish cities, in a way that was reminiscent of the Bolshevik rampages through Petrograd. Such violence was a source of serious discord within the Social Democrats, and, in late November 1917, the party leadership held a conference at Workers' House (nowadays

Paasitorni) in Siltasaari to try to resolve the matter. These top Social Democrats still backed reform rather than revolution, and their calls for law-abiding action formally won the support of the meeting. Ultimately, however, this was a hollow victory: in the absence of a non-partisan police or security force, both the Red Guards and the bourgeois White Guards had been feverishly amassing a stockpile of weapons, bringing the prospect of a nationwide power struggle ever closer.

One of the attendees at Workers' House was the as-yet-unknown Bolshevik Joseph Stalin, who gave an impassioned speech exhorting his Finnish comrades to soon seize power. He confirmed that the Bolshevik government would, in accordance with Lenin's promise, recognise Finland's independence. But, for this to result in true freedom for the working class, a revolution was necessary. Referencing Georges Danton, the great orator of the French Revolution, Stalin urged the hesitant assembly to act with "daring, more daring, unending daring", and assured them of brotherly help if required.

On 6 December 1917, parliament accepted the newly appointed bourgeois Senate's declaration of independence. This decision was enabled by the policy of the Bolshevik government in Petrograd, but, paradoxically, it was also influenced by the German government in Berlin. In fact, at this time, both foreign governments were increasingly attempting to steer the course of events in Finland, which they viewed as the gateway to Petrograd. They did this largely by inciting their Red or White allies to take action and claim power for their side. Over the autumn of 1917, bourgeois forces in Finland had established closer contact with the German government, which was actively calling for the country to declare its independence. This encouragement did not, however, stem from any kind-hearted concern for the fate of the Finns. Germany was on the verge of peace negotiations with the Bolsheviks, and was planning to demand that Russian troops be withdrawn from Finland so that it could better secure its hold over the country.

When the Bolsheviks formally recognised Finland's independence on New Year's Eve 1917, they were similarly motivated by self-interest. Their aim was to hasten the spread of the revolution, both to Finland and to other quarters of Europe, but equally important in their decision were the Baltic Sea Fleet's sailors that were still stationed in Helsinki. The Bolsheviks were aware that a civil war could well break out in Finland after Russia and Germany struck a peace deal, and they realised that these Russian troops could be a useful tool for the Reds. As a result, the Bolsheviks intensified their destabilisation efforts, while generously plying the Finnish Red Guards with weapons taken from the Russian garrisons in the country.

Their agitation bore fruit. In the evening of 27 January 1918, the Red Guards, following the orders of the Social Democrat leadership, lit a red lantern in the tower of Workers' House in Helsinki. This was the signal that the revolution had begun in Finland. The Reds claimed control of the capital city and southern Finland without any difficulty, but it was not long before they were met with resistance. For its own safety, the bourgeois Senate hurriedly moved to Vaasa, on the west coast of Finland, which also happened to be where the Headquarters of the White Guard were located. The Whites had disarmed Russian troops in this region, Ostrobothnia, on the same night as the Reds had launched their revolution. Within a matter of days, the conflict had escalated into a full-blown war, which, a little over three months later, ended in victory for the Whites. In Finnish and international histories, including this very book, the conflict is nowadays typically referred to as a civil war, but, as has been shown, it was more of an offshoot of the Russian Revolution and the First World War. In Helsinki, residents called it the

Red Uprising from the very start, regardless of which side of the political divide they belonged to.

That the turning point of the Finnish conflict took place a thousand kilometres south of the country further reinforces the idea that it was part of a wider series of struggles and upheavals. The decisive shift occurred in the Belarusian city of Brest-Litovsk, where Germany and Russia had been embroiled in peace negotiations since late December 1917. In early March 1918, they finally reached an agreement, by which the Bolsheviks undertook to withdraw the rest of their troops from Finland without delay and to stop destabilising the country's government, that is the bourgeois Senate that was then still based in Vaasa. This sealed the fate of the People's Delegation, the Reds' revolutionary government in Helsinki. The ink had barely dried on the peace treaty when the German Army captured the Åland Islands, and, in early April, a German division disembarked in Hanko, southwest Finland. The ramshackle Red Guards stood little chance against these troops, who were hardened veterans of the Eastern Front. The Reds' dire situation was compounded by the fact that the Senate's White Guards had surrounded their stronghold, the industrial city of Tampere, only a few days earlier.

Everyday life in Red Helsinki was, for obvious reasons, marked by a deep distrust and recurrent disputes between the revolutionaries in charge and those inhabitants with bourgeois sympathies. They included the vast majority of the city's public officials and clerical workers, who immediately went on strike, disrupting not just the municipal and state administration, but also banking and the bulk of Helsinki's commercial life. The bourgeoisie involved in food and energy distribution cooperated with the Reds at first, but, in late February, they, too, withheld their labour. Little by little, the White Guards left in the city began to engage in active resistance, which involved espionage, hijacking ships and military exercises in preparation for the moment when they could directly intervene in the conflict.

During these times of strife in early 1918, the People's Delegation assembled in the Senate building, while the Red Guards' General Staff was based in the former residence of the Russian Governor-General on Etelä-Esplanadi, which they had seized three weeks before their revolution began. This building has been known as "Smolna" ever since, for the Bolsheviks in Petrograd had set up their command centre in a renowned girls' school with the same name. The most prominent sign of the revolutionary rule in the city was, nonetheless, the thousands upon thousands of Red Guards in its streets. These left-wing Helsinki residents had been, from the outset, the foundation of the revolution, and they took on a central role in all the fighting that ensued.

In common with the rest of the revolutionary army, these Red units in Helsinki lacked a professional command. This made it harder to coordinate large operations, all the more so as discipline deteriorated over time. There was also a high turnover among guard members, which no doubt had something to do with the fact that their units were mainly made up of trade union chapters and local labour associations. Such was the case with Helsingin Jyry, the renowned athletics club: its members formed their own company, which was first used for political campaigning at the start of the war, but was later dispatched to the front, where it took part in a number of battles, including the defence of Tampere.

The arrival of the Germans on Finnish shores in early April— first at Hanko, then at Loviisa—had a devastating effect on the morale of the Red Guards. As the German troops made their way towards Helsinki, the Russian Navy based in the capital unhurriedly lifted anchor and set sail for Kronstadt. Germany had guaranteed the vessels free passage on the condition that any

Russians left in Helsinki would not participate in the fighting. The defining moment of the conflict was fast approaching. As the whistles from the departing Russian vessels sounded across the city, a German aeroplane appeared in the sky and dropped leaflets over Senate Square. They informed Helsinki's residents that the German Army was intervening in the war for humanitarian reasons.

In the afternoon of 12 April 1918, the German forces took control of the centre of Helsinki after having overcome pockets of dogged resistance. They turned their guns on Siltasaari, for the Red Guards had entrenched themselves at the northern end of Pitkäsilta Bridge. That evening, a fierce battle took place, during which the Germans used the Red Guards they had captured as human shields. In the dimming light of the dusk, thirty-something Red prisoners were killed by fire from their own side. The next day, German artillery on the west shore of Töölönlahti Bay fired on Workers' House in Siltasaari. After a number of direct hits, the tower that had launched the uprising was sent crashing down into the flames of the burning building. This was the signal for the majority of the Red Guards to retreat to Sörnäinen and Hermanni, where they continued to fight over the course of the following day, before finally surrendering. Nonetheless, isolated incidents of resistance still occurred after this point, and there were sporadic exchanges of fire in different parts of the city. Shots were even fired in anger at the start of the Germans' grandiose victory parade to Senate Square on 14 April.

The bourgeois Helsinki residents greeted the Germans' arrival with great relief. In the flush of victory, many gave free rein to both their pro-German and their anti-Russian feelings. Among those strolling euphorically around the city was Tekla Hultin, the Young Finn politician who had been hoping for a German victory from the earliest days of the First World War. She filled her diary with rapturous descriptions of the pomp and circumstance of the parading German soldiers, noting the cascade of floral tributes and cheers they received. "The mere fact that one no longer has to see a single Russian soldier on the streets," she observed, "is a cause for quite unparalleled and unexpected joy."

Among the captured Red Guards and their families, however, the mood was very different. Many were fearful of being severely punished for having taken part in the uprising. The liberal author, Juhani Aho, who had stayed hidden in Helsinki for the duration of the revolution, shared their disquiet. In the Swedish-language newspaper *Hufvudstadsbladet*, which had resumed publication after the cessation of hostilities, he noted a poem by a German officer that had included the expression "der rote Unverstand", that is, "the Red folly". In contrast to the many Finnish poets who were then penning verses about revenge and punishment, Aho saw that this outsider understood that the uprising had not stemmed "solely from villainy and hooliganism, but also from folly and thoughtlessness".

On 5 May 1918, the last remnants of the former revolutionary army surrendered in southwest Finland. A week later, Suomenlinna was handed over to the Finnish authorities by the Russian commanders. The circle was now complete: just as it had 110 years earlier, the proud sea fortress, so integral to Helsinki's destiny, had surrendered without a fight. And, just as before, its surrender was a chain reaction to a war between the European Great Powers into which the city's inhabitants had been dragged, the inadvertent audience to a surrealist geopolitical drama.

5

THE HEART OF THE REPUBLIC

The Driving Forces of Democracy

On 2 May 1918, the country's bourgeois Senate returned to Helsinki from its exile in Vaasa. Upon disembarking from their train in the capital, the senators were met with a large welcome delegation on the station platform. Prominently placed were the Commander of Germany's Baltic Sea Division, Rüdiger von der Goltz, and his general staff, all kitted out in their gleaming *pickelhaubes*, the Imperial German Army's spiked parade helmets. The message, like their headwear, was impossible to miss. The Germans had liberated Helsinki and would, therefore, have the last word about what Finland's immediate future would be. The country's own White Guards had not yet even arrived in the vicinity of the capital city. Down at the South Harbour, the Germans' warship lay anchored in front of the erstwhile Russian Imperial Palace.

All this was a source of utmost irritation for the Commander of the White Guards, Gustaf Mannerheim. He had risen to the rank of lieutenant-general during his career as an officer in the

Imperial Russian Army, so was certainly not enamoured by the idea that Germany might emerge triumphant from the First World War. The bourgeois Senate had, however, been entirely reliant on Germany's backing since the late autumn of 1917, and it was convinced that this support had to continue if Finland's fledgling and extremely frail independence was to be secured. The Finnish government might have been wary of Mannerheim's affinity for Russia, but they also realised that the White Guards under his leadership had made a significant contribution to the bourgeois cause. Since these troops had missed the Germans' victory celebrations, the Senate saw no reason not to give them their own day in the sun.

As such, on 16 May 1918, the White Army held its own victory parade in Helsinki. A total of 12,000 troops marched into the city to a euphoric reaction from the bourgeois residents. The spring sun shone shyly in the sky as Mannerheim rode at the head of the jubilant White forces. Marching among them was a 17-year-old grammar school student from Kajaani in the north of Finland: future president Urho Kekkonen. This was the young White volunteer's first-ever visit to the capital; four decades later, he would regularly be whisked through the same city districts in his presidential limousine, but on this day, he was wide-eyed and soaking in every detail. One thing that caught his attention, and became the object of his ire, were the flags hoisted by Helsinki residents. In a report he wrote for his local paper, he complained that so many of them were flying the traditional red-and-yellow lion flag, which indicated, Kekkonen argued, that the pro-Finnish blue-and-white version was not particularly popular in this strongly Swedish-speaking area of the country.

As the White Army was strutting proudly through Helsinki's streets, across the country the captured Reds were being subjected to depraved conditions and vindictive punishments. It was not uncommon for those on trial to be condemned to death, often on extremely flimsy grounds. All the while, roughly 80,000 Red prisoners of war were crammed together in big internment camps in southern Finland, which were set up in the garrisons and castles handed over by the Russian troops. In the Helsinki region, there were, at their peak, a total of 13,400 captive Reds, the majority of whom were concentrated on Suomenlinna and in the military area in Katajanokka. Nonetheless, until the autumn of 1918, thousands of prisoners were also awaiting their sentences on Santahamina and out among the recently constructed coastal fortifications on Isosaari, a remote island over five kilometres south-east of Suomenlinna.

The conditions in the camps were appalling, and not just because there was an acute shortage of food. They were overcrowded and extremely insanitary, which led to the outbreak of assorted epidemics. The deadliest of these was the global pandemic—which became known as the Spanish flu—that ripped through Finland that same spring. Rumours of the atrocious state of the camps quickly started to spread, and the prisoners' plight even received international attention. However, since the authorities reacted much too slowly, the situation degenerated into a humanitarian catastrophe. Of the 38,000 people who died as a result of the Finnish Civil War in 1918, 15,000 of them succumbed in the Red prison camps or as a direct consequence of incarceration.

In the Helsinki region, a total of 1,600 Red Guards lost their lives during or after their spell in the camps, including 140 who were executed out on Santahamina. The highest death toll was recorded on Suomenlinna, where 934 prisoners passed away from sickness and malnutrition. The majority of them were buried on Santahamina, as were most of those who were killed by firing squad. The sheer number of victims combined with the complete lack of any official intervention fostered suspicions and misgivings among the working class towards the bourgeoisie and elite that would linger long after the last Red Guards had served their sentences or received pardons. Kekkonen himself witnessed the abject misery on Suomenlinna while working briefly as a camp guard there. A long time later, he expressed his shame at having spotted an acquaintance from back home imprisoned on the other side of the barbed wire.

In the summer and autumn of 1918, Finland was governed as a vassal state of Germany. Mannerheim was forced to resign as the army's commander, and the so-called Stump Parliament (*tynkäeduskunta*) consisted almost entirely of bourgeois representatives. They rushed through legislation to make Finland a constitutional monarchy, and chose a German prince to become the King of Finland. But then, in November 1918, the bottom fell out of their plans. Germany's surrender brought an end to the First World War, and the victorious powers demanded that Finland change its government, organise new elections and enact a more democratic constitution. In return, they would send shipments of food supplies and recognise the country's independence. Finland was in no position to refuse, and so, in July 1919, the newly elected parliament voted for the lawyer and Young Finn politician K. J. Ståhlberg to become the first president of Finland.

In the space of less than two years, Finland had been transformed from an imperial Grand Duchy to a democratic republic. Both its foreign trade network and national security policy needed a comprehensive realignment after the rupture of relations with Bolshevik Russia. Although the two countries struck a peace deal—the Treaty of Tartu—in the autumn of 1920, their relations remained frosty throughout the interwar period. This acrimony had military consequences, but it also meant that the Finnish paper industry had to find new markets in the West. The political map of the whole of Europe had been redrawn and, in the hullabaloo that ensued, cities like St Petersburg,

Vienna and Constantinople lost much of their former lustre and influence as their empires came tumbling down around them.

For other cities, the collapse of these vast political units was, on the contrary, a stroke of good fortune. Suddenly, Warsaw and Prague gained capital city status once more, and, in their slipstream, a whole host of new national capitals emerged in the eastern half of Europe: Bucharest, Kaunas, Riga, Tallinn and Helsinki. Their new political roles necessitated a series of practical and symbolic adjustments interconnected with the formation of a nascent nation state. These countries had to establish their own diplomatic services and defence forces post-haste, while dealing with the disassembly of all the shared infrastructure and markets that had existed under imperial rule.

The new capitals often bore the brunt of these changes, and Helsinki was no exception, even though it had already been Finland's administrative centre for over a century, and the main stage for national politics and civil society for over fifty years. The railway connection to St Petersburg—that had proved so crucial to Helsinki's economic development—was almost completely severed. The spirit of the city was transformed by the removal of the Russian military presence and by the creation of Finland's own form of government, with its own national traditions and symbols.

The country's defence forces took over Helsinki's Russian military barracks, the President moved into the Imperial Palace and many Russian-sounding street names were changed: Nikolainkatu became Snellmaninkatu and Wladimirinkatu became Kalevankatu. The city's central axes of Aleksanterinkatu and Unioninkatu were, however, allowed to keep their original identity. And, in spite of vociferous protests, Alexander II's statue was permitted to stay standing in Senate Square. Even today, some tourists are surprised to come across it in the symbolic heart of Helsinki. Indeed, this broad-minded display of mercy was unusual at a time when monuments were torn down with abandon across Eastern Europe. It can be explained, however, by the fact that Alexander II's rule (1855–81) stood out in Finnish history as a time of numerous positive developments for the country.

Helsinki's residents otherwise showed scant desire to preserve the memory of the city's time under Swedish or Russian rule. In May 1918, Sveaborg was given a new Finnish name: Suomenlinna, or Finland's Fortress. The very next year, the island's Orthodox church had its onion domes removed and was converted into a Lutheran place of worship. While the Empress's stone was left undisturbed on the Market Square, no one had any interest in replacing the Russian double-headed eagle that revolutionary sailors had ripped down during the revolution. The city's Russian-speaking population were also aware that Finns could now freely express their negative feelings towards anything and everything Russian, and so many of them chose to Fennicise their surnames. So, too, did a number of people with Swedish-language surnames, either for ideological reasons or to help them advance in their career.

The political climate in the young Republic was deeply polarised all the way until the late 1930s, and its schisms were most clearly on display in Helsinki. Many on the right supported the extra-parliamentary influence of the White Guards, while many of the most committed socialists harboured thoughts of revenge, even after the bulk of the Red Guards had been pardoned. On the whole, it was the liberal and social democratic circles who tried to find a middle ground between the two opposing sides. It was also they who drove through the republican constitution, and who were most unfaltering in their defence of Finland's representative democracy.

In February 1922, Heikki Ritavuori, the liberal Minister of the Interior, was murdered outside his home on Nervanderinkatu

1. Gustav Vasa, King of Sweden (1523–60).

2a. The town's shoreline and topography during the seventeenth and eighteenth centuries. The core of the town was located on the peninsula to the north and east, which was only connected to the mainland in the south and west by a narrow isthmus.

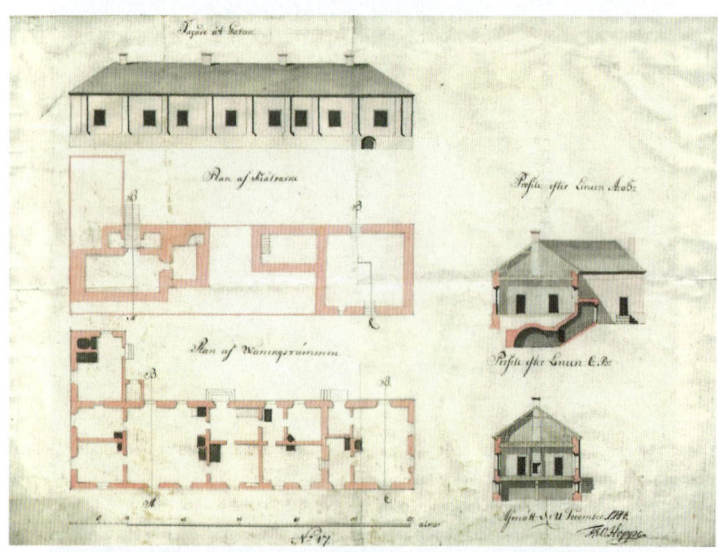

2b. Torsten Burgman's house, the first-ever stone building in Helsinki, was constructed in the late 1690s. Architectural plan from 1748.

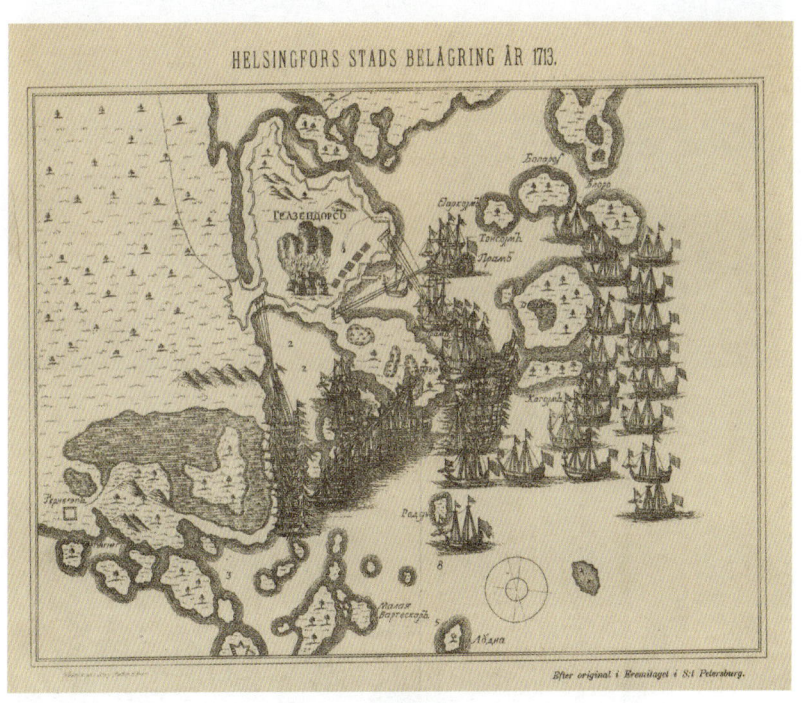

3. The Russian Navy's siege of Helsinki in May 1713.

4a. The construction of Suomenlinna's shipyard.

4b. Dancing on Suomenlinna in 1764.

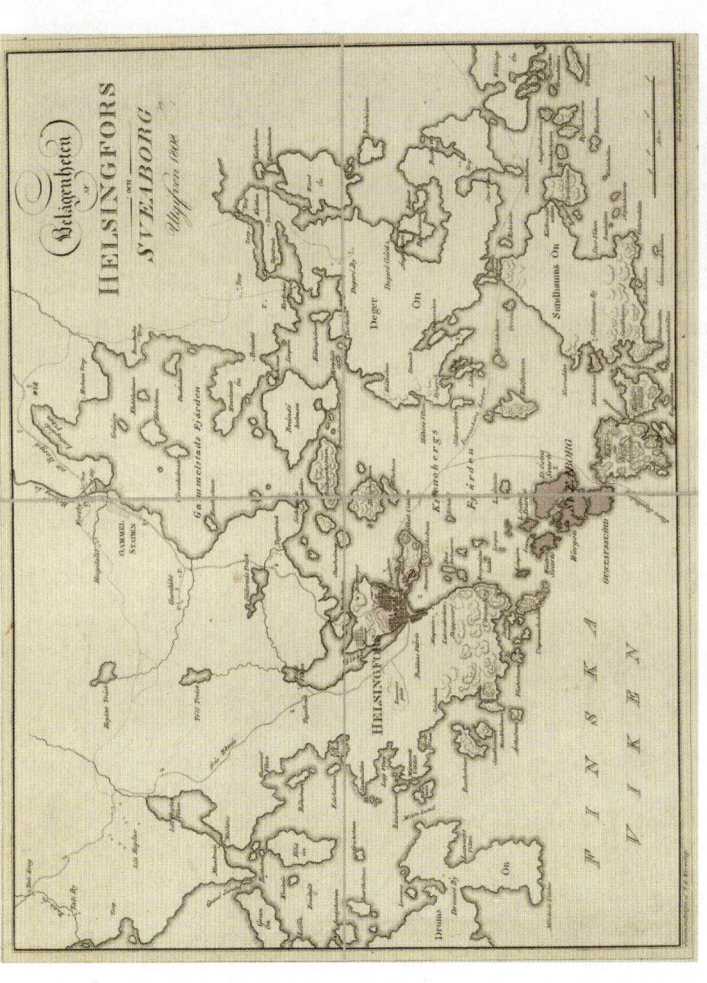

5. Helsinki, Suomenlinna and their environs in 1808, just as Finland's time under Swedish rule was coming to an end.

6a. The view looking south towards Helsinki from the Häme customs house at Pitkäsilta. Under Swedish rule, such toll gates were built in the 1600s to collect custom duties on domestic trade taking place in towns and cities. Under Russian rule, this practice was discontinued, and such buildings were instead used as guardhouses.

6b. The sights of Senate Square in 1838. The university building stands on the left, its library in the centre, and St Nicholas's Church on the right, with the Main Guard Post below it. Within a matter of years, this latter building would be replaced by a broad flight of stairs climbing up to the church.

7a. Kaivohuone—the well house—and its baths opened for business in Kaivopuisto in 1838.

7b. *Bombardement de Sweaborg* (The Bombing of Suomenlinna).

8. Nyländska Jaktklubben (The Nyland Yacht Club) in the South Harbour.

9a. The working-class street scene on Hämeentie in 1908, looking
down towards Hakaniemi Square. On the horizon is the newly
built rectangular tower of Workers' House (*Paasitorni*),
designed by Karl Lindahl.

9b. Crowds of demonstrators packed onto Pohjoisesplanadi during
the General Strike in Helsinki in early November 1905.

10a. Russia's Baltic Sea Fleet lay anchored in the North Harbour until the German Army wrested control of Helsinki from the Reds in April 1918. Behind the boats, across the frozen sea, are the islands of Korkeasaari and Mustikkamaa.

10b. German soldiers assembled at the Stone of the Empress monument on the Market Square in April 1918.

11. *Havis Amanda*, Ville Vallgren's statue and fountain by the
Market Square, has repeatedly been voted the most beloved
artwork in Helsinki.

12a. Stockmann department store in 1932, two years after its long construction process had finally come to an end.

12b. Emil Zátopek, the Czechoslovakian long-distance runner, on his way to victory in the 10,000m at the Helsinki Olympics in 1952. He would go on to win three gold medals over the course of the fortnight.

13a. Traffic at a standstill where Keskuskatu intersects with Aleksanterinkatu, which was then being trialled as a pedestrianised street.

13b. Fashionable and spirited youths at the Potato Square—as the plaza in front of Old Student House is known in city slang—in 1968.

14. President of the United States Gerald Ford (second from right) and Secretary of State Henry Kissinger (third from right) in the main auditorium of Finlandia Hall. They were attending the decisive meeting of the Conference on Security and Cooperation in Europe that was held in Helsinki in the summer of 1975.

15a. Once Kalasatama's construction is complete in 2035, the city district will be home to an estimated 25,000 residents and 10,000 jobs.

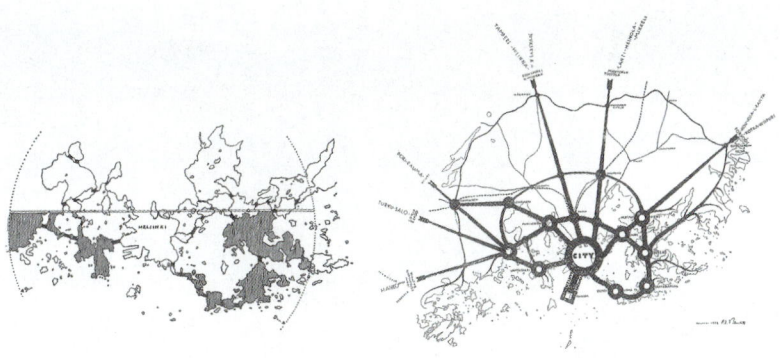

15b. Architect Pauli E. Blomstedt's plans for Helsinki's future expansion in 1932. His vision of the metropolitan area extending further out into the archipelago remains highly relevant to this day.

16a. The new faces of Helsinki.

16b. A memento of the Ice Age: the erratic boulder in the Haltiala
nature reserve in Helsinki Central Park.

in Helsinki by a radical right-wing activist. In this same period, police authorities were monitoring an intensifying communist agitation, coordinated from Moscow, in many of the city's factories and workers' associations. Finland's thriving economy during the 1920s helped to keep a lid on these antagonistic forces, but, in the autumn of 1929, an anti-communist movement flared up in the Ostrobothnian municipality of Lapua. Adopting some elements of fascism, the Lapua Movement launched a systematic campaign of terror against the political Left, carrying out assaults, abductions and even murders. In July 1930, it organised the so-called "Peasant March" on Helsinki, filling Senate Square with over 12,000 anti-communist protestors. The movement's leaders wanted a law that banned all communist activities in the country, and were furious that parliament had not sufficiently acquiesced to their demands. They used threats and more kidnappings to force a change of government and new elections, which resulted in the legislation being passed later that same year.

The culmination of the movement's terrorist activities came in October 1930, when it abducted the former president, K. J. Ståhlberg, and his wife. They had been out for a walk near their home in the garden city of Kulosaari, just east of Helsinki, but were bundled into a car and driven all the way to the eastern border of Finland before being freed. Up until this point, many among the bourgeoisie and upper class had shown understanding towards the movement's anti-communist agitation and activities, but this kidnapping tipped the scales of public opinion against it. After launching a failed coup—the Mäntsälä rebellion—in early 1932, the Lapua Movement was formally banned and its leaders were imprisoned. Over the years that followed, the country's representative democracy began to develop in a more stable direction, and, in 1937, the first cross-bloc majority government was formed. It was certainly not predestined that democratic principles and compromise would triumph, for almost all the other newly formed states in Eastern Europe ended up going down a more authoritarian path.

One significant factor behind Finland's political system holding fast under pressure, in spite of everything, was that its institutions and legislative body had a far longer tradition than, for example, those of the Baltic states. Many of the members of parliament had been active in politics during Finland's time as a Grand Duchy, and three of the country's first four presidents had actually sat in the Diets of the Estates, where they had learned that even profound disagreements could be solved through patient legislative processes.

At a symbolic level, the credibility of parliamentary democracy was strengthened by the inauguration of the new Parliament House in early March 1931, which had been built on Arkadia Hill in Etu-Töölö. Its construction was a torturous process: countless debates, reports and preliminary plans which all, for a variety of reasons, came to nothing. Finally, in 1926, work began on an imposing granite edifice designed by J. S. Sirén. The end result was, without a shadow of a doubt, the grandest architectural creation in Finland during the interwar years.

The building is a pre-eminent example of Nordic neo-Classicism. Its exterior follows a strict symmetry, with a monumental colonnade forming its facade. Its classical interior has art-deco trappings, and its parliamentary function is embodied in the cylindrical plenary chamber, where all Finland's presidents since 1931 have sworn their oaths of office. It is where all subsequent governments have defended their policies, and where various weighty motions have been debated and adopted. With the opening of Parliament House, the political epicentre of Helsinki slowly began to shift from the core of the old town to the brow of Arkadia Hill.

It would, however, take eighty years for the milieu around Parliament House to offer the same sort of evocative and harmonious framing that Finnish politics had enjoyed in Senate Square and the environs in front of the House of Estates. The entrance to the new parliament building was indeed impressive, but the view from the top of its steps had long been the congested traffic on the main road out of the centre and the grimy railway yard further in the distance. It was only in the 2010s that parliament's surroundings were upgraded: the busy Mannerheimintie remains, but behind it there now lies a wide and inspiring meeting place, Kansalaistori (Citizens' Square). This is bordered on three sides by architecturally striking cultural institutions: Musiikkitalo (Music Centre), Oodi (Helsinki Central Library) and Kiasma (Museum of Contemporary Art).

A Little Big City

Why did parliament, the beating heart of the Finnish state, not do something about its shoddy and half-finished surroundings sooner? Well, to cut a long and knotty story short, the sorry state of the government's finances and the reticence inherent to democratic decision-making both played their part. City planners and authorities were so invested in creating a comprehensive and symbolic context for the nascent Republic's political core that one proposal after another failed to get off the ground, dismissed as either too expensive or too problematic. On top of this, it proved difficult to find a suitable place for the relocation of the large railway yard.

Post-independence, the first ambitious proposal for a new city layout was drawn up in 1918 by the country's leading architect, Eliel Saarinen. It involved building a 3-kilometre-long and 90-metre-wide parade that would run northwards straight over Töölönlahti, with the idea that this "King's Avenue" would become the backbone of the city's commercial and public life. The plan also entailed the replacement of Helsinki's brand-new railway station, that Saarinen himself had designed, with a much larger one at the northern end of the avenue.

The Finnish government opposed such an expensive project, and, when the next city plan was presented by architect Oiva Kallio in the mid-1920s, the parade over Töölönlahti had been shortened and the Central Railway Station was kept in its original place. Kallio had also included the forthcoming Parliament Building on Arkadia Hill, proposing that it should have an eponymous square built to its east, which would open up on to the aforementioned parade. As the plan continued to be refined, Finland's younger architects began to increasingly criticise the idea of making Töölönlahti Bay and its surrounding green space into part of a compact stone city. Kallio's design ultimately went nowhere, as did a whole range of plans that succeeded it; one after the other, they were all turned down. Even Alvar Aalto's, the architect who defined the post-war period in Finland, was scuttled. Drawn up in the early 1960s, his centre plan imagined the area east of Parliament House as an open, fan-shaped terrace on three levels.

Nonetheless, upon close inspection of Kansalaistori and its surrounding environs today, it becomes evident that the finished design contains elements not just from Aalto's plan, but also from some of the others that fell by the wayside. The same incorporation of old ideas can be discerned in urban planning across the city. Even if Saarinen's "King's Avenue" was abandoned as quickly as Finland's mooted monarchy, he supported the successful proposal to make the islands to the south-west and north-east of the city centre into two big harbours. These would both be in use all the way until the early 2000s, when Vuosaari Harbour, on the eastern edge of modern Helsinki, was finally completed. In much the same fashion, the demands that Töölönlahti and its nearby green space should be preserved contributed, in no small part, to the fact that the Olympic Stadium (1938), Finlandia Hall (1971) and the Opera House (1993) could be built on spacious sites close to the city centre.

As the plans for its centre were being drawn and redrawn in the interwar years, Helsinki's built environment expanded steadily to the north and the north-west. The shortage of small-sized accommodation had become increasingly acute, and in the 1920s a whole new city district—Käpylä—was built, situated just north of Hermanni and Vallila, working-class neighbourhoods that had sprung up in the late 1800s. Käpylä's most striking feature was, at first, the beautiful wooden house quarter, built in understated neoclassical style along Pohjolankatu. During the next two decades, low-rise functionalist apartment buildings were also constructed there, some of which were intended to house athletes for the Helsinki Olympics in 1940. The sporting competition was, unsurprisingly, cancelled on account of the Second World War, which meant that Käpylä's Olympic Village never fulfilled its original purpose. However, in the years before the games were finally held in Helsinki in 1952, the district had a new competition village (*Kisakylä*) constructed, which did get the chance to host a large number of the visiting athletes, and thus live up to its name.

In terms of population density, the city's biggest expansion of the period took place in Taka-Töölö and Meilahti during the 1930s and 1940s, when a uniform stock of multi-storey buildings was erected. The openness of the functionalist architecture and the proliferation of green spaces were in sharp contrast to the tightly packed buildings of Etu-Töölö, which dated from the 1910s. Taka-Töölö and Meilahti's construction was restricted in the north and the east by the main road connecting Helsinki to Turku, which was rechristened Mannerheimintie in 1942. The long, straight section running through Meilahti became a favourite of urban photographers after the Second World War. Its tall apartment blocks—diagonally oriented to the street on the northern side—were seen to symbolise modern Helsinki. Back in the 1910s, there had even been plans to move the whole of the University of Helsinki out to Meilahti; although these were shelved, the institution's medical faculty did gradually start to concentrate its activities there.

Another enduring consequence of the urban planning of the early 1900s is Helsinki Central Park, a 10-kilometre swath of forested green space extending north from the heart of the city. Its southernmost section, just above Töölönlahti, became the most important sports park in Helsinki. The park had, in its time, been leased by Henrik Borgström—the same self-made businessman who founded the spa and health resort in Kaivopuisto—with the intention of establishing a zoo there, among other ventures. And this, therefore, is why the area is today called Eläintarha (or Animal Park), even though the city's actual zoo was set up on Korkeasaari in the late 1880s. It is also why the athletics stadium that was built in the park in the 1910s is still referred to as the Eläintarha sports field.

In the 1920s and 1930s, many world records were set in long-distance running on the red brick dust of Eläintarha's track, not least by Paavo Nurmi. He remains Finnish running royalty to this day, and, according to legend, his unofficial fee for racing on the track was a mark per metre. A little before Nurmi's heyday, in 1915, the city's first grass football pitch was opened on the western edge of Eläintarha. A few years later, in 1921, work began on Brahe Field (*Brahenkenttä*) in Kallio, although it was first built as an athletics pitch, and would only later be converted into a home for football. The previous year, the city had leased out a vast, flat tract of land in the north for harness racing and other equestrian sports. Until the late 1970s, it was known as Käpylä Trotting Track (*Käpylän ravirata*), but today it is home to a variety of pitches and goes by the name of Käpylä Sports Park.

The premier sports arena in Helsinki—and, indeed, the country—would, nonetheless, end up being the Olympic Stadium, which was inaugurated in Eläintarha in the summer of 1938. Finland was then gearing up to host the games in two years' time, and expectations were sky high after the country's sports stars' stellar medal hauls in all of the interwar Olympics. Perhaps even more important than athletic success was the competition's soft-power potential, for hosting offered a unique opportunity for the young Republic to show off its cultural and economic vitality to the world. The Olympic Stadium became, therefore, a matter of national interest: an architectural competition was organised to find the best design, with the young talents Yrjö Lindegren and Toivo Jäntti emerging as winners. Their strict functionalist proposal with its big, white surfaces and high tower set the tone for the other sports complexes that were constructed in the city before the games.

Symbolising the increasingly ill-disguised prejudice of the period, a spiteful incident occurred at the stadium's first athletics meet in June 1938. The crowd witnessed the sprinter Abraham Tokazier cross the line first in the men's 100-metre race, yet, when the results were announced, the Jewish runner had been dropped to fourth place. Many rightly suspected that this was due to anti-Semitism, which was then still deep-rooted in Finnish society, as elsewhere. The day after the race (22 June 1938), both *Helsingin Sanomat* and *Hufvudstadsbladet* published a photograph that clearly showed Tokazier had won, but the results were never amended.

In the second half of the 1930s, Helsinki's residents could admire a number of other functionalist public buildings that had been constructed around their city. Three of these rose up in the quarter just west of the Central Railway Station. The first was the low-rise Lasipalatsi (Glass Palace), which was taken into use in 1936, having been built on the site where the Turku Barracks had stood during Russian rule. Two years later, Postitalo, the main office of the Finnish postal service, opened almost directly opposite it. This was an unusually tall building for the time, and its light brick facade, in combination with its modern interior design, soon made it something of a landmark in modern Finland. In this same period, ground was broken on Hotel Vaakuna, which was constructed in anticipation of the flood of tourists for the Olympic Games. Like the sporting spectacle, the project was delayed by the outbreak of war and was only finished in 1947.

Despite the difficulties of trying to drive through a comprehensive urban plan, Helsinki's commercial centre had, slowly but surely, begun to shift towards the blocks closest to the Central Railway Station and further west along Läntinen and Itäinen Heikinkatu. These were two sides of the same street, separated by an avenue lined with linden trees until 1935, that formed the first section of the main road running north from Erottaja out of the centre. The second section was Turuntie, but it would not be long before the two parts were officially united as Mannerheimintie. The Central Railway Station's commercial prospects had been improved back in the 1910s, when its eastern approach had been made more accessible by the construction of Kaisaniemenkatu, the new street's diagonal path tearing up the city's long-established grid plan. As for Heikinkatu, it had benefitted from the opening of Stockmann's huge department store on the corner it shared with Aleksanterinkatu in 1930.

In common with a number of other large building projects in the city, the plans for the department store had been conceived prior to the First World War, when economic growth seemed to know no bounds. The business's German founder, G. F. Stockmann, had set up shop back in 1862 in premises near Senate Square, but these had become too small by the 1910s, so his sons, now in charge, decided to construct a large department store. It would, they envisaged, occupy an entire block, and be built in the same style as the great department stores on the Continent. Bit by bit, they bought up the block alongside Itäinen Heikinkatu, and, with the help of an architectural competition, they settled on a plan for a seven-storey building proposed by Sigurd Frosterus. The end result is today widely considered to be the versatile architect's best work: its core idea was an open, light atrium in the middle of a shopping complex, with unfussy interior decoration, capacious lifts and an abundance of escalators. This was all designed to aid the flow of customers from one floor to the next.

The construction process stuttered forward in stages, so, by the time the department store stood in all its finished glory in 1930, the next generation of architects viewed it with a critical eye, deriding its monumental facade of dark burnt brick as hopelessly out-of-date. For Frosterus, however, keeping up with architectural trends mattered less than staying true to the original design. And his approach was vindicated, for the building's inviting shop windows combined with the dazzling product displays to quickly make Stockmann a hit with retail-hungry residents and tourists. The department store's concerted efforts to appeal to a broad clientele certainly contributed to its success, as did its careful efforts to avoid getting embroiled in the language feuds that repeatedly flared up in the 1930s. During these, the nationalistic "real Finn" (*aitosuomalainen*) movement exhorted consumers to boycott shops that were deemed too Swedish in character.

While only a tiny minority of private individuals could afford to buy their own car in the interwar years, different kinds of motor vehicles still started to appear on Helsinki's streets. At a local level, public transport continued to consist of train and tram services. However, as transit technology developed further, buses emerged as a viable alternative, and they were soon an increasingly popular mode of travel, even over longer distances.

As a result, it took far less time than ever before to go between Helsinki and the surrounding rural districts. The city's territory had grown somewhat through individual incorporations in the early 1900s, but it was only in the 1940s that it expanded at scale. Until then, its borders had, on the whole, remained unchanged from those that had been delineated when the city had been moved to Vironniemi from its home by the rapids 300 years earlier. Tightly built settlements with their own industries and related services sprang up further and further from the city's outskirts in the nearby countryside, especially in the vicinity of railway stations.

Another mass transit medium that dawned in this epoch was civil aviation: air travel evolved at a lightning pace in the 1920s, and by the 1930s the industry was starting to establish norms for passenger flights. Until 1936, when Helsinki-Malmi Airport opened just north-east of the city, Helsinki's air traffic had consisted solely of hydroplanes that landed on the sea by the south-eastern point of Katajanokka. Two years later, the airport's terminal was inaugurated: it was a functionalist round building that was intended to serve as a welcome place for tourists and athletes during the Olympic Games. As we know, these would end up being postponed until 1952, but this disappointment did little to diminish the Finns' immense pride in their new airport. It is no coincidence that a number of feature films from the period shot scenes with its shining white architecture and plane hangar in the background.

Aeroplanes also made it possible to see Helsinki in a whole new light, offering a bird's-eye view of its structures, streets and shoreline. One of the first impressions of Helsinki from the sky was shared by the young architect Alvar Aalto in a column for the satirical paper *Kerberos* in early 1921. He had been invited to take the dizzying trip by a famous fighter pilot, and, once the roaring machine had carried him skywards, he was struck by how the whole capital opened out before his eyes, and his thoughts instinctively turned to "the art of town planning". He recorded his scattershot impressions: people on Esplanadi looked so "terribly small"; the Helsinki laid out by Ehrenström and Engel was "actually a beautiful arrangement"; hopefully Saarinen's "King's Avenue" would one day come to something. He then observed, scathingly, that "an aviator can see where the monkeys have been and destroyed so very much."

Collective Growing Pains

This would not be the last time that Aalto would express his dissatisfaction over how incoherently Helsinki seemed to be growing. One reason for this was parliament's parsimonious attitude towards big investments, another was the housing sector's overriding concern with profit. Just as often, however, the sluggish and largely risk-averse urban planning had its roots in the city council that decided on Helsinki's affairs. Since the first democratic municipal elections in the late autumn of 1918, it had been made up of varied and frequently competing political priorities, which were rarely sufficiently unified to affect large-scale changes in the street plan of the city.

The turnout of Helsinki residents in these elections remained modest throughout the whole interwar period. The exception was the year of 1920, when nearly sixty-five per cent of eligible voters went to the ballot box. This high turnout benefitted the parties on the left, who garnered fifty-four per cent of the vote. In the other municipal elections, the bourgeoisie parties won clear majorities, with the Swedish People's Party of Finland (SPP) at their head, which diminished the city council's willingness to implement social reforms or tackle income inequality. The SPP's popularity in the interwar municipal elections was not simply due to the fact that a significant proportion of Helsinki's population (twenty-eight per cent) was still Swedish-speaking in the late 1930s. It was also because these Swedish speakers comprised substantially more of the city's middle and upper class than any other population group, and it was this demographic, with its bourgeois mindset, that was most assiduous in exercising its right to vote.

Municipal elections notwithstanding, the linguistic shift in favour of Helsinki's inhabitants registered as Finnish-speaking occurred in tandem with the city's overall population increase. Between 1920 and 1940, Helsinki experienced a population growth of over 90,000 people, from 160,000 to 252,500. In absolute terms, this growth rate was more rapid than anything Helsinki had ever experienced, but, in relative terms, it did not quite reach the same level as the increase around the turn of the twentieth century, when the city's populace doubled in a similar time frame. The interwar boom was even greater if the growth of the built-up areas in Helsinki's surrounding municipalities is taken into account, for the capital city region's population rose by, in all, 110,000 people, from 179,000 to 289,000. Such an explosive upsurge had, of course, a huge influence on all sections of society.

As before in Helsinki's history, a large part of the population increase was due to a cascade of migrants from other regions of Finland. The extent of this can be seen by the fact that only a third of Helsinki's inhabitants during the interwar years were native to the city. While the majority of new arrivals continued to hail from elsewhere in Uusimaa and various districts in and around Häme, the number who came from the provinces of Vyborg and Kuopio increased significantly. These migrants from eastern Finland soon made up twenty per cent of Helsinki's non-native residents, whereas they had previously accounted for just a tenth. The closure of the eastern border was the fundamental reason for their increase, for it had strangled the regions' trade with Petrograd and other parts of Russia. It had also put an end to cross-border employment opportunities.

Besides the influx of Finns from the east, the geopolitical realignment had other consequences for everyday life in Helsinki. The onset of Bolshevik rule caused a mass exodus from Russia, part of which passed through Finland. Scant few of the Russian émigrés stayed in the country, however, choosing instead to travel further afield onto the Continent. Before they went on their way, many sold off their jewellery and other valuables on the Finnish art and antique market. This soon gave rise to a thriving trade in smuggled artefacts and artworks, which the ousted elite of Imperial Russia were desperate to sell on before they could be confiscated by the Bolsheviks.

These exclusive goods served as a nostalgic reminder of just how bountiful the selection of luxury products had been in pre-revolutionary Petrograd. Indeed, long into the second half of the twentieth century, many Finnish middle- and upper-class homes contained furniture, artwork and household articles that had been imported from Russia during Finland's 108 years as a Grand Duchy. The memory of the Russian era, consequently, was kept alive in this way. Indeed, it should be noted that, although the vast majority of Finns welcomed and valued their country's independence, by no means everyone materially benefitted from its newfound freedom.

Some of the biggest losers were the highest-ranking civil servants and officials, whose real wages had sunk dramatically during the First World War and would never again return to what they had been during Finland's time as a Grand Duchy. Left-wing and centrist members of parliament showed little compassion towards "the gentlemen's" pay demands, with the result being that their real wages in the late 1930s were almost one third less than they had been prior to the Great War. Nevertheless, things could have gone much worse for the social elite. In most other states that emerged in the war's aftermath, the old bureaucratic elites were quickly replaced by a new breed of official. In contrast, those in Finland were only removed from their posts if they could not demonstrate a sufficient grasp of the Finnish language.

Still, for the lion's share of Finns, national independence was unquestionably a change for the better. One group that saw instant and tangible benefits was Finland's Jewish minority: in 1917, they were allowed to become Finnish citizens for the first time, and, within a year, their community in Helsinki had registered as a religious society. Immediately thereafter, it founded its own school, which helped make many of Finland's 1,300 Jews feel more secure about their future in the country. The vast majority of them were, until the Second World War, Swedish-speaking. This was a consequence of the fact that they had previously only been permitted to live in Helsinki, Turku and Vyborg, and only allowed to make a living in the mercantile profession, which, in those cities, necessitated a knowledge of Swedish. The influence of Swedish was especially pronounced in Helsinki's Jewish community, with its roughly 1,000 members. This began to shift in 1933, when the Jewish school's language was gradually changed to Finnish, in order to ensure financial support from the state. Over time, Finnish became the dominant language among the country's Jews.

This linguistic transition did not present much of an issue among the Jewish community, most of whom were proficient in multiple languages. It also helped that it happened at a time when the Finnish-speaking population of Helsinki was becoming increasingly dominant, totalling seventy-two per cent of all residents in 1940, which, in turn, made knowledge of Swedish less and less necessary. The city had formerly been a place where the active use of both languages had been embraced, yet the growing monolingualism created a degree of friction between

Finnish and Swedish speakers. The latter were still a prominent and vociferous part of city life, not solely because of their often-elevated social status, but also because of their strong traditions and networks. And although the proportion of Swedish-speaking residents shrank in respect of the total population size, their number increased in absolute terms over the interwar years, from 54,000 to 80,000.

As the split between Finnish and Swedish widened, so, too, did the division between the associations and cultural institutions linked with each language. It also led to the demand from the "real Finn" movement, spearheaded by the ultra-nationalist Academic Karelia Society (AKS), that teaching at the University of Helsinki should be conducted solely in Finnish. For obvious reasons, this was opposed by the Swedish-speaking Finns, not least because they made up a larger proportion of the students at the university than they did the population as a whole. Even late in the period, between 1936 and 1940, they accounted for 16.5 per cent of all students, whereas in 1940 they numbered just 10.9 per cent of all Finns.

In common with past language feuds that had been waged in the city, the conflict was also plainly imbued with regional prejudices and class-based animosity. Nearly ninety per cent of AKS members came from Finnish-speaking districts outside of Helsinki, which goes some way towards explaining their irritation over the fact that the country's capital was still so "un-Finnish". Matters were not improved by the background and character of the Swedish students: they were, on the whole, Helsinki natives from the upper social strata, who often acted with the entitled expectation that the world would bend to their will.

During the 1930s, this schism manifested itself in "real Finn" demonstrations, along with calls for people to boycott Swedish-speaking shopkeepers and to Fennicise their surnames. For a number of years, on 6 November, violence flared during the annual celebration of Finnish Swedish Heritage Day (*Svenska dagen*) in Helsinki, with rival gangs of Finnish and Swedish-speaking boys brawling in the quarter closest to the Swedish Theatre. Finally, in the spring of 1937, the government managed to pass a new law which laid much of the bile and vitriol to rest. Finnish was made both the language of the university administration and the principal language of tuition, but, at the same time, the legislation established a minimum quota for the number of professors that had to offer teaching in Swedish.

Yet, for all the furore, this was a language war fought mainly in middle- and upper-class circles, with even its fiercest clashes eliciting little more than a shrug from the majority of Helsinki's residents. It was still very common for people to live a bilingual—or even a multilingual—existence, and, among the working class, the dispute was rightly viewed as a trivial issue. Just as in the past, their primary concern was establishing a degree of security in daily life, which typically meant finding and keeping a steady job that could support a family. And, in the years after the abominable civil war of 1918, it was hard for the Finnish working class to keep their heads above water, which further reduced their desire to get embroiled in a bourgeois squabble over language.

In Helsinki, the trade unions and other labour organisations had played a significant role in the revolution. As a result, many of their members spent the subsequent years languishing in prison camps, and only gradually regained their civil rights. Those that suffered the most were the working-class families whose fathers had perished, whether killed in the war, executed in its aftermath or finished off by the brutal conditions of imprisonment. The Whites' attitude towards the workers' movement was often sceptical at best and outright hostile at worst, which did little to help facilitate reconciliation between the two sides. Many among the bourgeoisie, particularly the members of the White Guards, were fearful that the socialists were busy plotting a new coup attempt.

Their suspicions were not unfounded, at least when it came to the Communists, who had maintained close contact with the Finnish revolutionary leaders who had fled to the Soviet Union. The majority of the city's working populace, however, gradually got behind the reformist policies that had been launched by Väinö Tanner in the autumn of 1918, the moment the labour movement had been permitted to resume its activities. Tanner was one of the few high-profile Social Democrats who had refused to take part in the revolution. As a result, he would go on to take a leading role in the slow process of reconciliation that took place between the country's socialist and bourgeois inhabitants.

In fact, the interwar period would develop into something of a golden age for the associational life and the cultural activities of the labour movement. This vitality stemmed, of course, from the prevailing belief among its members that a socialist future was at hand. Just as important, however, was Finland's economy recovery, which led to higher wages for manual labourers, and the introduction of the eight-hour workday. These workers had more opportunities for leisure time than ever before, and many took part in the manifold activities organised by the labour movement. The events put on by associations could even become the springboard for careers in singing and acting, as was the case for the brightest stars of the Finnish silver screen, Ansa Ikonen and Tauno Palo, who both debuted at the Helsinki workers' theatres.

Around fifty-three per cent of the city's working-age residents were classified as blue collar at the outset of the 1930s. This suggests that the working-class proportion of Helsinki's overall population had shrunk slightly from the early 1910s, when it was about sixty per cent. The shift can, in part, be explained by the fact that industries had established themselves across different regions of the country in ever greater numbers. At the same time, many of Helsinki's labourers had been pushed out of the city to the surrounding municipalities by its housing shortage and extortionate rents. In addition, a number of industrial branches had successfully incorporated machinery into their production processes, leading to more and more labourers seeking work in the trade, transport and warehouse sectors.

Approximately a third of Finland's foreign trade continued to pass through Helsinki, which necessitated the expansion of Katajanokka's port and warehouse capacity, as well as the construction of the West Harbour in the early 1920s. This latter project involved connecting the islands of Munkkisaari and Jätkäsaari, via a process of reclamation, to the south-western edge of mainland Helsinki. Another striking continuity in trading patterns was that around three quarters of Helsinki's port traffic still comprised shipments of imported goods, which were then distributed onwards, for a healthy profit, to other parts of the land.

Operating in the shadow of the above-board foreign trade was an extensive smuggling network in illicit spirits. This had sprung up along the Uusimaa coastline after the prohibition law, which had originally been approved by Finnish parliament in 1907, finally came into effect on 1 June 1919. The practice would also endure for some time after prohibition was repealed in 1932. The legislation had been introduced to combat the destructive levels of spirit consumption across the country. Its effect, however, was quite the opposite: having hit a record low during the civil war of 1918, per capita alcohol consumption actually rose steadily in the years after prohibition. Police attempts to curtail the illegal sale of alcohol were often toothless, not least because it was the only way a significant portion of Finland's restaurants could make a profit. And many politicians were moved to speak out publicly against prohibition, complaining that it only served to erode ordinary citizens' respect for the law.

The smuggling process was facilitated by, among others, Estonian and German cargo ships that dropped anchor off the Finnish coast. They would be met by fast and mobile motorboats, which would load up with canisters of spirits before setting off for suitably sheltered harbours in the Helsinki region. Upon landing, the illicit cargo would be loaded into cars and vans, which would then discreetly deliver it to public houses and private households. It was undoubtedly a risky business, and not just because of the threat of arrest: in the wake of spirit smuggling there came a crime wave that, at its most serious, involved shootings and murders. However, it was also extremely profitable, and so it became the principal means of making a living for many small-time criminals and local fishermen.

One of the most renowned spirit smugglers was Algoth Niska, whose portfolio of misdeeds included delivering spirits to the social elite in Helsinki. It took a number of stints in prison before his black-market business became unprofitable. Over time, Niska became something of a folk-hero in Finland, helped in no small part by the publishing of his action-packed memoirs *Mina äventyr* ("My Adventures", 1931). In these, he made a point of stressing how few of his contemporaries actually thought that smuggling was criminal: "It is nothing that people get worked up about, it sooner provokes a good-natured smile." Niska was also famed in the city's sporting circles for his football skills, having played for the Finnish national team, which came fourth at the Stockholm Olympic Games in 1912.

Past Memories and Present Sentiments

Just as in many other cities, Helsinki's residents became more interested in the history of their urban surroundings as their education level increased. The first account of the city's past to be written with a general audience in mind was published back in 1888 by journalist Rafael Hertzberg, in the work *Helsingfors för trehundra år sedan och i våra dagar* ("Helsinki 300 Years Ago and in Our Present Day"). The historical overview was, however, only a short introduction to the impressionistic texts and vibrant images of everyday life and environs in the contemporary Helsinki of the author and his illustrator, Alex Federley. In the early 1900s, historian Petrus Nordmann published a compendium of primary sources from the city's first two hundred years in Swedish, but this, as the subject matter might imply, did not give a coherent account of Helsinki's history either.

The past was made significantly more accessible to residents in 1911, when the Helsinki City Museum was founded. Until the 1980s, it was housed in Villa Hakasalmi, a large Empire-style property from the Russian era, which is today directly opposite the National Museum of Finland. After the First World War, the city museum gradually expanded its activities, putting on a number of well-received exhibitions and putting out a publication series about Helsinki's history. The museum's most popular exhibit was a three-dimensional 1:500-scale model of Helsinki in 1878, which revealed how small and picturesque the city had been before it had been overcome by the irrepressible advance of industrialisation. The miniature Helsinki can still be found on display in the museum, which today is located in the Sederholm House on the southern edge of Senate Square.

The 1910s were also when the first plans were made for an academic anthology of the city's history. In the early 1930s, the city's decision-makers got on board with the idea of publishing such a work, and allocated a budget to help make it happen. However, even with their backing and the many capable historians engaged in the project, it took more than thirty years for the whole nine-volume anthology to come out in both Finnish and Swedish. The delay was partly a product of the war years, and partly down to the sizeable turnover of the researchers involved, but the finished work certainly served its purpose.

Besides adding substantially to the pool of knowledge about Helsinki, it had a tangible impact on public interest in the city's remarkable journey since its creation by Gustav Vasa. In recent decades, between 1997 and 2025, a new anthology of the city's history has taken shape: at ten volumes, it is even more extensive than its predecessor and casts an even more illuminating light on Helsinki's tumultuous past.

Another example of the city's budding understanding of its cultural memory in the early decades of the twentieth century was the foundation of Helsinki-Seura (The Helsinki Society) in the spring of 1934. This voluntary organisation of city residents would come to generate plenty of interest in Helsinki's cultural heritage. Mention should also be made of the Pro Helsingfors Foundation, established by businessman Julius Tallberg in 1917. Among other initiatives, this was responsible for the erection of sculptor Felix Nylund's Three Smiths statue (*Kolmen sepän patsas*) at the western end of Aleksanterinkatu in 1932. After the Second World War, there were also a large number of city district associations set up; each, in its own way, helped to shape and strengthen Helsinki's collective cultural memory.

During the 1930s, the Three Smiths statue was joined by many other public artworks in the city. Almost none of them, however, had any direct link to Helsinki's history, which perhaps reflected the need of the time to demonstrate that the city was the heart of the new Finnish Republic rather than a former imperial outpost. The sole exception was an obelisk commemorating Gustav II Adolf's visit to Helsinki in 1616. This was erected in 1932 in Vanhakaupunki, the former home of Helsinki, at the spot where the King had held Finland's historic meeting of the estates. In a similar spirit, a monument to the city's founder, Gustav Vasa, was unveiled at Vanhakaupunki in the summer of 1950, as part of Helsinki's 400-year jubilee. It was, nonetheless, telling that there was no interest in making space for the memorial in the modern city centre, where reminders of the Swedish era were almost non-existent.

An important conduit for the memories and emotions that stemmed from urban existence was the written culture of the period, whether the daily press, the weekly papers or the various trade publications. At the outset of the 1920s, they already contained reports and articles that described both the vanished and the current Helsinki with heartfelt sentiments and an expert eye. The weeklies' photographs were typically printed on better paper than the dailies' pictures, and were also subject to a more painstaking selection process. Nearly every issue of the leading political publication of the age—*Suomen Kuvalehti* ("Finland's Picture Magazine")—included photographs of events in Helsinki where politicians, soldiers, authors or sports stars were framed against the backdrop of the city's recognisable sites and streets.

Another vibrant reflection of Helsinki's emotional landscape were the contemporary novels and modernist poetry of the epoch, some of which produced fine depictions of the urban environs and class markers found within them. The most read of these literary portrayals of Helsinki were those by author Mika Waltari, who grew up in the city and paid close attention to its physical transformation and the eclectic fates of its inhabitants. In the 1936 novel *Surun ja ilon kaupunki* ("The City of Sorrow and Joy"), Waltari takes the reader through a day and a night in the pulsating Finnish capital. In the midst of his journey, he comes to a halt in the vicinity of Stockmann department store, and captures the spirit of Helsinki's commercial centre in a few snapshots:

> [...] cars empty from the parking spaces on the streets, on the tram stop at Old Student House people push and shove, [...] soon the shops' doors will be shutting too, the movie theatres' neon lights are already glowing shyly in the sunshine [...] on the tram stop a woman's painted nails glow against the green of a packet's wrapping paper [...]

In the same decade, the poet Katri Vala lived in the proletarian district of Sörnäinen, in what was then Helsinki's largest apartment building: Marjatan talo (Marjatta's House). This stood next to the rocky ridge of Vilhonvuori, which offered a view all the way out to sea. After her death, the location was christened Katri Valan puisto (Katri Vala Park) in her memory. One poem from her 1934 collection *Paluu* ("The Return") is entitled "Kesäilta laitakaupungissa", or "Summer Evening on the Edge of Town". In only a couple of verses, she evokes the peculiar mixture of raucousness and melancholy that consumed Marjatan talo in those moments:

> The big house tinkles like a musical box,
> The songs of the South Sea, the rhythms of the dance,
> The songs of sweetness arm-in-arm with the marches.

> People unfurl themselves out of windows,
> Look out to sea with eyes of mystery,
> Listen to the footsteps on the street,
> Dream of parties and of beautiful hearts,
> Of happiness, which never comes.
> On the rock opposite an armless youth ambles
> Staring ceaselessly out to sea.
> Empty sleeves fluttering
> Like feeble wings.

In common with Waltari, Vala had begun her writing career in the modernist literary group Tulenkantajat (The Torch Bearers), which had formed in 1920s Helsinki. As time progressed, however, the pair's ideological outlooks grew further and further apart. During the Second World War, Vala was periodically interrogated for her contacts with the Communists, while Waltari wrote rollicking reports of the police's hunt for these left-wing agitators. Even with their divergent politics, both authors' repertoires are alike in that a number of their other writings include references to Helsinki. The bilingual Katri Vala regularly reviewed and translated the modernist works of her Swedish-speaking Finn contemporaries, in which the Finnish capital often featured in one way or another. Waltari, for his part, wrote numerous film scripts in the late 1930s, some of which contained scenes set at famous locations in the city centre or its surroundings.

The breakthrough of the talkies (films with sound) in the early 1930s created a demand for scripts with believable dialogue and effective one-liners. With his background in the advertising industry, Waltari knew how to turn a phrase, and his first script to be made into a film was the action-adventure *VMV 6* (1936). Its protagonist was an enterprising coast guard officer aboard boat *VMV 6*, who was on the hunt of a gang of spirit smugglers; after various mishaps, he managed to capture not only the ne'er-do-wells, but also the heart of his love interest. Although the movie centred on smuggling operations out at sea, the director was able to insert a number of scenes set in the attractive environs of Kaivopuisto and in the orderly blocks of high-rises of Etu-Töölö.

Helsinki features even more prominently in the 1934 comedy film *Minä ja ministeri* ("The Minister and I"). This was based on a Finnish theatrical farce from the 1920s and directed by the rising star Risto Orko, who would soon become one of the biggest and most in-demand names in Finnish cinema. The film's plot itself is relatively banal, but this is counterbalanced by its value as a historical source, for it is sprinkled liberally with some of Helsinki's most recognisable sights. These include Aleksanterinkatu with Stockmann in the background, the Market Square and the south quay, the plaza at the House of the Estates, the main entrance to Helsinki Central Station, the modern functionalist blocks and, of course, the city's trams. Although the critical reception was sharply divided on the film's quality, it was united in respect of its urban cinematography, which everyone agreed was the finest that a Finnish filmmaker had ever produced.

For all their beguiling shots of the city, these feature films do not exactly give a realistic picture of Helsinki in the 1930s. The urban sequences were carefully engineered to emphasise the city's aesthetic qualities, and the films' lead roles were played, of course, by charismatic and articulate actors. That said, these motion pictures were made with an audience in mind, so in that sense they were showing a version of Helsinki that its contemporary inhabitants wanted to see. They also reflected the fashions of the era: the clothes, the jokes and the expressions that were then prominent among the denizens of the capital.

A more authentic depiction of everyday life in Helsinki could be found in the short newsreels that were screened before every feature film. The practice continued in the capital's movie theatres until the 1960s, as it afforded tax breaks to the proprietors. The aim behind the newsreels was to strengthen the audience's social consciousness and faith in the future. Rather than stage events for the camera, the film crews tried to capture what was actually happening in the city's bustling street life and workplaces. As such, their footage is a fairly true-to-life snapshot of quotidian Helsinki. Take the news reel made in the summer of 1933, by the pioneering Finnish documentary filmmakers Aho & Soldan, about the lively commerce on Market Square. It also contains a series of shots that show how the tree-lined avenue running between Läntinen and Itäinen Heikinkatu (today the start of Mannerheimintie) was being ripped up to make room for tram tracks. Such a scene is a far cry from the picturesque Helsinki of the period's movies, but it is far closer to the lived reality of urban life, for road works and construction sites are perpetual features of every city.

War and Peace

With the benefit of hindsight, it is hard to watch the light-hearted films of the late 1930s and not reflect on the darkness that was just around the corner. Finland's economy was thriving, living standards were steadily increasing and the prevailing hope was that the deteriorating relations between Europe's Great Powers would, despite everything, prove a temporary blip. It did not. Hitler, the dictator of Nazi Germany, would stop at nothing in his nationalist project to expand his country's territory, or *Lebensraum*. Stalin, his Communist counterpart in Moscow, did not take much convincing to join in with the Führer's brutal land grab, and the secret Molotov–Ribbentrop Pact of August 1939 divided Central and Eastern Europe into German and Soviet spheres of influence. This resulted in the Second World War, and the death of 54 million Europeans.

In contrast to the previous world war, this time around, Finland numbered among those countries that were struck first and suffered worst when the conflict erupted in the autumn of 1939. The two dictators, working in cahoots, first invaded Poland, then Stalin forced the Baltic states to let the Soviets establish military bases on their soil. He made similar demands of Finland, too, including a readjustment of the Finno-Soviet border, but the country's leaders refused to comply. As such, on 30 November 1939, Stalin ordered the Red Army to launch an invasion. He was driven not just by an imperialistic desire to establish a Greater Russia, but also by a pressing issue of national security. In order to protect Leningrad and its million-plus inhabitants, Stalin understood that he needed to have control of the Gulf of Finland's waters, which thereby meant taking control of Finland itself. The ink may barely have dried on the German-Soviet pact of non-aggression, but Stalin realised that a war with Germany was fast approaching.

And so, once again, Finland was dragged into a war between Great Powers due to its long coastline on its eponymous gulf and its proximity to its eastern neighbour's erstwhile capital on the mouth of the Neva. And, as so often before, Helsinki was the urban area behind the front lines that was worst affected by the enemy's attack. On the very same morning that the Red Army's troops swarmed over the border on the Karelian Isthmus, the Soviet air force began its bombardment of Helsinki. The planes were spotted on their approach, which gave the air raid sirens time to sound their warning over the city before it was rocked by explosives. A few hours later, however, a second wave of Soviet bombers appeared suddenly out of the clouds above the city, and dropped their deadly cargo before the sirens could alert the inhabitants.

The third Soviet barrage came the very next day, after which authorities were able to take stock of the damage. The Finnish capital and its inhabitants had been subject to widespread destruction: ninety-one people had been killed, many hundreds injured, and numerous houses had suffered direct hits and been burned to the ground. The death toll would have been greater had not many residents sought shelter outside of the city before the bombing started. Fifteen other localities in Finland were also targeted by air raids, five of which were, like Helsinki, densely built districts on the south coast.

In spite of the chaos the bombings caused, it would be wrong to claim that the outbreak of war had come as a complete surprise. Universal military service for Finnish men had been in place for almost as long as the country had been independent, and many of these reservists had already received their mobilisation orders from the Finnish Army in October 1939. That same month,

Helsinki authorities had started to make preparations for a war-induced food shortage by handing out ration cards to the city's populace.

After the early days of the war, the situation at the front gradually started to stabilise, and the aerial assaults against Helsinki and other coastal urban centres abated. Nonetheless, the three and a half months of the Winter War came to be a profoundly damaging experience for almost all Finns. It was difficult to come to terms with the sharp contrast between the optimism and hope of peacetime and the unforgiving reality of war: the fallen soldiers, the blown-up homes, the lost territories. Just as terrible, too, was the inaction of the Western world: there might have been a groundswell of sympathy for Finland in many countries, but this failed to translate into substantial military support. For a large number of the Finnish populace, the horrible realisation that their country would be left to fend for itself against a far larger aggressor would live long in the memory.

After a certain amount of vacillating when the Winter War broke out, the Finnish government resolved to stay put in Helsinki, reasoning that doing so would help maintain morale. Throughout the conflict, it held its meetings in the Bank of Finland's bomb-proof vault, which was a location befitting the new prime minister, Risto Ryti, who had been the bank's governor. In contrast to the government, the parliament was evacuated out of Helsinki to the western town of Kauhajoki, in Ostrobothnia, from where it would carry out its business until February 1940. Its impact on the course of the war was limited, however, as all critical decisions were made by the government in collaboration with the Commander-in-Chief of the Finnish Army, Gustaf Mannerheim. At the age of 72, and after two decades in the reserves, he had been recalled to lead the country's military effort at this dire time. During both the Winter and the

Continuation Wars against the Soviets, he would direct Finland's defence from the Headquarters of the Finnish Army, which were established in the inland city of Mikkeli, north-east of Helsinki in South Savo.

Mannerheim also had a private train car and he used it regularly to travel to Helsinki for discussions with Finland's other wartime leaders. On his trips to the capital, it is likely that he, in common with many other Finnish decision-makers, patronised Hotel Kämp. This prestigious establishment on Pohjoisesplanadi took on an unlikely role in the Winter War when around a dozen foreign journalists booked rooms there a little over a month before fighting began. They had heard reports of how badly the Finno-Soviet negotiations had been progressing in Moscow, and wanted to be on location if the situation escalated further. The Finnish authorities had nothing against their presence. On the contrary, when the second floor of the fashionable hotel was turned into a press centre, the state made sure that its information and propaganda departments were also accommodated there. By the time the war actually broke out, there were already some fifty international journalists based in Hotel Kämp and eager to report on Finland's desperate fight for its future.

This sudden burst of interest in Finland was partly a consequence of the lack of action in the trenches on the Continent in the winter of 1939–40. On the hunt for more drama, many journalists made the trip to Finland, since its existential defensive struggle against a more powerful enemy had all the ingredients of a heroic tale. One of the first on the scene when the bombs started to strike Helsinki was American ace reporter Martha Gellhorn, the sweetheart and future wife of Ernest Hemingway. Among her contemporaries, she was best known for her reports from crisis-hit regions across the world for *Collier's*, the American weekly magazine.

After the second air strike on Helsinki, Gellhorn made her way out onto the city's streets and in the direction of the burning buildings. At Kamppi's bus station, she encountered the wreckage of a number of cars and a bus in flames, beside which lay a man's headless corpse. In her article, Gellhorn paid attention to his repaired leather shoes. Stalin's propaganda claimed that the Red Army was coming to the aid of the Finnish working class, yet the war's first victims were some of the very people he was meant to be saving. A large number of the innocent civilians slain at the bus station were women and children, who had been awaiting evacuation from the city.

As the weeks turned into months, the international press corps became increasingly irritated by the Finnish war censorship, and the difficulties in gaining access to the frontline. When the Finnish government was forced to make a harsh peace deal with the Soviet Union on 13 March 1940, the journalists quickly turned their focus back on the heroic spirit of the Finnish people. Their stirring reports described the peace treaty as a realistic outcome, but this was a far cry from how the populace saw its bitter terms, which required that Finland cede large swaths of land in the east to the Soviets. Disappointment hung in the air over the nation, embodied by the white-and-blue Finnish flags hung at half-mast across Helsinki. It could be seen in the daily papers, where the treaty was outlined amidst the death notices from the front, the vindictive peace terms an injustice to the fallen soldiers' sacrifice. It could be heard in Minister for Foreign Affairs Tanner's announcement of the peace on the radio, in both Finnish and Swedish. He defended the state leadership's decision to accept the deal with the caustic remark that "the democratic states could not or did not want to help us in this unequal conflict."

Nerves were frayed and hackles were raised, but the Finnish nation, as a collective entity, had to maintain its composure to make an orderly transition from war to peace. Keeping things together was especially crucial when the Soviet threat still loomed large, so much so that many suspected another war was just around the corner. Yet it was understandably hard to move on from the Winter War, when almost 25,000 soldiers had lost their lives fighting and a further thousand civilians had been killed in the bombing. Moreover, many of the fallen troops were still awaiting burial, many of those with serious injuries were still receiving treatment, and the evacuation of everyone living in the annexed areas still had to be organised. During the ensuing fifteen months of so-called "interim peace", the prevailing atmosphere in Helsinki was therefore a strange mixture of relief, unrest and dogged determination, which caused some of the residents to party and live their lives as though every day was their last.

On Sunday 19 May 1940, a national day of remembrance was organised for the war dead for the first time. The Finnish flag was flown in their honour across the country and wreaths were laid in almost every churchyard. At the same time, the Whites' victory parade, which had been held annually on 16 May ever since the civil war, was henceforth discontinued. Even two decades after the domestic conflict had finished, the march remained a source of bad blood between the working class and bourgeoisie. Its abolition was thus an attempt to foster a spirit of national unity. The defence authorities had ensured that the deceased soldiers were returned to their home regions, where they were interred in heroes' graves that had been reserved for them. These heroes' graves came to form lasting monuments to Finland's war years between 1939 and 1945. The largest of them was established at the northern end of Hietaniemi Cemetery in Helsinki, where a total of 3,164 fallen soldiers from the capital were laid to rest. In February 1951, Mannerheim himself would be buried next to them, making their memorial into something akin to a national shrine.

In the summer of 1940, it was certainly not taken for granted that this day of remembrance would become an annual tradition, nor that the fallen soldiers' heroic legacy was assured. Stalin was then busy incorporating Estonia, Latvia and Lithuania into the Soviet Union, but he had not given up on the idea of invading Finland. In fact, as the Red Army was overthrowing the Baltic governments, he began to turn up the heat on the Finnish leadership in Helsinki. Among other threats and intrusions on Finland's sovereignty, Moscow encouraged its loyal Finnish Communists to organise demonstrations in Hakaniemi Square in July 1940 to protest against their government's unwillingness to accommodate the Soviets' sharpening demands. It was during these weeks of strife and unrest that Finland and Germany first opened up top-secret lines of communication, with the aim of establishing closer relations. This mutual diplomatic effort would culminate in Finland and Germany, together with Romania, launching a carefully planned attack on the Soviet Union in June 1941.

One of the first visible signs of Finno-German cooperation was the organisation of a three-way athletics meet between Finland, Sweden and Germany at Helsinki's Olympic Stadium in early September 1940. As the national teams marched out onto the field, those in attendance certainly took note of the German swastika hoisted up alongside the Nordic cross flags, although not a word was uttered in the press about the event's political symbolism. The focus was resolutely on the sporting performances, and it was those of Rudolf Harbig that earned the biggest reaction from the crowd. The German running star arrived in Helsinki as the recently crowned 400m and 800m world-record holder, and he won his races in both distances at a canter.

Over the coming winter of 1940–1, Finland and Germany covertly intensified their military and economic collaboration.

In early June 1941, the Finnish state leadership informed the chairmen of each political party's parliamentary group that a war between Germany and the Soviet Union could well be on the cards. Finland should, therefore, mobilise its own army in order to protect its national security. The political and military leadership were, of course, actively downplaying Finland's involvement in the forthcoming conflict: in reality, they were making preparations for a coordinated assault on the Soviet Union. The Finnish Army's firepower had been doubled by extensive arms purchases from Germany, and the northern half of Finland's eastern front would be defended by German troops arriving from northern Norway. As the Finno-German cooperation became increasingly hard to conceal, the majority of the Finnish populace were relieved that their land no longer stood alone against the Soviet Union. Only a tiny fraction of them felt particularly drawn towards Nazism itself; for the rest, the ideology was simply of secondary concern in Finland's vulnerable position. On Sunday 22 June 1941, Germany launched its attack on the Soviet Union, but the Finnish Army remained on standby: the plan was that it would join the war only after the Red Air Force had targeted southern Finland with bombing raids. When this happened three days later, the government could confirm that Finland was at war again.

On this occasion, the centre of Helsinki was spared, but it was a different story north of Pitkäsilta Bridge. In early July, an air strike hit Kallio and Alppila, killing more than thirty people. The destruction might well have been worse if the city's anti-aircraft defences had not been considerably strengthened by German military technology. It was now protected by seven heavy anti-aircraft batteries, whose gunfire was coordinated, along with the rest of the capital's air defences, from an underground command centre built beneath the fire station's hilltop tower on Korkeavuorenkatu. As the summer progressed, the war's focal point shifted further and further from Helsinki. And once the Germans had captured Tallinn at the end of August 1941, the Soviet bombers no longer had such a convenient location from which to embark on sallies against Helsinki, with the upshot being that they targeted the city far less frequently.

The situation in Helsinki was, in other respects, noticeably calmer than at the outbreak of the Winter War. As part of the bolstered anti-aircraft defences, acoustic detection of the city's airspace had significantly improved, and new bomb shelters had been built during the brief period of interim peace. Moreover, the threat of Soviet raids had provoked less panic in the streets this time around, as many families had already travelled to the countryside for the school holidays. The undisguised stationing of German soldiers in the city also served as a timely reminder that Finland was not fighting this war alone. During the next three years, the German Ambassador to Helsinki, Wipert von Blücher, regularly made public appearances with the Finnish state leadership. Von Blücher's office was then the elegant German embassy building that had been built in east Kaivopuisto in the late 1920s, but the war's disastrous end for both Finland and Germany would see it pass into Soviet ownership. Today, it functions as a school for the children of the staff at the Russian embassy.

By the autumn of 1941, it had become apparent that the war would go on for a lot longer than initially envisaged. Particularly during the conflict's first winter, this led to food shortages and the strict rationing of wood and gas. A significant factor behind the scarcity was that such a large share of the male labour force had gone to the front. In an effort to combat this, duty-to-work legislation was enacted in the spring of 1942, by which all citizens over the age of 16 could be conscripted to take on jobs essential for the day-to-day function of the country. As a result, many Helsinki residents had to quickly learn how to chop wood, and a sizeable number of them were sent out of the city to work the land during the autumn harvest.

The specific demands of the tasks varied, but such obligatory employment shaped the daily lives of most of the city's population for the next two years of war. Although the conflict largely took the form of positional warfare on the Finnish section of the front, the number of fallen soldiers continued to rise every day. In Helsinki, those looking to escape the constant stream of sorrow and despair often turned to the cinema. German movies were screened regularly, and so, too, were American ones, since the United States—in contrast to Britain—had not declared war on Finland after the Finnish collaboration with the Nazis became public. Movie theatres were a welcome distraction from frontline news, but they were not immune from the horrors of war: on Sunday 8 November 1942, tragedy struck a children's screening in the Edison Cinema at Kolmikulma, right in the centre of Helsinki. Reacting to the air raid sirens that went off mid-way through the film, the audience were hurrying out of the movie theatre towards the closest shelter when a bomb from the lone Soviet plane hit the rail of the tram tracks at a nearby street corner. This sent shrapnel flying over a far wider area than usual, leading to the deaths of around fifty people.

The next year, Helsinki's defences were further reinforced with German anti-aircraft equipment. The most important were two large radar stations, which were able to intercept the signals of approaching Soviet planes from a distance of up to 200 kilometres. With the help of these and four smaller radar apparatuses, the anti-aircraft system could track the bombers' flight paths with precision, and fire off targeted flak into the sky just as the planes entered the city's airspace. The machinery was tested regularly, and was in full working order when, late in the afternoon on 6 February 1944, it picked up signals that a large fleet of Soviet aircraft was on its way to attack Helsinki.

At 6.15pm, the so-called silent alarm went off. This entailed disabling the electricity supply for a few moments, shrouding the entire city in complete darkness. It also stopped all trams and trains in their tracks, giving their passengers the opportunity to seek shelter. The sirens' piercing wail rang out across the city at 6.51pm, but it was ignored by some citizens, including groups of youngsters out on the ice-skating rinks around the city centre. Their mistaken assumption that it was just another false alarm would have deadly consequences. When the first bombs fell in the vicinity of the Central Railway Station half an hour later, a number of schoolchildren skating on the ice in Kaisaniemi Park were killed by flying shrapnel.

This was the opening salvo of three nights of Soviet air raids on Helsinki, which were designed to force Finland's increasingly uncooperative government to begin peace negotiations. By pure coincidence, the attacks took place at exactly ten-day intervals, on 6–7, 16–17 and 26–7 February 1944. This was because the night sky over Helsinki was completely cloudless on these dates, which made it easier for the bombers to find their pre-agreed targets. Starlit skies notwithstanding, the Red Air Force's bombardments did not see much success. The flak from the Finnish anti-aircraft guns proved such a deterrent that over half of all the dropped bombs fell into the sea. Moreover, the Soviet pilots were clearly unused to carrying out such precision bombing missions, as only four per cent of their explosives struck Helsinki's high-rise districts.

Nevertheless, from the perspective of most of Helsinki's residents, and most of the home front more generally, these three night raids comprised the most terrifying experience of the entire Second World War. The total death toll came to 146 people, while 109 buildings were completely destroyed. Certainly, this was only a fraction of the devastation that the Western Allies' bombing campaign wreaked on Germany, but not a single Helsinki inhabitant would have believed their city would escape so lightly on those hellish nights, when the sirens howled and the bombs whistled and roared all around them. Indeed, the first night raid provoked such fear that a substantial proportion of the city's children and adolescents were evacuated to the countryside in its immediate aftermath.

The final night raid was the most furious of all. The University of Helsinki's main building, on the west side of Senate Square, took a direct hit, which turned the Great Hall, replete with its collection of artwork, to ashes. In such perilous circumstances, scarcely anyone dared to head out into the streets to capture all the destruction on camera. One exception was the anonymous photographer from the military authorities, who snapped a famous shot of the burning university with Alexander II's statue standing tall and perfectly intact in the foreground. This picture has featured, almost without fail, in every published work on the bombing of Helsinki in 1944.

As a new spring began to blossom in 1944, so, too, did renewed hope among the Finns that the worst was perhaps over. They were sorely mistaken: in June 1944, the Red Army launched a large offensive on the Karelian Isthmus to try and break Finnish resistance once and for all. The Finns clung on to their defensive positions by the skin of their teeth, and prevented the Soviets from marching on their homeland. This came at a heavy cost, however: 12,000 Finnish soldiers had lost their lives, and Stalin had done enough to force Finland to cut ties with Germany. On 19 September 1944, the Finnish government was forced to enter into an even harsher armistice agreement than that of March 1940, although many Finns feared that this was just a precursor to a new Soviet invasion. They were again mistaken: when the war ended less than a year later, Finland had survived as an independent nation. In fact, there were only three capital cities of combatant countries in Europe that ultimately avoided occupation: London, Moscow—and Helsinki.

6

COLD WAR CLIMATES

Great Annexations

In late September 1944, Helsinki's position did not look particularly rosy. The world war was still in full swing in Central Europe, and one of the harsh ceasefire conditions was that Porkkalanniemi, a peninsula just 30 kilometres west of the capital, had to be handed over to the Soviet Union for use as a military base. The residents of the area were given a mere ten days to evacuate. In order to ensure that the Finnish government adhered to the strict terms of the treaty, the Allied Control Commission arrived in Helsinki in early October, under the direction of Stalin's right-hand man, Colonel-General Andrei Zhdanov. The commission's members made Hotel Torni their headquarters, which could, as the city's only high-rise building, generously be described as a skyscraper.

One of the control commission's first observations was that Helsinki had emerged surprisingly unscathed from the war. The Soviet representatives were forced to acknowledge the relatively limited success of their bombing campaign, while their British colleagues expressed amazement at how well-dressed and healthy the city's population looked compared to that of London. In fact, during the final winter of the war, things would only get worse for a large number of the European capital cities still embroiled in the fighting. Warsaw's old town was blown to smithereens, while Budapest and Berlin would soon be in ruins, as would many medieval quarters in both Tallinn and Riga.

The reason that Helsinki—and the whole of Finland—had made it through the war largely intact was down to the country's conscript army, with German support, holding firm against Soviet pressure. Its fate was also determined by the push and pull of bigger geopolitical forces. When, during the winter of 1944–5, Stalin began hurriedly bearing down on Berlin, the country's location north of the Gulf of Finland became, for the first time, a blessing. It was now more trouble than it was worth for the Soviets to try and launch an offensive from Finland onto the Continent. The Finnish Army was not quite done fighting, however: in the spring of 1945, it began waging war up in Lapland against the Germans, its erstwhile brothers in arms. Nonetheless, this conflict—and the havoc it wreaked—was far smaller in scale than the blood-soaked scenes down on the Continent.

The main focus of most Helsinki residents, however, was on the transition from war to peace, which demanded a number of adjustments. Alongside accommodating the demobilised troops and the civilian population from the territories annexed by the Soviets, the battle-scarred city itself required a fair degree of rebuilding, and would not be fully restored until well into the 1950s. As a result, the housing shortage in Helsinki became increasingly acute, compelling the Finnish government to dramatically redraw the boundaries of the city. From the start of 1946, Helsinki's area increased five-fold, from 30 to 165 square kilometres, through the incorporation of both the surrounding countryside and the smaller urban centres in its vicinity. Twenty years later, it would further integrate a sizeable chunk of Helsinki Rural Municipality, namely the eastern coastal region of Vuosaari.

This process was facilitated by the fact that the city had begun making plans for such incorporations back in the 1920s, and had, therefore, already acquired almost half of all the land that would comprise its new area. Even so, it was met with a certain amount of opposition, not least in Kulosaari, which had formed its own rural municipality in 1922. The garden city's spokesman was Finland's first president K. J. Ståhlberg, who owned a villa on the island. Referencing the constitution that he himself had helped bring into being, he demonstrated that the incorporation was in contravention of Finnish law. His efforts were in vain, however, for constitutional legality did not carry much weight with the politicians in power during the years straight after the war. It was a time when they were often forced to drive through decisions that went against the Western concept of justice. The most flagrant example of this was the long prison sentences handed down to Finland's wartime president and seven ministers in February 1946; the convictions had their basis in a retroactively passed and grotesquely misinterpreted law.

Both the government and the city's leadership were under pressure to find a rapid solution to Helsinki's crying shortage of housing. They were fortunate, then, that Helsinki's city planners had, for decades, had designs at their disposal that showed how the expansion could be carried out. The most important of these was a city plan from the 1910s signed by Helsinki's zoning architect Bertel Jung. With a few tweaks and additions from Eliel Saarinen's visionary proposal from 1918, Jung's plan would prove the surprisingly dominant guiding force for the city's large building projects all the way up to the 1990s.

In spite of the acute lack of building materials, the city planners and decision-makers set about realising these designs with vim and vigour. Over the next two decades, the city underwent its biggest transformation since its industrialisation in the late nineteenth century. The large majority of its new territory had belonged to Helsinki Rural Municipality and lay, in the main, to the north and the east of the city's former boundaries. The exception was Lauttasaari, an island just west of the city: in common with Kulosaari, the island on the east side of the centre, it gradually gained a stock of high-rise buildings. Both islands were also firmly tied to Helsinki by the construction of multi-lane highways running through them into the inner city.

The steady growth in car and bus traffic allowed Helsinki to expand in a more unrestrained fashion than ever before, as the new city districts could be built further apart from one another. And just as with the densely packed population hubs that popped up around the railway stations on Helsinki's outskirts in the late 1800s, the post-war suburbs were connected to the city centre via their transport arteries. This time it was main roads, rather than rail tracks, that were in vogue, and these were straightened and widened into multi-lane thoroughfares in the 1960s and 1970s. The first large-scale suburbs of this sort were Lauttasaari, Munkkivuori, Pohjois-Haaga and Herttoniemi, whose central areas stood ready in the mid-1950s. They would become the template for the city's future suburbs: the core of each was built around high-rise flats, schools, a shopping centre, sports grounds and a library, which all also served the inhabitants of the terraced and detached houses in the vicinity.

In the 1960s, the focal point of home construction moved, slowly but surely, to the eastern half of the city's recently incorporated regions. Until this period, these suburbs had been distinctly rural areas, as suggested by names such as Pihjalanmäki (Rowan Hill), Myllypuro (Mill Brook) and Kontula (from the Swedish *Gårdsbacka*, loosely meaning Farm Hill). The next urban expansion in the east took place in Laajasalo and Vuosaari, both of which became popular locations for terraced and detached houses thanks to their long coastlines. As might be expected, the overall effect of this development was that these eastern suburbs experienced the fastest population increase in Helsinki, while the inner city's oldest districts saw their resident numbers shrink drastically.

In addition, at the outset of the 1970s, closely packed housing blocks were erected in Helsinki's neighbouring municipalities: Espoo to the west and Helsinki Rural Municipality (renamed Vantaa in 1972) to the north. Fewer and fewer of the capital region's inhabitants moved through the city centre on a daily basis, so their home districts came to assume an increasingly prominent role in defining their identity. A similar process, it is true, had taken place in the 1800s when the city's first suburbs had sprung up on the outskirts of the centre. Back then, just as in post-war eastern Helsinki, these inhabitants were usually first-generation Helsinki residents.

Helsinki's largest population increase occurred, naturally enough, in tandem with the great incorporation of 1946. Overnight, the city's total inhabitants shot up by 65,000 people, from 276,500 to 341,500. And yet, in the decades immediately thereafter, their number continued to climb steeply, a product of both the record baby boom after the war and the sweeping urbanisation of Finnish society. By around 1970, Helsinki's population had risen to 524,000 people, but, from this point on, the trend turned sharply in the opposite direction, with the capital region's residents increasingly choosing to live beyond Helsinki's boundaries, in Espoo or Vantaa. From 1970 to 1990, Helsinki decreased in size by over 33,000 people, all the while the two municipalities next door grew by 162,000, from 169,000 to 331,000 residents.

A comparable shift from the busy and crowded city to the quiet and calm of the surrounding towns and suburbs happened in all

Western countries. The reversal of the cities' fortunes can largely be explained by the improved transport infrastructure and a growing need for reasonably priced housing. This resulted in many young families in Finland's capital city region eschewing Helsinki for Espoo or Vantaa. The majority of them had been born and raised in other areas of the country, but had migrated to Helsinki to seek work or to start their studies. Typically, they would initially live in the city itself, before readily moving out to new and more roomy housing after finding a partner and having children. Finland's youth did not just descend on Helsinki, however: a significant number emigrated to Sweden between 1950 and 1980, with a total of 300,000 staying on in the country for good.

In Helsinki, the scale of this population shift can be seen from the fact that, in 1950, only thirty-eight per cent of residents were born in the city. The largest category of migrants, at 12.4 per cent, consisted of those who hailed from the regions annexed by the Soviet Union after the Continuation War, with Karelians featuring most prominently among their number. Almost as abundant were those who had moved from other parts of Uusimaa and Häme, who comprised the second-largest migrant group in the city. Over the decades to come, the inflow of people from the regions would level out while the proportion of native-born residents began to creep up, so that the latter accounted for forty-three per cent of all inhabitants by the late 1980s.

Just as in earlier epochs in the city's history, the accelerating waves of new arrivals brought with them new customs, linguistic norms and class signifiers that were absorbed into the collective everyday experience of Helsinki. The three decades immediately after the war were, to a great extent, characterised by the baby boom. The first signs of this were the city's packed-out playgrounds and sports fields, then the division of the school day into morning and afternoon shifts as the only way to accommodate all the pupils. As they got older, these young people flooded Helsinki's secondary schools, workplaces and entertainment venues. On a national level, the population explosion was greatest between 1945 and 1954, but in Helsinki it only reached its peak in the 1960s, following the construction of the large eastern suburbs, when a total of 80,000 children were born.

Another vibrant force among the throngs that swirled through post-war Helsinki were the Karelian migrants and their offspring. At the start of the 1950s, a little over ten per cent of the city's population, or 41,400 people, were originally from Karelia. The proportion with such heritage was, of course, greater still, since there were plenty of children born into Karelian families in the city. A significant number of arrivals from this province came from its urban centres, particularly the Vyborg region. This meant that, in contrast to more rural migrants, many of them had been keenly involved in commercial and associational life, and they quickly threw themselves into similar activities upon moving to Helsinki.

One of the Karelian businesses that came to the capital was Wiipurin Korsetti ("Vyborg's Corset"), which had begun selling ladies' lingerie in Vyborg's medieval quarter just before the Second World War. After setting up shop for a few years in the city of Mikkeli, the owner decided to open a branch of the store in Helsinki, at 8 Arkadiankatu in Etu-Töölö, where it remains to this day. Another Karelian business that is still a landmark in modern-day Helsinki is Restaurant Lehtovaara, which also originated as a fashionable establishment in Vyborg's old town. It relocated to the capital following the evacuation of Vyborg during the Winter War in 1940; only a matter of months later, in summer that same year, it began serving customers from a new functionalist building at Sibelius Park in Etu-Töölö. It is still widely considered to be one of the best restaurants in Helsinki.

The central organisation for all evacuated Karelians in Finland—*Karjalan Liitto*—similarly started its operations in

Helsinki in the aftermath of the Winter War. As did Viipurin Suomalainen Kirjallisuusseura (Vyborg's Finnish Literature Society), a cultural institution founded back in 1845. These two associations would together play an important role in upholding Karelian cultural traditions and representing the ethnic group's political interests. The most nostalgic exiled Karelians long clung to wistful hopes that their home region would be repatriated by Finland, but the majority were more concerned by everyday economic matters. In particular, the associations were expected to look out for the financial security of smallholders, for Karelians had, in many parts of the country, been compensated with parcels of land after the war. Two of their spokesmen became high-profile figures in domestic politics: leader of the Agrarian League (which became the Centre Party in 1965), Johannes Virolainen; and Veikko Vennamo, who established the populist Finnish Rural Party in 1959.

Although Vennamo was a skilled public speaker, it was rather Virolainen who became known for his Karelian accent. This could well be due to the fact that the latter's father had actually toiled the land in Karelia as a farmer, whereas the former was the son of a bank manager, a less traditionally Karelian profession. As a rule, the Karelians who moved to Helsinki quickly got into the habit of speaking a more standardised version of Finnish outside of the home, as the capital's residents did not exactly adore the various Finnish and Swedish dialectical pronunciations they encountered. Moreover, by this time, the everyday Helsinki Finnish had already been profoundly shaped by the Häme and West Finnish vernaculars that previous generations of migrants had brought with them.

A similar kind of standardisation also took place within written Finnish. Up to the Second World War, this had been shaped by the priorities of the Fennophile social elite, who aimed to create a standard Finnish that was unadulterated and well-articulated. As both geographic and social mobility increased, this formal manner of writing and speaking slowly morphed into something more fluid and flexible, which is immediately apparent when the early Finnish-language radio broadcasts and films are compared to those of the 1960s. A broadly equivalent linguistic standardisation occurred in Swedish-speaking circles in the city, but at a notably slower rate, since they ended up using Finnish increasingly often in their everyday interactions, as their number began to decline.

To be precise, the total of Swedish-speaking Helsinki residents fell steadily from 71,000 in 1950 to 45,200 in 1980. Not only was the birth rate substantially lower among Swedish speakers, many of them also chose to move further afield during this period, whether to Espoo, Kauniainen or all the way to Sweden. Indeed, it should come as no surprise that they were, proportionally, hugely over-represented among the residents of Helsinki who emigrated west to Sweden. Besides which, the camaraderie and shared destiny brought about by the war years had been an efficient way of diffusing tensions between the language groups. This resulted in a growing number of marriages across the former language divide, and made the linguistic identity of the progeny of such unions less hotly contested. Up until the 1970s, the majority of these children were registered as Finnish-speaking and sent to Finnish-speaking schools. But since then, the opposite has occurred, and today most bilingual families choose the Swedish educational path for their children.

Set in a wider context, both the internal migration to Helsinki and the emigration to Sweden were representative of the same patterns of movement that occurred in many other parts of Europe after the Second World War. The young workforce in the provinces was attracted by the opportunities in the bigger conurbations in their homelands, and many soon went seeking better-paid industrial work in foreign countries, whether

Sweden, Great Britain or West Germany. To a considerable degree, this improved mobility was enabled by the better transport connections both within countries and between them. This development was not entirely without its downsides, and Helsinki's residents in the 1960s had to quickly learn to live with the new everyday phenomena of tailbacks and traffic jams. Early the next decade, the first car ferries began running regular voyages between Helsinki and Stockholm. In the Finnish capital, they departed from the South Harbour, which was a source of dismay for many who saw the constant stream of through-traffic as undermining the area's urban charm.

The Olympic Spirit

This shoreline south of the city centre was given a huge boost in conjunction with the preparations for the Helsinki Olympics at the end of July 1952. A few days before the games' opening ceremony, a combined passenger and freight terminal began its operations in the South Harbour's western quay. The elegant, functionalist building, with its yellow-brick facade complementing its light interior, would later be christened the Olympic Terminal in recognition of its original purpose. Prior to its inauguration, a promenade had been laid out along Kaivopuisto's coastline, starting from another new premises constructed especially for the Olympic tourists: Café Ursula. A few blocks to the north, just west of Market Square, the Finnish Employers' Confederation had just finished Palace, its building complex on Eteläranta. According to one contemporary arbiter of taste, its modernist style and smart decor had a Cosmopolitan charm that was "in some way American". The building served as a hotel for the duration of the Olympics, and still houses one of Helsinki's best restaurants.

These new builds were far from the only necessary investment when the city was re-awarded the games in 1947. Many of

Helsinki's sports facilities had, it is true, been constructed already in the 1930s, in preparation for the postponed 1940 competition, but both the Olympic Stadium and the nearby Messuhalli (today *Töölön kisahalli*) still had to be enlarged. The hosting duties stretched well beyond the venues themselves, of course, and entailed extensive building projects, such as the new, larger airport north of the city in Helsinki Rural Municipality. Today it is known as Helsinki-Vantaa Airport, the hub of international air travel in Finland. Alongside this, there was a concerted effort to rejuvenate the city after the fatigue and adversity wrought by the years of war and reconstruction. There was not enough time, however, for everything to come into place. Two blocks west of the resplendent new Palace, the Guards' Barracks still lay in ruins, having been decimated during the Soviet bombardment of February 1944.

The would-be Olympic Village in Käpylä (*Olympiakylä*) had already been taken into use by domestic residents. This led to the construction of a whole new city quarter, Kisakylä, just south of the original development, where most of the foreign athletes would be housed. Finland's own Olympians had to make do with their accommodation at the Military Academy out on the island of Santahamina in the south, while the teams of Soviet and Eastern Bloc athletes stayed at the Helsinki University of Technology's new campus west of the city in Otaniemi. It was not a coincidence that the communist athletes were based in this remote student housing, but rather a stipulation by the Soviet Union, for it did not want its sportsmen and women mingling with their Western counterparts any more than necessary.

The Soviet Union's demand was met without complaint by the Finnish organisers, not least because its interest in participating in the games, for the first time ever, had been a crucial factor in the choice of Helsinki as host city. Indeed, if the Soviets had disapproved of the idea, then the competition would almost certainly have been held elsewhere. When the International Olympic Committee made its decision on the matter in June 1947, the Allied Control Commission was still operating in the Finnish capital. It was only after the Paris Peace Treaty came into force in late September 1947 that the commission left Helsinki, but its departure did little to diminish how dependent Finland was on the Soviet Union's whim. That same year, Moscow pressured the Finnish government into declining the invitation to participate in the Marshall Plan, through which the United States provided economic support for Europe's post-war reconstruction. Furthermore, the Soviet military was still located ominously close to Helsinki, since Porkkalanniemi, a little to the city's west, remained under Moscow's control as a naval base.

The Finnish government therefore saw the Helsinki Olympics as a unique opportunity to show the world that the country had survived the Second World War with its independence intact. Helsinki's decision-makers shared this goal, but they also understood that the games gave the city the chance to promote itself as an attractive tourist destination. For the country's sporting bodies, organising almost two weeks' worth of athletic events was naturally a great responsibility, but it was also a once-in-a-lifetime experience. Every sport had to take place in a venue that met international standards, and every contest had to be overseen by officials who knew the discipline's rules down to the smallest detail.

On 19 July 1952, the opening ceremony was held at the Olympic Stadium in the midst of a torrential downpour, which did put something of a dampener on proceedings. Still, the fleet-footed arrival of Paavo Nurmi, the superstar of Finnish running in the 1920s, certainly caused a sensation. He entered the arena at a brisk jog with the glowing Olympic torch in his hand, and kindled the Olympic flame in front of the spectators. From there, the torch was carried on to the Stadium Tower outside, at the top of which stood a second Olympic cauldron waiting to be lit. This time, it was another legendary long-distance runner who got to do the honours: Hannes Kolehmainen, a double-gold medal winner from the Stockholm Olympics in 1912.

Then happened something completely unplanned. Just as the Archbishop of Finland was about to bless the games in Latin, a young woman clad in a long white dress rushed past him to the rostrum. She managed to utter "Ladies and gentlemen" in English before Erik von Frenckell, Finland's organiser-in-chief of the games, grabbed hold of the microphone. He was heard to say "Nein, you can't speak it," before politely escorting her away. The incident provoked great excitement in the stands, where many guessed that the woman was none other than Armi Kuusela, the Finnish beauty queen who had won the inaugural Miss Universe competition earlier that same year. They were mistaken, however, and while the journalists began feverishly writing their reports of what they had just witnessed, the woman was taken to the nearest police station.

It seems that one of the policemen there tipped reporters off as to her true identity, since the article in the next day's *Helsingin Sanomat* made no mention of Kuusela, but instead described the detainee as "an enterprising, fanatical German lady who is apparently suffering from delusions of grandeur". During questioning, it had come out that she was a 23-year-old German student called Barbara Rotbraut-Pleyer, who had travelled to Helsinki alone for the purpose of delivering her message of love to the whole world at the Olympic opening ceremony. After having tried, in vain, to secure an audience with Finnish President J. K. Paasikivi, she had snuck into the stadium at the same time as Paavo Nurmi was running out onto the field. Her motive had been entirely apolitical: she had been carrying a manuscript, later confiscated by the police, which made clear that she simply wished to appeal for freedom and peace for all.

When the truth surfaced, Rotbraut-Pleyer was nicknamed "the angel of peace", but she was not given another chance to spread her spiritual word in Helsinki. The morning after the incident, she was discreetly transported to the airport and put on a flight back to her homeland.

By then, the packed competition schedule had already taken much of the limelight away from her antics. The stand-out performance from the Helsinki Olympics was produced by the Czech athlete, Emil Zátopek, who claimed three gold medals in long-distance running, the final one coming after he spontaneously decided to run his first-ever marathon. To cap it all off, his wife, Dana Zátopková, took home a gold of her own after securing victory in the women's javelin. While no one on the Finnish team could match Zátopek's heroics, the country still came away with a haul of twenty-two medals, which was similar to the twenty-four it had won at the London Olympics in 1948. Nonetheless, there was a sense of disappointment among the Finnish public, particularly because their athletes had seen only modest success in track and field events, which, before the war, had been Finland's forte. The prevailing excitement around hosting the games at least softened this blow to national pride, with many Finns savouring the stunning feats of athleticism that were on display in the numerous Olympic venues.

As with Finland's athletic performance, Helsinki's concerted efforts to attract tourists for the games failed to yield the desired result. The number of visitors was only half of the hoped-for total, which was probably due to the city having comparatively little to offer foreign sightseers or pleasure-seekers. Its remote location, far from the world's more densely populated regions, did little to add to its appeal. The international sporting event, therefore, ended up making a considerable financial loss, but this was mitigated by the state guarantees for the games' budget. These had been loosely defined from the outset, which made it possible to cover the debts with revenue from the state-owned gambling company, Veikkaus, that was then becoming an increasingly important source of government funds.

This economic setback was understood, quite simply, as the price Finland had to pay for the positive attention the games had generated in the world's press. It is debatable whether Helsinki ever again enjoyed such global goodwill as during those two weeks of sporting competition. In part, this was down to the international situation being relatively stable and the international news cycle being relatively slow when compared to later decades. For Finland's own population and, most of all, for the Helsinki residents who were immersed in it, the sporting festival became a cherished lifetime memory, a perennial rose-tinted lens through which they could reminisce about their city and its history.

The appeal of the Olympics was certainly not limited to those Helsinki inhabitants who closely followed the sporting contests, although there were, of course, a good number for whom the defining experience was the athletic drama itself. For the majority of the residents, however, it was rather all the big public events and the various other entertaining diversions held across the city that lived long in the memory. As ever, it was the *Helsingin Sanomat* cartoonist, Kari Suomalainen, who captured the prevailing public sentiment. Published on the day of the opening ceremony, his cartoon depicted a giant statue of "Ericus", the alias of the games' chief coordinator Erik von Frenckell, stood in the middle of Helsinki's hustle and bustle. Holding aloft the Olympic torch, he was gazing with satisfaction as the whole city underwent a commercial metamorphosis. In the foreground was a market stall bearing the English-language sign "Hollywood Bar", next to which a young woman was becoming intimately acquainted with a dark-skinned tourist; in the background could be seen a large Coca-Cola advert, while the cartoon's finishing touch was another English sign—"Snack Bar"—that had been affixed to the roof of the Parliament Building.

During the Olympics, the American company Coca-Cola donated over 700,000 bottles of the fizzy drink to the event organisers, after they had promised to pledge the bulk of the sales profit to the Disabled War Veterans' Association of Finland. The PR stunt was made possible by the fact that Coca-Cola production had recently begun in Central Europe, in tandem with the Marshall Plan's economic measures. The drink sold like hot cakes, and its popularity functioned, like so many other American products, as an excellent advert for the "Free World", to use the Cold War parlance for the West. Of course, enjoying "ice-cold Coca-Cola" did not mean swallowing the aspirational Cold War message whole. One of the salesmen at the city's Coca-Cola kiosks was the 15-year-old upper secondary school student Matti Klinge: he would grow up to be a distinguished historian, yet he never became a big fan of sports or, for that matter, the United States.

Car or Metro?

The memory of the Helsinki Olympics was also rose-tinted in the minds of many Finns because it marked a turning point for the country, when its economy and national identity entered an optimistic new era. In early February 1951, over 100,000 Helsinki residents turned out for the grand state funeral of Gustaf Mannerheim, Finland's great military leader and a powerful unifying force during its armed conflicts with the Soviet Union. His passing was widely interpreted as the moment when the country bid a definitive farewell to the war years. In September 1952, Finland bid a far less sombre farewell, when it dispatched its last trainload of war reparations across the border to the Soviet Union. And, with Stalin's death in the spring of

1953, a lot of the knotty issues in Finno-Soviet relations were straightened out. Particularly significant was the decision by Moscow in the autumn of 1955 to relinquish the Soviet military base on Porkkalanniemi. The peninsula was formally returned to Finland in late January 1956.

At this time, Western Europe was entering into a period of prolonged and abundant economic prosperity. Finland would feel the effects of this boom, and it would also manifest itself in Helsinki's shops and urban milieu: Continental fashion trends took hold, coffee substitutes were replaced by the real thing, new cigarette brands appeared, and there were even sightings of a new Volkswagen or two in the city's streets. The war reparations had, without question, been a drain on the state's finances, but they had also given a shot in the arm to the country's metal industry, which had long been the biggest manufacturing branch in Helsinki. As a result, when freight transport to the Soviet Union reverted to a normal trading relationship in the early 1950s, the city's metal and mechanical engineering industries came to represent a significant share of Finland's eastern exports.

All the way up to the turn of the millennium, the metal industry consistently remained Helsinki's largest industrial employer. Its workforce accounted for between forty and forty-five per cent of all industrial labourers in the city. Their number was, however, shrinking fast over this period, as all the more manufacturing was moved out to neighbouring municipalities and an increasingly large portion of Helsinki residents were employed in the commerce and service sector. As such, the proportion of industrial labourers in the city's employed population fell from forty per cent to a little over nine per cent.

As would be expected of a capital city, Helsinki had a burgeoning public sector, but the fastest growth of all took place in its financial and insurance services. Their share of the employed population increased almost fourfold over the second half of the twentieth century, from five to nineteen per cent, although this has since doubtless fallen as a consequence of the recent wave of digitalisation. Amidst these labour market shifts, two features of the city's economic life remained a constant: Helsinki was always Finland's leading import harbour and, with the exception of the metal industry, the majority of its manufacturing and service sectors were always directed towards the domestic market.

These changes in the city's economic structure had tangible consequences for its class composition. Between 1960 and 1985, the size of the working-class population fell by forty per cent, from 177,000 to 106,000 residents, while the number of white-collar workers went in the opposite direction, rising from 183,000 to 215,000, an increase of nearly twenty per cent. The share of students and pensioners likewise increased, which further accentuated Helsinki's middle-class character.

The shifts in the inhabitants' social standing had, in turn, repercussions for the balance of political power in Helsinki. At the start of the 1950s, the Social Democrats and the Finnish People's Democratic League, which was even further to the left, had a combined share of almost forty-seven per cent of the vote in the municipal elections. Half a century later, this had dropped to barely twenty-nine per cent. They were not the only ones to suffer a decline: the Swedish People's Party shrank until it was only a minor player in local politics, while the Liberal People's Party, founded in 1965, spent fifteen years as the standard-bearer of Helsinki's enlightened middle classes before falling dramatically out of favour in the 1980s. In its stead came the Green League, who, since the 1990s, have enjoyed a similar level of support in the capital as the Social Democrats, each typically garnering twenty to twenty-four per cent of the vote. Since the 1970s, however, the conservative National Coalition Party has most often been the biggest party in the capital, reflecting the growth of the middle classes. It typically secures over twenty-five per cent of the Helsinki electorate's support.

Just as before, a resident's income and wealth dictated where they could live in the city. The new suburbs in the north and the east were mainly populated by the working and lower-middle classes. Their commutes, school runs and other trips to the centre grew steadily in the 1960s, until they reached such a level that traffic was regularly at a deadlock. Drastic solutions were required. The city's two-lane arterial roads into the centre had been built out in every direction, but the traffic flow was stymied by the capital's geography. With the core of the city lying out in the sea on a peninsula, there was, until the 1970s, only a short collector road between it and the main roads, which contributed to even longer tailbacks during rush hour. As did, of course, the rapid increase in private automobility, which was sent soaring to even greater heights after the state significantly lowered the import duties on personal cars from Western Europe in 1962.

In the space of a decade, the number of private automobiles in Finland tripled. The development was no less dramatic in the capital city region: between 1960 and 1970, the number of personal cars per thousand Helsinki residents increased from 64 to 167. Tellingly, the growth was even steeper in the city's neighbouring municipalities. As the region's public transport services became increasingly sluggish, more and more people chose to commute in their own vehicle, which only made the congestion worse, and finally forced the city leadership to take action. They had been mulling over various traffic management solutions since the mid-1950s, but it was not until the summer of 1965 that the city council decided to fund the construction of a metro line between the centre and Puotinharju in east Helsinki. Before going ahead with the proposal, however, they tasked city planners with producing a comprehensive development strategy for all modes of transport in Helsinki.

The right wing of the city council was sceptical of the need for a metro, and would sooner have solved the issue of traffic bottlenecks by building motorways that would scythe through the city centre. To minimise municipal squabbling, responsibility for the comprehensive city plan, therefore, ended up being delegated to outside consultants. After three years, they delivered their proposal for a traffic system that elicited delight among the petrolheads on the council. The city's transport links would prioritise the needs of car drivers, even if an abridged metro line was included in the plan. Slicing through the centre of the city would be a multi-lane highway, which would connect to the existing road network with the help of three colossal multi-level junctions built on pillars and a tunnel running under South Harbour.

The most audacious detail in the proposal was the new road network's southernmost tentacle, which would run from Hietalahti straight across the city to South Harbour, and would require that all the city blocks that lay in its path be razed to the ground. In late November 1968, *Helsingin Sanomat* published a bird's-eye perspective of how this would look. Drawn up by the newspaper's multi-talented artist, Henrik Tikkanen, it must have created quite the public outcry, at the very least from those who lived in the vicinity of the proposed new road. The motorway's brutal impact on the urban landscape was startling: directly to its south, the twin towers of St John's Church were still visible, but many other historic buildings and sites had been wiped out. Gone were the revered Finnish and Swedish lyceums, the Topelius monument in Koulupuistikko Park, and the German Church, to name but a few.

If, up to this point, there had been a fairly equal split in the city council between the car enthusiasts and the metro advocates, opinion now swung firmly in the latter's favour. Perhaps this had even been the purpose of the commissioned plan all along.

In May 1969, a large majority of the councillors voted to build a metro line between Kamppi and Puotinharju. This was finally opened for passengers in the summer of 1982, after over a decade of extensive construction, technological investment and diverse problems along the way. Alongside the metro project, the city began developing an electrified local train network in cooperation with nearby municipalities and the state-owned railway company, Valtionrautatiet (today called VR Group). Its positive effect on Helsinki's public transport system was at least as pronounced as that of the metro.

The Social Democrat group on the council had been fervent supporters of the metro project. In the same period, it also created a single-issue movement called *Enemmistö* (The Majority), with the aim of preserving Helsinki's old urban environment and defending the rights of pedestrians against the surge in personal automobility. It was not merely the traffic jams and the parking problems that had started to get on city-dwellers' nerves, for hot on the tail of the increasing stream of cars came the building contractors who wanted to remodel the city around the automobile. They intended to replace the older houses in the centre of the city with complexes of buildings that were tailored, first and foremost, to the motorists' needs. Even at the time, these constructions were not considered beautiful.

The most contested example of this sort of architecture was a large retail and office building directly opposite the main entrance to Helsinki Central Station. This stood finished in 1967, and almost instantly acquired the nickname "Sausage House" (*Makkaratalo*), on account of the cylindrical bulge that ran along the edge of its second-floor carpark. Everything about the building had been designed to make life easier for the motorist. The parking bay was reached via large and conspicuous access ramps, while pedestrians were sent down into tunnels. These took people to an underground concourse of shops and kiosks, from where they could connect to various tram stops and the central railway station. The Sausage House has the dubious honour of having been named the ugliest building in Helsinki on multiple occasions, but it has been preserved largely intact, with the exception of the long-gone access ramps, as a monument to the epoch's car-centred architecture.

The most unrelenting critique of everything that the Sausage House and its tunnels represented was most likely the polemic published by the young pair of architects, Vilhelm Helander and Mikael Sundman in 1970. Entitled *Kenen Helsinki?* ("Whose Helsinki?"), their booklet argued that the building was sad and emphatic proof that the unchecked car culture had started to destroy the city's architecture. Yet, the Sausage House was, for the authors, also symbolic of other insidious developments. They discerned the influence of big business behind it, which consciously strove to transform the whole inner city into a commercial centre that aimed to function solely for the benefit of private car drivers and divest itself of its inhabitants. When squeezed out of the heart of the city, people would have no choice but to move out to the poorly planned suburbs.

Helander and Sundman's last jibe was unjustified. Those who moved to the suburbs typically did so willingly. They came from either the countryside or from the cramped and dated housing of the inner city, which meant that they were inclined to appreciate the modern conveniences and more spacious living conditions of their new homes. Otherwise, the pair's scathing assessment was well-founded, although it came just as the worst excesses of both the car craze and the demolition fever started to subside. A clear sign that the winds of public opinion had started to change direction was that Alvar Aalto's grand plan for a modern city centre around Parliament House—which included a largely car-oriented overhaul of Helsinki's main traffic routes—was given up for good. The only building that ended up being constructed as intended was Finlandia Hall, the large and undeniably magnificent event centre just south of Töölönlahti. Completed in 1971, it got to play host to the final session of the Conference on Security and Cooperation in Europe in 1975, when the Helsinki Accords were signed in an effort to thaw the icy relations between the East and West.

While Alvar Aalto's visions for a cultural corridor by Töölönlahti never came into being, those seeking examples of his architecture in Helsinki will not be left disappointed. During the 1950s and 1960s, five trademark Aalto buildings were erected in different parts of the city. Completed first, in 1955, was Rautatalo (Iron House), an office complex on Keskuskatu, closely followed in 1956 by the headquarters of Kela, Finland's Social Insurance Institution, in Taka-Töölö. Finalised next was Kulttuuritalo (Culture House) in Alppila in 1958, which a collection of left-wing organisations, including the Finnish People's Democratic League, had commissioned Aalto to build. In 1962, the head office of the Finnish forestry company Enso-Gutzeit opened for business in the South Harbour; Aalto had designed it specifically to form part of the city's distinguished shoreline silhouette. Last but not least, Kirjatalo (Book House) was built as a home for the Academic Bookstore on the corner of Keskuskatu and Pohjoisesplanadi in 1969. Over the years, its well-preserved functionalist interior has developed into an oasis for Helsinki's bibliophiles. If these edifices alone are not enough, a visit to Alvar Aalto's home and architectural office in Munkkiniemi is surely in order, for they today serve as a museum to the world-renowned Finnish designer.

A well-functioning city cannot solely be based on refined aesthetics and finely tuned logistics, however. It also requires a careful and considered approach to its environment. The rising number of private cars also increased awareness of another urban problem: the city's growing air pollution. Car exhaust fumes still contained large quantities of lead in the 1960s, but they were not the only culprits. When a study was undertaken to determine the cause of the worsening air quality in Helsinki, it found that the collective furnace heating and waste burning of individual households accounted for at least as large an amount of heavy metals in the inner city's atmosphere. The worst perpetrators were shown to be the lead bottle tops that were thrown away with the rest of the rubbish. When this trash was burnt, it sent six kilograms of lead fumes spewing over the city every hour. As a result, household furnaces were almost completely scrapped in the mid-1970s, and waste started to be transported to Kyläsaari's incineration plant in the north-eastern part of the city. This markedly improved the air quality of the inner city, if not of the Helsinki region as a whole, for the smoke from Kyläsaari's huge industrial chimney dissipated over a far wider area.

Indeed, it was not long before these flue gases stoked outrage among Helsinki's residents, which led to the incineration plant being shut down completely in 1983. All the waste was initially transported to the tip in Vuosaari instead, but, from 1987, the majority of the capital region's waste disposal has been concentrated in Ämmässuo in western Espoo. This has acquired the dubious honour of being the biggest dump of its kind in all the Nordic countries. Although the ability to separate out harmful materials in the disposal process has improved considerably, the volume of refuse managed at the site has continuously grown over time, as it has started to treat increasingly large quantities of construction and industrial waste.

By the mid-1970s, over half of the city's properties had moved onto district heating, that is the supply of houses with hot water from a centralised thermal energy source through insulated pipes. Authorities had also set a significantly tighter limit on the lead content in motor fuel. While these were steps in the right direction, Helsinki's issues with pollution were a long way from resolved. A significant share of the household district heating was produced by the city's coal power station, which, in tandem with the car exhaust fumes, continued to emit great quantities of carbon into the atmosphere. As environmental concerns gradually entered the public consciousness, Helsinki's residents became increasingly unnerved by the sheer amount of carbon dioxide and other polluting particles their combined activity produced on a daily basis. By the early twenty-first century, emissions would be a central topic of debate in municipal politics.

Helsinki's water supply also required concerted action in this period. Until the end of the 1960s, the city had sourced its tap water exclusively from the Vantaa River. In spite of a laborious purification process, there were still times when it left an unpleasant taste in residents' mouths due to the eutrophication brought about by the agricultural and industrial discharges in the river. To solve the issue, the city built a 120-kilometre-long rock tunnel from Lake Päijänne, which manifestly increased the supply of clean water to the whole Helsinki region when it was taken into use in 1982. In tandem with this development, the sewage treatment works of the capital and its neighbouring municipalities gradually transitioned from mechanical to chemical water purification. The improvement was soon such that swimmers and bathers could return to the waters of the Vantaa. The city's original lifeforce was, once again, a place of vitality rather than a symbol of its environmental destruction.

The Golden Age of the Nation-State

So geographic expansion, demographic shifts and infrastructure overhauls reshaped the capital city region in this period, fundamentally changing the everyday life of Helsinki's inhabitants in the process. At the same time, however, there were many facets of the residents' quotidian existence and urban experience that survived intact, or, at least, that developed irrespective of the city's growth. The old public buildings and artworks in the inner city represented one such element of continuity. They had mostly made it through the war in one piece, and those that had not were, in time, rebuilt anew. The University's main building and the Guards' Barracks had been severely damaged in the Soviet air raids of February 1944, but both were repaired within the next decade. In the latter's case, this admittedly meant constructing a whole new administrative building for the Ministry of Defence behind the old facade. Yet, in terms of preserving the city's cultural heritage, even restoring the exterior of the former military quarters was a significant achievement, not least as the charred ruins of the Turku Barracks had been torn down in the 1920s. The third of Engel's monumental military constructions, the Naval Barracks, benefitted from a comprehensive renovation in the late 1980s, when it became the new home of the Ministry for Foreign Affairs. Until this point, the ministry had been housed in the eastern wing of the Government Palace on Senate Square.

During the interwar years, there had been a conspicuous absence of new monuments erected to honour the young Republic's leading statesmen. This was, of course, partly because of the truncated time period, but it was also because, in a democracy, it is not always easy to agree on who is worth remembering. The first of the monuments that came to decorate the city in the decades after the Second World War was the statue of Finland's first president, K. J. Ståhlberg, standing tall holding a legal tome, which was unveiled in front of the Parliament Building on the seventh anniversary of his death in September 1959. However, it was, in many respects, the second monument to appear that carried the most symbolic significance: Mannerheim's equestrian statue, unveiled on the Marshal of Finland's birthday on 4 June 1960 after more than two decades' debate and planning. It stood between Postitalo and his own street, Mannerheimintie, which had been rechristened on the same date eighteen years earlier, as a 75th birthday present to him from the city. The former White General was still a source of lingering resentment in Communist circles, but the majority of the Finnish populace remembered him fondly as a figure who had unified the nation, not least because he had, as president, helped the country survive the transition from war to peace.

Crafted by sculptor Aimo Tukiainen, the equestrian statue was certainly not received with universal praise in art circles. The abstract aesthetic had already come in vogue, so a true-to-life representation of a horse-riding Mannerheim was seen by many as rather old-fashioned. Among the general public, however, the monument was met with almost universal acclaim. In the coming years, the statues of two other former presidents— P. E. Svinhufvud and Kyösti Kallio—were also erected outside the nearby Parliament House. Taken together with Ståhlberg and Mannerheim, they form a fine cavalcade of figurative monuments to the leading men of the nascent Republic. A couple of decades later, in the autumn of 1980, J. K. Paasikivi's abstract monument was unveiled next to Lasipalatsi, directly opposite Mannerheim's equestrian statue. Over the years, nearly all of the country's other presidents would be commemorated in a similar style, with non-figurative memorials along or in the vicinity of Mannerheimintie. This stretch of statues and sculptures has thus come to function as independent Finland's counterpart to the chain of imperial monuments between Market Square and Esplanadin Puisto.

The formation of this ever-extending series of presidential monuments was, in its own way, an expression of how Finland had begun to reach maturity as a nation-state, after its dramatic birth and turbulent youth. The country's economy was growing steadily, sweeping social reforms were underway and its relations with the Soviet Union were in order. By the late 1960s, a growing number of the population considered that the Second World War belonged to a past chapter of Finnish history. The younger generation, in particular, were sick of hearing about it. This desire to move on could be seen in the Republic's fifty-year jubilee festivities in December 1967, such as in the speech given by President Urho Kekkonen on the eve of Finnish Independence Day at a large public celebration in Helsinki's recently opened Jäähalli (Ice Hall). In the presence of the heads of state from Sweden and the Soviet Union, Kekkonen talked at length about independent Finland's economic and social development, but skimmed over the war years with the brief acknowledgement that there were lessons to be learned from them.

On Independence Day itself, 6 December 1967, a great fireworks display was organised in Helsinki. This received plenty of coverage, as did the Independence Day Reception at the Presidential Palace, where Kekkonen and his wife shook hands with a long procession of the great and the good of Finland. The traditional handshake ceremony was first televised in the late 1950s and, to this day, remains the most-watched programme each year in Finland. In 2023, the show's estimated audience was over three million Finns, or more than half the country's whole population. Another enduring custom on Independence Day is the student unions' torchlit procession, although in 1967, this was rather more fiery than it had been in the past, as the nation's youth were then stirred up by new demands and expectations. At the procession's starting point, the war heroes' graves at Hietaniemi Cemetery to the west of the centre, the students' spokesman gave a heartfelt address. After the usual patriotic rhetoric, he reminded his audience that Finns were not the only ones in the world who had been forced to put their lives on the line to fight for their freedom. As such, it was now Finland's duty to support other people's struggles for independence. When the students had marched to Senate Square, they were greeted by another speaker, who, for his part, castigated the Finnish government for its modest contribution to international development aid.

These critiques were largely inspired by the student movement in Western Europe and the United States, which had started directly challenging governments and elites to take action on various issues, from the environment to women's rights. Its common denominator was a growing frustration over the lack of effort by the West to address the social and political injustices that prevailed across the world. In the early 1960s, the movement had been focused principally on peace and reconciliation, but it radicalised across the decade, as television became established as a medium for mass communication. Through the footage broadcast on the evening news, people could follow the civil wars in former European colonies and the civil rights protests in the United States in real time, which certainly contributed to the student protests developing a more revolutionary rhetoric.

In the late autumn of 1968, inspired by the actions of their brethren overseas, students in Helsinki occupied Old Student House. They were not only protesting against the academic establishment, but also against the student union's leadership, which was accused of being oligarchical in nature and mired in corruption. In the moment, the occupation was not considered an especially sensational event, yet it would later be framed as a turning point in the Finnish student movement's history. Not long after this direct action, many of its leaders would take several steps further left and attach themselves to the Stalinist faction of the Finnish Communist Party. In so doing, they convinced a good number of the ideologically and artistically inclined students to join them.

Although much of this revolutionary fervour had subsided by the late 1970s, the cultural legacy from the epoch lived on for decades. Remnants of it could even be found in Helsinki's streets, such as the plaques that were put on the facades of the apartment buildings to commemorate the places where Lenin had stayed in 1917. Most of these were, however, hurriedly taken down in the spring of 2022 after Russia launched its war of aggression against Ukraine. The next year, Helsinki city council voted in favour of changing the name of Lenininpuisto (Lenin Park) in the northern city district of Alppila. The park had acquired its appellation in 1970, on the centenary of the revolutionary leader's birthday. Pandering to the Soviets, President Kekkonen also used the occasion to honour Lenin, reminding that the socialist figurehead had recognised Finland's independence on New Year's Eve 1917.

These modern efforts to strip away an emotionally charged layer of Cold War culture from Helsinki are not only quite unnecessary, but they are also damaging to our collective historical memory. It will be even harder for us to understand the prevailing mood of the era if we can no longer see how fundamentally important it was for Finland to maintain good relations with the Soviet Union. A central tool in shaping public opinion at that time was the state's TV and radio monopoly, the Finnish Broadcasting Company (Yle). Its news and current affairs programmes were careful to avoid discussing the downsides of the USSR too openly. The Finnish people were aware, of course, that this soft censorship was taking place, but it was generally accepted that it was a necessary evil. Successive Finnish presidents had made it clear that the policy was a prerequisite in the fractious geopolitical climate. More than that, the majority of Finns who had lived through the war years were grateful that the existential threat the Soviet Union posed to their nation could be moderated by such means, even if the price was a fawning rhetoric of friendship and self-censorship. The Western press would soon come up with a pejorative term for this practice: Finlandisation.

In fact, the decades between the end of the Second World War and the 1980s came to be the high point for Finland's cultural homogeneity. Contributing to this were the state's role in forming public opinion, including its control of the media, the widespread social reforms that made the country into a Nordic welfare state, and the large amount of funding poured into all levels of education. As a consequence, the Finnish language assumed a more dominant position in public life than at any other point in the country's history. Over these years, Finland was a typical European country of emigration: while hundreds of thousands of Finns went abroad—mainly to Sweden—in search of work, the country took in very few immigrants, since its eastern border was closed and its job market was such that there was little need for foreign labour.

Nevertheless, it is unlikely that the average Helsinki resident would have characterised their daily life in this period as particularly monolingual or culturally isolated. The city's Swedish-speaking population shrank during the Cold War, from 71,000 in 1950 to 34,000 in 2000, but its influence in the older districts of Helsinki remained surprisingly undiminished. This can be attributed to how well it maintained its own branch of the education system, as well as its network of associations, each with their own deep-rooted customs and traditions. Swedish speakers actually increased in Helsinki's neighbouring municipalities, although their proportion of the total population still fell as these areas further urbanised. In Espoo, for example, their number rose from 10,000 in 1950 to 20,000 in 2000, all while their relative size as a population group plummeted from forty-three to nine per cent.

Finland's capital was less culturally homogeneous in other respects, too. As discussed above, Finnish students were influenced by trends and movements from abroad, and Helsinki was still home to the leading institutions of higher education in the land. It was also the best place in Finland to access foreign media and consumer goods, it had excellent transport links with other countries, and it welcomed a steady—if modest—flow of tourists. All of this had a diluting effect on the Finnish monoculture, as did the wide selection of foreign TV shows that became available in the 1960s, along with the growing market for Western pop music and youth fashion. These went hand in hand with new forms of sociability and less inhibited sexual morals, and would eventually result in rather strong Anglo-American dominance in Finnish popular culture.

Nonetheless, this was not a linear process, as shown by the variety of films on offer in Helsinki's movie theatres during this period. By the 1970s, cinemas were to be found in nearly every city district, and they screened a considerable amount of films from the Continent; far more, in fact, than were shown on the nation's two TV channels. Their movie selection was, to some extent, influenced by the cost: it was far cheaper for small cinemas to rent and distribute French and German films, along with individual Italian, Russian and Swedish ones, than it was to get the big Hollywood productions. But their listings were also a result of the improved quality of the Continental film industry: after the Second World War, it had developed from light-hearted hobbyist productions into a serious art form, one that captured the interest of Helsinki's cultured middle classes and students.

The culmination of this craze for European movies came in the late 1960s, and in the year 1968 in particular, when over 300 film premieres were registered in Helsinki. These included hits like Jean-Luc Godard's *A Married Woman* and Aleksandr Zarkhi's *Anna Karenina*. During this same period, a new style of domestic film production also broke through, in which the urban experience was presented without undue moralising. In December 1967, one such movie, Mikko Niskanen's *Lapualaismorsian* ("Girl of Finland") premiered at a number of cinemas in Helsinki.

It told the story of the capital's young students and their growing protests against social injustices both at home and in other parts of the world. This movement was personified by a young student played by the 21-year-old Kristiina Halkola. Following the French New Wave style, the director inserted realist shots of various Helsinki environs in amongst the film's more plot-driven scenes. Although disconnected from the story, they imbued the production with a strong sense of place, laying bare the diverse and chaotic elements that composed the city: a vessel being launched from Hietalahti's shipyard; the throng of humanity around Old Student House; the labour movement's May Day march from Hakaniemi Square; the sleet and the slush in the streets; and the billowing flags in the wind.

In a similar vein, author Pirkko Saisio's work of autofiction, *The Red Book of Farewells* (2023), captures atmospheric snapshots of 1970s Helsinki and its Stalinist art scene. It is full of tobacco smoke, spirits and work clothes, of inns where the air is thick with cooking fat and where the carefree students and the war-worn veterans rub shoulders with each other. It likewise describes Saisio's first lesbian lovers, and how covert these relationships still had to be in the early 1970s. Homosexuality was only decriminalised in Finland in 1971, and continued to be stigmatised long after the law had changed. Salvation for Saisio took the form of a speakeasy on Kalevalankatu: when her fictional alter-ego finally manages to slip inside, she sits down on an old bus seat and experiences a strange feeling of having reached her destination. The stream-of-consciousness narrative acknowledges her arrival with the line: "Lawbreaker, this is your secret home."

The European Security Conference

As noted above, the concept of Finlandisation emerged as a means to describe the political culture that developed in Helsinki during the Cold War. Just as in other nation states, the country's capital was the place where the political, financial and cultural elite came into contact with the foreign diplomatic corps, many of whom were engaged in intelligence operations. This was especially the case for the diplomats of the Soviet Union and the United States, who did not merely conduct surveillance in these elite circles, but also tried to use them to influence Finland's foreign and national security policies.

The foreign corps of diplomats had been involved in intelligence work in Helsinki ever since Finland first gained independence in 1917. Their covert activities, however, became far more extensive after the Second World War, due to Finland's delicate position in a geopolitically divided Europe. The Soviets' influence was swiftly established after the signing of the Moscow Armistice in 1944. To ensure that Finland adhered to the terms of the agreement, an Allied Control Commission was stationed in Helsinki until the autumn of 1947. At its head was one of Stalin's most-trusted men—Andrei Zhdanov—and its body was largely comprised of Soviet representatives, who vastly outnumbered their British counterparts. This allowed the Soviet intelligence service to quickly foster connections with both Finland's leading Communists and other key figures in its society.

During J. K. Paasikivi's ten-year stint as president, from 1946 to 1956, many of the right-wing and Social Democrat politicians adopted a reserved attitude towards these Soviet agents. However, during Kekkonen's long period in power (1956–81), and even during Mauno Koivisto's first term (1982–8), it became customary for Finland's leading politicians and many of their advisors to maintain regular contact with KGB officers from the Soviet embassy. These agents started to be called "house Russkis" (*kotiryssät*) in political circles. The practice was permitted largely because the president's principal means of communication with Moscow was also through the embassy's high-ranking representatives from the KGB. Indeed, the presidents themselves referred to it as "the party line". Finland's own security services tried their hardest to keep tabs on this duplicitous activity when it occurred in public, but so much of it took place behind closed doors that their surveillance efforts were not particularly effective.

Helsinki's geography was intimately tied to the epoch's political culture, for the most influential powers in Finland—the President and the Soviets—became known by their respective code names "Tamminiemi" and "Tehtaankatu". Across his twenty-five years as head of state, President Kekkonen preferred to carry out most of his duties from Tamminiemi, his official residence in Meilahti in western Helsinki. With its picturesque shoreline setting, this large Jugend-style villa had been donated to the Finnish state by the media mogul Amos Anderson during the Second World War. It was here that Kekkonen often took receipt of citizen groups, organised cocktail parties for the cultural elite, and liaised with some of his domestic and foreign contacts. In addition, it was the location from which Kekkonen handled the formation and appointment of new Finnish governments. The longer he remained president, the more common it became for people in political circles to reference a phone call from "Tamminiemi" in order to get something dealt with post-haste. Even after his resignation from office in the autumn of 1981, Kekkonen was allowed to continue living in the villa until he passed away six years later. The property has since been turned into a popular house museum.

In a similar fashion, an invitation to or a message from "Tehtaankatu" signalled that something important or ominous was afoot. During the interwar years, the Soviet embassy had operated out of a fashionable high-rise building on Bulevardi. This was destroyed, ironically enough, by the Red Army's bombing in February 1944, but, by the terms of the armistice agreement, it was Finland that was duty-bound to rebuild it.

A few years later, Moscow communicated that it would rather have its new embassy constructed in the vicinity of Kaivopuisto's diplomatic quarter. The long-vacant plot of land at Tehtaankatu 1 B was chosen, and, in June 1952, the large, Stalinist-style embassy building was finished, and handed over to the Soviet Ministry of Foreign Affairs.

From this point, it did not take long for "Tehtaankatu" to become a synonym for the Soviet Union's concerted efforts to keep Finland in line with Moscow's national security interests. This could involve actively interfering in Finland's domestic politics. If a politician was considered to be anti-Soviet by Tehtaankatu, then they had, in practice, absolutely no chance of ever obtaining a position in government. Without a shadow of a doubt, this was the most troubling consequence of Finlandisation. Yet it should not be overlooked that, for many Finns of the period, this deference to Soviet wishes was clearly a price worth paying for their country's improved national security and open economy, which thereby also resulted in a relatively free society.

Indeed, unlike all other countries in the eastern half of Europe, Finland remained a Western free-market economy. Through deft negotiations with both the Soviet Bloc and Western European countries, Finland was able to secure agreements that allowed it to send its exports in both directions. This gave rise to rapid economic growth, the fruits of which were distributed more equally across society than on any other occasion in the country's history. In such circumstances, most among the Finnish populace had little cause to complain about the fact that Kekkonen was able to be re-elected four times, often using underhand means to shore up his position in the process. However, equally important for his popularity was his role in a series of Finnish foreign policy milestones in the first half of the 1970s.

Relations between the two global superpowers were just starting to thaw at this time, which offered Finland excellent opportunities to raise its profile in matters of European security. Helsinki, for example, was the backdrop for many of the US–Soviet disarmament talks between 1969 and 1972. The Finnish government, for its part, began negotiations to normalise relations with East and West Germany in 1972, and managed to reopen diplomatic channels with both countries in early 1973. This success ultimately paved the way for Helsinki to host a decisive meeting of the Conference on Security and Cooperation in Europe in 1975, during which the American, Soviet and European heads of state signed their final accords.

The formal endorsement took place on 1 August in the main auditorium of Finlandia Hall. The signatories from thirty-five countries all accepted the state borders that had been drawn up in Europe after the Second World War. This was, in other words, official acknowledgement not just of the division of Germany, but also of the Soviet Union's political and military grip on the eastern half of Central Europe. That it was signed by no less than the United States, Canada and the Western European NATO members, along with the Continent's neutral countries, infuriated many foreign policy hawks in the West. They asserted that the Helsinki Final Act was a Soviet propaganda victory, through which Moscow could undermine NATO's capacity to stand up to the USSR, as well as the need for the military alliance to exist at all.

As a counterbalance to this geopolitical demarcation, the resolution also contained pledges to increase cooperation across the iron curtain in respect of trade, technological research and environmental policy. On the Western Powers' insistence, additional terms were included in the accords, which bound each signatory state to guarantee a better quality of life and freedom of association for its own citizens. This was, if possible, an even vaguer agreement than that promising greater international collaboration. Nonetheless, the Western camp was satisfied that its inclusion in the final act amounted to an acceptance of fundamental human rights, and, in short order, it did come to have a tangible impact. Namely, the special Helsinki Monitoring Groups set up by political dissidents in the Eastern Bloc, which started to report on their governments' authoritarian conduct that contravened the pledges of the conference's accords.

Following the fall of the USSR sixteen years later, it was asserted in some quarters that these increasingly active Helsinki Monitoring Groups had helped hasten the empire's demise. The attention they drew to the systematic abuse in Communist regimes contributed to the Western Powers stressing the inviolability of human rights at the follow-up meetings of the security conference in the late 1970s and the 1980s. The eventual collapse of the unstable Communist leadership in Moscow was, however, brought about by the coming together of multiple conflicting forces, of which human rights advocacy only formed a very small part. Scant few observers could have foreseen this confluence of circumstances, and fewer still could have imagined that things would fall apart so peacefully.

In early August 1975, such a seismic event was certainly not part of the prospects for the thirty-five heads of state assembled in Helsinki. As they signed the final act, the shared expectation was that it would serve to cement the geopolitical balance in Europe for a long time to come. This suited both the host country and its president perfectly. Indeed, Kekkonen's welcome speech gave him a unique opportunity to highlight to the world Finland's policy of active neutrality, the premise of which had now been accepted by all parties to the accords.

It is doubtful if Helsinki has ever been subject to greater political attention than in those three sweltering summer days in 1975. At that moment, there were no other global events to divert the international media's spotlight away from the city. Moreover, the personal attendance at the conference by some of the most renowned heads of state in the world made the occasion even more of a draw for journalists. President Gerald Ford himself made the trip to Finland from the United States. Following the American military's ignominious withdrawal from Vietnam in the spring of 1975, he wanted to demonstrate to the electorate that their country still stood up for the "Free World" and its fight for human rights. The US presidential elections were only a year away, and Ford must also have been conscious that directing attention to issues abroad might help distract voters from the Watergate scandal that had ousted Nixon, his predecessor, in 1974. His Soviet counterpart, General-Secretary Leonid Brezhnev, did not, of course, need to court public opinion in his homeland or its satellite states to anything like the same extent. In the run-up to the summer conference, however, he had suffered a serious stroke, from which he would never fully recover. He was, consequently, a pale shadow of his former self in Helsinki, and kept his bilateral meetings with other countries' presidents and prime ministers to a minimum.

Notable among those other world leaders were the recently appointed heads of France and West Germany, President Valéry Giscard d'Estaing and Chancellor Helmut Schmidt. The conference was the first time that Schmidt would meet his East German counterpart, Communist Chairman Erich Honecker, face-to-face. Lots of European prime ministers were also in attendance, including the full complement from the Nordic countries. After the summit's second day of meetings, on the evening of 31 July, all the heads of state and government gathered for a reception at Kalastajatorppa, a high-end restaurant right on the shore of Munkkiniemi in western Helsinki. As they mingled on its broad sea-facing terrace, President Kekkonen was captured by press photographers having an intimate conversation with Prime Minister of Sweden Olof Palme.

The conference preparations had been many years in the making. When it became clear that the participants were going to be from the highest political echelons, the security measures were ratcheted up to an even more rigorous level. The conference went like clockwork, and even the notoriously unpredictable Finnish summer played ball. Indeed, the weather was almost tropical, which contributed to great hordes of people gathering around Finlandia Hall and along Mannerheimintie in the hope of catching a fleeting glimpse of one of the Great Powers' leaders as they swished past in their black limousines. The Finnish population could also get a comprehensive run-down of the summit's events from its domestic press, with *Helsingin Sanomat* even publishing the final act in full as a double-page spread.

The summit would go down as the finest achievement in President Kekkonen's career as a statesman. It would also go down in history as one of the shining success stories of Finnish diplomacy. Harmony and accord never last in Great Power politics, however, and the follow-up security conferences were again buffeted by colder winds. Over the acrimonious course of the second follow-up summit, held in Madrid between 1980 and 1983, the Eastern Bloc's flagrant disregard for human rights became a highly contentious issue. The protracted talks did little to diffuse tensions, and, when the Soviet military shot down a South Korean passenger plane in the concluding days of the meeting, in September 1983, there seemed little hope of diverting international relations from their increasingly hostile path. And yet, it would only be a matter of years before the political scene in Europe was completely transformed.

The Finnish state leadership was careful not to react too quickly as events unfolded in the late 1980s and early 1990s. It was only at the outset of 1992, following the Soviet Union's dissolution in December 1991, that the Finnish government made three quick and decisive moves. In January, it struck a new treaty with Russia to replace the one that had been in place since 1948, thereby enabling Finland to give up its long-standing national security obligations to its eastern neighbour. Barely a month later, the Finnish government submitted its membership application to what would soon be christened the European Union. And in early May, it drove through a resolution in parliament to purchase sixty-four ultra-modern American fighter jets (F/A-18 Hornets). The acquisition was justified entirely in technological terms, but everything points towards the fact that this was Finland's first conscious step towards military cooperation with the United States. Thirty years later, in 2023, with the prevailing national security climate having again been tipped on its head, Finland would become a member of the NATO military alliance.

In contrast to the great turning points of Europe's past, which had all entailed dramatic consequences for Helsinki, the city's residents could, at the end of the Cold War, observe the geopolitical commotion from a relatively safe distance. Russia's instability was a cause for concern, while Finland's EU membership was a source of pride, but that which affected daily life in the capital most of all was the Baltic States' new-found freedom. In the space of just a few years, the amount of ferry traffic and trade between Helsinki and Tallinn increased many times over.

From the mid-1960s until the end of the Cold War, the only passenger service over the Gulf of Finland had consisted of a single Estonian ferry. For many Finns, however, it was the two countries' contrasting mentalities during this period that made their Baltic neighbour seem a world apart. This sense of separation faded fast once Estonia had regained its independence in August 1991. There has since been an explosive increase in tourist trips and the movement of workers between Tallinn and Helsinki, a vibrant maritime exchange that bears more than a little resemblance to the symbiotic relationship the two cities had established during the sixteenth and seventeenth centuries.

7

THE NORTHERN EUROPEAN METROPOLIS

Capturing the Coastline

A wave of optimism and prosperity swept across Europe in the second half of the 1990s. The Cold War had, in the main, been brought to a peaceful conclusion, the European Union had formed in its wake, and the global economy was showing positive signs of growth as the digital revolution quickened pace. There was, it is true, a bitter civil war underway in the former Yugoslavia, which ought to have served as a reminder of the fragility of peace in Europe. Instead, as so often happens in the aftermath of great crisis or upheaval, most people preferred to believe that humanity was now wiser, and on the verge of a more enlightened future.

For Finland, too, the sky seemed to be the limit at this time. The country had climbed its way out of a severe economic depression in the early 1990s, and had recently gained fresh impetus from the success of Nokia, which was riding high late in the decade as the world's leading mobile phone manufacturer. On 1 July 1999, it was Finland's turn to take on the mantle of

EU Presidency for the next half year. In preparation for this honorary role, which required the country to welcome a steady stream of EU delegations and European heads of state, Helsinki's public places and venues were spruced up, to ensure that they were fitting for their high-profile guests. The most visible improvements were made to Esplanadin Puisto, where both the flower beds and the sand paths were given a complete face-lift.

Beyond the city's immediate revamp for the imminent EU Presidency, far bigger building projects were starting to kick into gear. Helsinki's population had, once again, begun to grow, and the city council had, after exhaustive studies and interminable debates, agreed to take decisive action. In the early 1990s, it began an historic restructuring and expansion of Helsinki's building stock in many parts of the centre and along the city's sprawling coastline.

The first large-scale project took place in the area between Töölönlahti and Kamppi, thereby finally fulfilling many elements of the various visions for Helsinki's new centre that had been piling up on the city planning office's drawing boards since the 1910s. Its focal point became Kansalaistori (Citizens' Square), a wide, car-free plaza laid out just east of Parliament House, around which a number of the city's pre-eminent cultural sights and spaces have been built: Kiasma Museum of Contemporary Art (1998), the concert and event venue Musiikkitalo (Music Centre, 2011) and Helsinki's flagship library Oodi (2018). The wavy facade of Oodi forms the eastern border of the new plaza, which has recently started to become the regular setting for a variety of public events and celebrations. And from Oodi's upper terrace, the visitor is afforded a fine view over the heart of modern Helsinki.

Just across Mannerheimintie, south of Parliament House, Kamppi was also turned into a pedestrian zone. The area had functioned as a military parade ground in the eighteenth and nineteenth centuries, before being taken into use as a bus station in the 1920s. After Kamppi had been made a stop on the metro line in the 1980s, it was decided to construct a shopping centre on the site and move the bus station underground. The seven-storey retail complex finally opened in 2006, with the plaza in front of it named Narinkka Square in memory of the Jewish traders who had kept their market stalls there during the Russian era and Finland's early period of independence. A few years later, on the square's western edge, a small Lutheran chapel opened, its unusual cylindrical shape and spruce-wood exterior standing in striking contrast to the blocky shopping centre's glass facade.

Alongside the metamorphosis of Töölönlahti and Kamppi, new construction sites began popping up all across the city, both in districts set far back from the sea and in those right out on the water's edge. Their proliferation in Helsinki mirrored a trend occurring in large cities all over the globe. A combination of logistical and environmental pressures led to the industries, ports and railyards disappearing from the city centre, thereby freeing up large parcels of land for new housing developments. Everywhere this occurred, it would have a transformative impact on the look and feel of the urban environment.

The most significant reorganisation of the city's mass-transit system was carried out between 1990 and 2020 at Pasila Station, the first stop north from Helsinki's central terminus. The station and its surroundings were completely rebuilt, and turned into a major interchange for the capital-city region's rail-borne passenger traffic. The end result was not a world away from the large northern station Eliel Saarinen had proposed for the top of the "King's Avenue" in his city plan from the late 1910s. Pasila's large shopping centre and station complex was completed in 2020, and, since then, the old railyards in the vicinity have continued to be replaced by office buildings, tightly packed residential apartments and a row of skyscrapers.

The first substantial seizure of the city's coastline took place already in the 1970s, when the old industrial workshops on the eastern edge of Hakaniemi were knocked down. In their place rose a dense collection of apartment buildings, which together formed the residential area of Merihaka. The next shoreline to be opened up to new inhabitants was the eastern end of Katajanokka, which was completed in the mid-1980s. Then, in the early 1990s, it was the turn of Ruoholahti, an old industrial and port area on the coast a little west of the city centre. In addition to the construction of residential housing, it also gained a cultural centre—Cable Factory—since one of its old factory complexes was spared demolition after having become a haven for the city's artists. In the mid-1990s, Helsinki's coastal expansion continued when work began on an even bigger city district at Arabianranta, due south of Vanhakaupunki. The shore here had been filled with industrial waste over the years, so it required an extensive operation to clean up the contaminated soil before any construction could get underway.

When Arabianranta at last stood ready in the early 2010s, there was no doubt that all the toil had been worth the trouble. The city had even decided to reserve a certain percentage of the construction budget for public artworks, which added a playful charm to its buildings, streets and parks. New residential districts on Herttoniemenranta and Vuosaari followed similar patterns. First, the sites of industry and shipping were razed to the ground, then the soil had to be decontaminated, before the construction firms could finally take the reins. In the early 2000s, with both areas more or less finished, they were garnering plaudits for their functional designs, safe environments and unimpeded sea views.

The 1990s also saw the start of perhaps the biggest spatial shift in Helsinki's history: the transfer of the majority of the city's sea-borne trade to a new freight harbour in eastern Vuosaari. The abandoned quays and port areas around the inner city were then converted into residential and recreational spaces. As was so often the case in shipping history, the driving force behind this development was an acceleration of the global economy, which, in the 1960s, had resulted in the containerisation of maritime trade. With the growth of international shipping came an increasing demand for a faster and more voluminous transit process, leading to the use of standardised containers for the loading, transportation and storage of freight. This simplified logistics and contributed to the construction of larger container ships in the 1980s, but it also required far more operating space than could be found in many inner-city ports.

In spite of vociferous opposition from the district's residents and environmental activists, the city council accepted the proposal to build Vuosaari Harbour in 1996. Sörnäinen's and Laajasalo's port operations were moved, along with Jätkäsaari's container traffic, to a new 240-hectare harbour area with its own rail link and a direct connection to Kehä III (Ring III), the city's outermost ring road. And once the first container ships had started to dock at Vuosaari in 2007, Jätkäsaari, Sörnäinen Harbour and Laajasalo's shoreline embarked on their decades-long transformation into large, new residential districts. As with many of the repurposed coastal areas before them, they all benefitted from expansive views over the Gulf of Finland.

The eastern quay of Jätkäsaari, which has been better known as the West Harbour since the 1910s, continued to function as a focal point of ferry traffic to and from Estonia. A new terminal was built there in the 2010s, doubling its passenger capacity. The rest of Jätkäsaari has gradually been filled with tightly built tower blocks, through which winds a wide and flowing green space out towards the sea. The new city district at Sörnäinen Harbour was christened Kalasatama (Fish Harbour), having earlier been the principal port for Helsinki's trawlers. Kalasatama's southernmost point, the harbour formed from the erstwhile islands of Sompasaari and Nihti, was relandscaped by cutting two slim canals horizontally across it. In another nod to the area's past, many of the streets have been given names with maritime associations, such as Kaljaasi Auroran Kuja (Galleass Aurora's Avenue) and Kapteeni Sundmanin Katu (Captain Sundman's Street).

Kalasatama's landmark has become a row of skyscrapers. The biggest—Majakka, or Lighthouse—extends skywards to the height of 134 metres, making it the tallest residential building in Finland. As its thirty-five floors were rearing up out of the ground, work was already starting on the city's next repurposed district: Kruunuvuorenranta, on the west coast of Laajasalo. This had formerly been the largest oil harbour in Helsinki, but was transformed into a new residential area with striking and unusual design elements, not least the works of light art incorporated into the construction process. The district's shoreline offers a fantastic view over Kruunuvuorenselkä, both west towards the city centre and south towards the Gulf of Finland. Yet the defining feature for the area will be the huge new tram, bike and foot bridge over Kruunuvuorenselkä that the city council have approved. Under construction at time of writing, it will connect the new neighbourhood—and the rest of Laajasalo—to Kalasatama and Hakaniemi, and looks set to open up Helsinki's island landscape in a quite radical way.

It does not take finely honed psychic powers to predict that Helsinki's urban environs may very well stretch further out into the Baltic Sea over the coming decades. South of Kruunuvuorenranta lies the large island of Santahamina, which has been exclusively used by the military for the past two centuries. The country's defence capacity is currently a more pertinent issue than it has been for a very long time, but the future utility of such an island base to Helsinki's defences is an open question. Over the following decades, it could even come to pass that not only Santahamina, but its adjacent islands of Kuninkaansaari and Vallisaari, end up being transformed into bona fide residential districts. Should this happen, then the dream of Helsinki's founder, Gustav Vasa, would finally be realised, for Helsinki would truly be a city on the sea.

The New Face of Helsinki

Helsinki's increasingly high building density has gone hand in hand with a significant jump in its population size. Between 1990 and 2023, the number of inhabitants rose by thirty-five per cent, from 492,000 to 674,500. And, since there was even greater room for growth in the municipalities surrounding the capital city, the overall population increase for the Greater Helsinki region during this same period was over forty-five per cent, from 1.1 to 1.6 million. The pattern was the same for all the other capital city areas around the Baltic Sea, with the consequence that each has come to comprise an ever larger share of its country's population total. In the mid-2020s, close to a third of all Finland's inhabitants (twenty-nine per cent) live in the Greater Helsinki region, which includes the neighbouring cities of Espoo and Vantaa, as well as ten other municipalities. All signs point to this trend continuing in the years to come.

The majority of Helsinki's new arrivals have, as in the past, moved to the capital from other parts of Finland. Since the 1990s, however, the number of foreign-born inhabitants has increased elevenfold, from 10,000 to 110,000, which means that over sixteen per cent of the city's population in the mid-2020s hail from abroad. If their children are included in this total, then twenty per cent (or 132,000) of all residents have a mother tongue that is neither Finnish nor Swedish. This development can appear dramatic, but it is happening at a clearly slower rate than the city's past linguistic shifts, whether the increase in Swedish speakers during the second half of the eighteenth century or the increase in Finnish speakers in the late 1800s. Such a perspective is crucial for a nuanced discussion of the changing face of the city, and it is equally important to keep this in mind when talk turns to how Finland's two national tongues will survive in Helsinki.

Moreover, the city's history demonstrates a manifest connection between Helsinki's economic growth and its language adjustments. Significant changes in the linguistic composition of its residents have, without exception, coincided with booms in the city's economy. This is not a great surprise: in times of prosperity, cities attract new migrants who often end up contributing to their growth, whether as sources of cheap labour, enterprising business owners, or innovators and creatives with international networks, such as researchers and artists.

A new feature in this iteration of the city's linguistic shift has been that a number of minority languages in the city have established relatively equal percentage shares within its population. The proportion of Swedish speakers among Helsinki's residents has continued to decline (5.1 per cent in 2023), but in absolute terms their number has actually marginally increased. The second largest linguistic minority were Russian speakers (3.1 per cent in 2023), followed by four languages that were fairly equally split: Somalian (2.1 per cent), Arabic and English (each at 1.5 per cent) and Estonian (1.4 per cent). In reality, this latter figure is a vast underestimate of the amount of Estonian speakers in the city. In recent decades, Estonians have formed a significant part of the workforce in Helsinki's construction sector, but they typically commute over the Gulf of Finland rather than live permanently in the city, and are hence under-represented in the statistics.

Until the early 2020s, Russian was also heard more frequently in Helsinki's streets than the population totals would suggest. This was due to the Finnish capital's popularity with Russian tourists, which had been helped in no small part by the opening of the high-speed rail connection between Helsinki and St Petersburg in December 2010. The so-called Allegro Service substantially reduced the journey time between the two cities, from 5.5 to 3.5 hours. It ran four times a day, and tempted over a million Russians to Helsinki each year for short breaks and shopping trips. All this came to a sudden halt with Russia's full-scale war against Ukraine in February 2022, when the flow of tourists was cut off abruptly. As the war continued, Helsinki's Russian-speaking minority became understandably cautious about using their mother tongue in public spaces. Since the outbreak of the war, Finland has taken in nearly 60,000 Ukrainian refugees, although the vast majority of them have received housing in other parts of the country. In early 2024, only 2,500 Ukrainian refugees were living in Helsinki.

Since the Second World War, the city residents' English-language skills have steadily improved, partly thanks to the school reform of the 1970s that made a nine-year comprehensive education free to all children, and partly thanks to Finland's increasing contact with the Western world. Entwined with these developments has been the immense pulling power of Anglo-American popular culture. One consequence of this Anglicisation has been a marked decline in the knowledge of German and French among Helsinki's more educated residents. Another has been the gradual growth of English as a lingua franca among the city's different language groups. Until the 2000s, English was principally spoken in commercial and academic circles, but since then it has started to percolate into a wide array of social and cultural contexts. The pace of change has been driven by the growth in immigration, but also by the increasing grip of a globalised digital culture on the human consciousness, and thereby on people's everyday existence.

A clear demonstration of the pervasive spread of English can be seen in the service sector, where it is often spoken in customer-facing roles that are typically the most accessible for immigrant workers. Helsinki's older generations might raise an eyebrow at this, but most younger residents fail to bat an eyelid. For some, changing languages can even be a form of relief, as it allows them to switch between different modes of expression. Indeed, for many residents, not only has English become an increasing feature of the workplace, but it has also taken on a similar significance to Finnish and Swedish in their private lives, as a language of emotion and sociability. A striking example of this trend is that interactions between Finnish-speaking and Swedish-speaking youths can even take place in English, as both groups understand the other best in that language.

In parallel with the seemingly inexorable rise of English, life for the city's linguistic minorities has also been made easier by the internet, through which they can readily keep contact with the people and culture of their former homeland. There are diverging opinions on how this closer connection will impact the migrants' integration into Finnish society. Some consider these digital communities to be an important means of ensuring cultural diversity, while others see them as a threat to national identity, since they can make it harder for new arrivals to assimilate and lead to greater social segregation between the different districts of Helsinki.

As in other big cities, immigrants in Helsinki tend to settle in the same suburbs as those who have come before them. The newcomers are most often low-income earners and might well be reliant on social support, which means that, in comparison to many other social groups, they have very little choice about where they reside. As such, the large majority of the capital city region's migrant population live in the eastern and northern suburbs of Helsinki and in Vantaa, since these are the areas that have, as a rule, the cheapest rental properties.

The city's authorities have actively tried to fight back against this segregation by ensuring that reasonably priced rental housing has also been constructed in more middle-class districts of Helsinki. Up until the mid-2020s, at least, they have been more successful in this endeavour than their counterparts in Stockholm, where severe segregation has led to serious social problems in immigrant-dense suburbs, including high rates of youth crime as well as criminal gangs with links to international terrorism. Only time will tell if Helsinki manages to avoid following a similar path to Stockholm.

One of the main meeting places for many in Helsinki's immigration population is Itäkeskus, a transport and retail hub in the east of the city. Its huge shopping centre underwent an extensive renovation in the early 2020s, and a stroll down its new indoor boulevard, flooded with natural light, offers some rays of hope for the city's future, as long as it can continue to develop in this direction. To do so, however, requires that both its municipal decision-makers and its residents have the sense to accept and support its linguistic and cultural diversity.

The Green City

Cities do not develop without direction. Some of their circumstances are set in stone, while others are dependent on the priorities and the expertise of their decision-makers. In respect of its municipal governance, Helsinki bears closest comparison with Stockholm: both are Nordic capitals with a stable tax base. Stockholm has, of course, been a big city much longer than Helsinki, and its population is still much larger, which is a central reason why social segregation is a far greater concern in the Swedish capital than in its Finnish counterpart.

The Finnish state has rarely had the same level of resources to dispense upon its capital city region as Sweden. Helsinki's sea-bound location, with its collection of peninsulas, islands and expansive bays, comes with a greater set of logistical challenges than in Stockholm, where the city's hinterland stretches out both to the north and to the south. The Swedish capital's decision-makers have, then, likely had an easier time carefully developing their city in collaboration with its neighbouring municipalities. Indeed, the cohesion between city and surroundings is reflected by the fact that, together, they form Stockholm County. Its subway system has expanded out in every direction, while Helsinki still only has a solitary metro line running east to west. It was not until 2006 that the capital's western neighbour, Espoo, acquiesced to let the line extend into its municipality. After myriad delays, the so-called West Metro (*Länsimetro*) finally began its operations in late 2017.

Helsinki's and Stockholm's municipalities do, however, have something significant in common: green political parties have been strongly represented on both city councils since the 1990s. The Green League has been the second biggest party group in Helsinki throughout the first quarter of the twenty-first century, which has expediated the city's investment in new bike paths and tram routes. It has also given rise to an ambitious target to make Helsinki carbon neutral by 2035, which requires an eighty per cent reduction in emissions compared to their level in 1990. In spite of the worthy aim, the strategy itself has proved controversial, as it has delayed funding for car tunnels that would relieve traffic congestion in the city centre.

Such differences of opinion concern, at their core, what sort of city people want to inhabit. The radical environmental activist might dismiss cities outright as "unnatural" places, but a more nuanced interpretation would be to regard them as urban ecosystems, where plants, animals and humans have learned to co-exist together. A great amount of flora and fauna has, it is true, disappeared or been displaced from the barren peninsula where

Helsinki's current centre was founded so many centuries ago. In its stead, however, a range of new species have emerged with the strengths and qualities to survive in an urban environment.

Until the late nineteenth century, a large proportion of the households in Helsinki kept their own livestock, which provided daily sustenance to their owners while, at the same time, sustaining a diverse plethora of insects and parasites. Dogs and cats have always been found in Helsinki's streets, and the same goes, of course, for the rats, which found alternative accommodation down in the sewers and in other nutrient-rich environments as the city's collection of livestock decreased and houses began to be built out of stone. Many species of birds, not least crows and gulls, have shown a similar capacity to adapt to the increasingly urbanised environment. One four-legged predator that continues to thrive in Helsinki is the fox, thanks to the wide choice of quarry in the city's green spaces, which includes rabbits, hares, roe deer and even white-tailed deer.

This latter variety was imported to Finland during the first half of the twentieth century, while rabbits only became a part of Helsinki's ecosystem in the 1990s, when a few fugitive bunnies fled their owners and made a new life for themselves in the wild. They have since become a real threat to the city's vegetation, as have the white-tailed deer: beautiful though these beasts may be, they are notorious for their insatiable consumption of flowers and vegetables. It was also in the 1990s that large flocks of barnacle geese, en route further north, began to descend on Helsinki and spread their excrement with abandon across the city's parks and shorelines. Irritation over these newcomers has fostered demands to prevent the proliferation of foreign species in Finland because of the threat they pose to the prevailing ecological conditions.

Throughout history, urban settings have constantly acted as an entry point for non-native animals and plants into countries. As hubs of transport and commerce, they have welcomed an endless stream of vehicles and vessels, from the horses and carts of centuries past to the trains of the industrial age. In among this stream, concealed in the cargo or affixed to the vehicles, have been species and microbes from all across the world. The majority of such new arrivals in Finland have not survived for long, as the unfamiliar climate and ecological environment is typically too harsh for them. Nonetheless, on occasions, the flora, fauna or bacteria have proved sufficiently resilient to successfully spread to other parts of the country. An unusual example of foreign species flourishing in Helsinki was the exotic vegetation found on the island Sompasaari. Until the early 1960s, when it was levelled, filled in and made a part of Sörnäinen Harbour, it had been an unloading place for schooners carrying sand, resulting in hundreds of different plants from more southerly latitudes taking root on the island.

In many cases, non-indigenous flowers and shrubs have intentionally been planted in the city's gardens and parks, from where their seeds have dispersed further. Two such species are hawthorn and lilac: according to legend, it was the Swedish officers on Suomenlinna who were responsible for planting the latter's first seedlings in Finland during the second half of the eighteenth century. Often, though, these kinds of cultivation efforts have come to nothing, on account of Helsinki's unforgiving sea climate. This was considerably colder during the city's first three hundred years (1550–1850) than it has been in the twentieth and early twenty-first centuries. The sea often froze as early as October, and, in the coldest springs, the ice only began to melt in early May. This, of course, was a key factor in Suomenlinna's surrender in 1808, for the sea ice prevented the Swedish Navy from arriving to rescue the sea fortress by the agreed-upon date.

Since the mid-nineteenth century and the Industrial Revolution, the greenhouse gases pumped into the atmosphere have caused an observable increase in temperature across the world. Global warming has had a palpable impact on the Helsinki region, particularly on its winters: between 1960 and 2020, the average temperature between December and February has risen by three degrees Celsius. The change can be difficult to perceive at the level of personal experience, for one winter is never the same as the next, and there is still a great difference between milder years and colder ones. Nonetheless, it is clear that the growing season of the city's vegetation has extended over time, starting earlier in the spring and concluding later in the autumn. The linden trees in Esplanadin Puisto nowadays rarely lose their leaves before the second half of October, two or three weeks later than they typically did in the 1960s.

The summer months have also become warmer, and the number of certifiably hot days—hot, at least, in Nordic terms—has been on the rise. Between 1960 and 1990, there was an average of ten days per year when the temperature exceeded 25°C; between 1990 and 2020, there was an average of sixteen days (a sixty per cent increase). Few Helsinki residents complain about these heat waves, even if they do have a negative impact on swimming at the cities' beaches, for higher water temperatures stimulate the growth of the toxic blue-green algae, cyanobacteria. While Finnish summers are still considerably shorter and cooler than those of more southern climes, this might ultimately boost Helsinki's appeal to tourists in an era when many parts of Europe are increasingly being afflicted by searing seasonal heat.

Helsinki also enjoys other advantages upon which its inhabitants seldom reflect. The sea climate can sting and bite without mercy, particularly during the late autumn, but in the summer's heat it is, more often than not, pleasantly refreshing. The brisk winds also contribute to Helsinki ranking as one of the best big cities in the world for air quality. That said, this is certainly not the case in early spring, when the studded tyres on cars and the grit on the pavements—both prerequisites for safe passage around the city in the winter—combine to fill the air with huge quantities of street dust, a serious health hazard. Over the coming years, however, this form of seasonal pollution will hopefully be alleviated somewhat by Helsinki's heavy expenditure on its tram and bike infrastructure.

Although Helsinki's building density has risen dramatically in recent decades, in an international context, the city is still an unusually green metropolis, containing large areas of unspoiled nature. The largest of these green oases is the 305-hectare nature reserve in Viikki and Vanhankaupunginlahti, which is situated almost exactly in the geographical midpoint of the city. Since the 1800s, Viikki's bird-rich wetlands have been an important research environment for ornithologists, and, in the 2000s, they started to become a breeding ground for many new species, such as grey herons and sea eagles. Their arrival was facilitated by policies of environmental protection, but also by the warmer temperatures resulting from climate change.

The Twists and Turns of Geopolitics

Just as with climate change, developments and crises in Great Power politics have consequences that, sooner or later, bring themselves to bear on daily life in most corners of the world. Helsinki's history is—as has hopefully become clear over the course of this book—an unusually overt example of this process. Nearly every time that the city has experienced a change in fortune, it has been as a result of a shift in Europe's geopolitical balance, whether acute bursts of wars and woes or gradual transitions into periods of continuity and cohesion. Until the early nineteenth century, the lives of Helsinki's residents were primarily shaken and stirred by the conflicts in Russo-Swedish relations. When war broke out between the two countries, it was almost invariably fought on Finnish territory. And when fighting took place in Finland, Helsinki was, as a rule, caught up in it, on account of the town's important maritime connections. Since the early nineteenth century, the continued existence of Helsinki and Finland has been threatened on multiple occasions by conflicts between Russia and other Great Powers in Europe.

When the Cold War came to an end, there was widespread hope that Russia would develop into a Western democracy in close cooperation with the European Union. The thaw in Russo-European relations lasted for two decades, from 1992 to 2014, and benefitted Helsinki in myriad ways, for its excellent sea and rail links with Russia helped boost its tourist trade and commercial interests. Another significant step forward was the regional cooperation between the three coastlines on the Gulf of Finland. Among other initiatives, the construction of a new water purification plant in St Petersburg, with financial and technical support from Finland, considerably reduced the city's pollution of the Baltic Sea.

Finland's warmer relations with Russia also contributed to the Finnish Defence Forces' decision to phase out their permanent coastal artillery, which was replaced in the 2010s with a mobile missile system. The decommission of these military bases, and their exclusion zones, on the islands in Helsinki's waters has opened up a sizeable new section of the city's archipelago for visitors to explore. Most popular among the new destinations have been Vallisaari and Kuninkaansaari, two large islands east of Suomenlinna that were made available for civilian use in 2016. Helsinki's residents and tourists alike can now easily access both via regular ferry services in the summer months.

Just as visitors were enjoying the sunshine on these sites of past military tensions, a fresh chill was descending over Europe. This culminated in the sharp freezing of geopolitical relations when Russia launched its war of aggression on Ukraine in February 2022, which sent both Finland and Sweden hastily scrambling to join NATO. The countries had, it is true, begun increasing their military cooperation with the United States long before this, but their newly formalised defensive partnership transformed the political atmosphere in their capital cities. Even before Finland's NATO membership was ratified in April 2023, Helsinki was visited by an American aircraft carrier and other military vessels from NATO countries. The arrival of the USS *Kearsarge* in August 2022 attracted a great deal of attention, but it was, above all, a reflection of the new geopolitical climate that had taken hold over the Gulf of Finland.

Life in Helsinki was also impacted by the wide range of economic sanctions imposed on Russia by the EU. Many Finnish businesses were forced to wind up their operations in their eastern neighbour, which made Finland, as a consequence, less attractive in the eyes of international investors. Together with other structural issues in the country's economy, it also contributed to a substantial downturn in Helsinki's property market. Although most prognoses suggest the Finnish economy is heading towards a tentative recovery, the foreseeable future still contains a raft of challenges for Finland, and, therefore, for its capital city as well.

Helsinki's economic development can, of course, diverge from how the rest of Finland fares. For example, the ongoing depopulation of many of the country's sparsely inhabited areas is providing the urban centres, and the Greater Helsinki region most of all, with an influx of new labour. However, the capital is certainly not detached from the fortunes of the country as a whole. The Finnish state's straitened finances and the heightened geopolitical tensions with Russia have inhibited significant investment in the capital region's infrastructure and cultural life, which are integral to making Helsinki a liveable and vibrant city. It has spent centuries being shaped by the maritime tides, but its vigour and vitality are not solely connected to the geopolitical stability of the Baltic Sea region. On the contrary, Helsinki lives and breathes with Finland.

Helsinki in 2050

How will the city look in 2050, when it celebrates its 500th birthday? Well, that depends on the opportunities, not to mention the slings and arrows, that fate flings Finland's way in the next twenty-five years. In 1725, Helsinki was struggling to recover from the ravages of fire and war; by 1750, the construction of Suomenlinna was in full swing. In 1825, the city was brimming with new-found stature and a newly built centre, which contributed to the subsequent twenty-five years of demographic, academic and cultural growth. And in 1925, the capital and the fledgling Republic were marked by political and linguistic divisions, but both would emerge from the turmoil of the 1940s more united and with forward-looking plans for their post-war development.

If there is anything to be learned from history, it is that Helsinki's future rests on the interaction of its ever-present forces—that is, its geography and climate—with a series of unpredictable events. These events are, of course, partly products of humanity's selfishness and greed, but they are also consequences of natural disasters, pandemics and unexpected chain reactions from technological innovations. Consider digitalisation and social media: many believed that their impact would strengthen democracy in the West and help the political system take root in other parts of the world. The development has gone in quite the opposite direction, however.

The fraught geopolitical atmosphere in Europe today has left Helsinki in an undeniably tricky position. There is cause to hope, however, that circumstances in Russia will, at some point, take a turn for the better. The carbon-filled atmosphere of the Earth poses another daunting challenge for Helsinki's residents, although solving the problems caused by the climate crisis will likely not be any more difficult in Finland's capital than in metropolises and megalopolises the world over. Caught as we are in the whirlwind of the Fourth Industrial Revolution, scientific discoveries and technological innovations are currently taking place at an accelerated pace, and there is often scant time wasted between their invention and their practical application. Although such breakneck speed brings with it added precarity and risk, rapid technological development can, in the best-case scenario, considerably improve people's daily lives.

Even in such an uncertain and rapidly changing world, Helsinki ought to have ample opportunity to develop into a city that can meet its housing, transport and energy needs with sustainable solutions. It ought to be able to take good care of its inhabitants, while also attracting creative and skilled migrants from different parts of the world. It has the potential to function as a model for other cities to follow, as an urban embodiment of the functionality, user-friendly and egalitarian elements of Finnish design. Whether it will or not, well, that's another story.

BIBLIOGRAPHY

1. The Harbour

Aalto, Seppo, *Krigsstaden: Helsingfors Gammelstads historia 1550–1639*, Helsinki: Otava, 2013.

——, *Kronostaden: Estnässkatans Helsingfors 1640–1721*, Helsinki: SKS Kirjat, 2016.

Aalto, Seppo, Sofia Gustafsson and Juha-Matti Granqvist, *Fästningsstaden: Helsingfors och Sveaborg 1721–1808*, Helsinki: Minerva, 2021.

Ehrström, Erik, *Helsingfors stads historia från 1640 till stora ofreden*, Helsinki: Tidnings- & Tryckeri-Aktiebolagets Tryckeri, 1890.

Hietala, Marjatta, Martti Helminen and Merja Lahtinen (eds), *Helsinki—Helsingfors: Historiallinen kaupunkikartasto*, Scandinavian Atlas of Historic Towns: New Series 2, Helsinki: Tietokeskus, 2009.

Hornborg, Eirik, "Ständermötet i Helsingfors år 1616", *Historisk Tidskrift för Finland*, 19 (1934), 76–83.

——, Eirik, *Helsingfors stads historia II*, Helsinki: City of Helsinki, 1950.

——, "Militär och krigshändelser", in Ragnar Rosén, Eino Jutikkala and Eirik Hornborg (eds), *Helsingfors stads historia III, första bandet*, Helsinki: City of Helsinki, 1950.

Jäppinen, Jere (ed.); *Burgman: Helsingin ensimmäinen kivitalo*, Helsinki: Helsingin kaupunginmuseo, 2007.

Kiiskinen, Terhi, "Sigfrid Aronus Forsius", in Henrik Knif, *Biografiskt*

BIBLIOGRAPHY

lexikon för Finland / 1: Svenska tiden, Helsinki: Svenska Litteratursällskapet, 2008, pp. 236–40.

Kuisma, Markku, *Helsingin pitäjän historia II: Vanhan Helsingin synnystä isoonvihaan, 1550–1713*, Vantaa: Vantaan kaupunki, 1990.

Kujala, Antti, *Miekka ei laske leikkiä: Suomi suuressa pohjan sodassa 1700–1714*, Helsinki: Suomalaisen Kirjallisuuden Seura, 2001.

Kuvaja, Christer, *Försörjning av en ockupationsarmé: Den ryska arméns underhållssystem i Finland 1713–1721*, Turku: Åbo Akademi University Press, 1999.

Laine, Esko, "Säätyvallan ja penkkijärjestyksen aika", in Marjo-Riitta Antikainen, Esko Laine and Anne Birgitta Yeung (eds), *Kaupunkilaisten kirkko: Helsinkiläisten ja seurakunnan kohtaamisia kuudella vuosisadalla*, Helsinki: Otava, 2006.

Marjomaa, Risto, "Ernst Johan Creutz", *Biografiskt lexikon för Finland / 1: Svenska tiden*, Helsinki: Svenska Litteratursällskapet, 2008.

Parland-von Essen, Jessica, *Affärer, allianser, anseende: Konsten att tillhöra eliten i Helsingfors ca 1740–1820*, Helsinki: Schildts, 2010.

Salminen, Tapio, *Vantaan ja Helsingin pitäjän keskiaika*, Vantaa: Vantaan kaupunginmuseo, 2013.

Villstrand, Nils Erik, *Sveriges historia 1600–1721*, Stockholm: Nordstedts, 2011.

Zetterberg, Seppo, *Viron historia*, Helsinki: Suomalaisen Kirjallisuuden Seura, 2007.

2. In the Glow of Suomenlinna

Aalto, Seppo, Sofia Gustafsson and Juha-Matti Granqvist, *Fästningsstaden: Helsingfors och Sveaborg 1721–1808*, Helsinki: Minerva, 2021.

Clarke, Edward, *Travels in Various Countries of Scandinavia: Including Denmark, Sweden, Norway, Lapland and Finland—Volume 1*, London: T. Cadell and W. Davies, 1838.

Ehrensvärd, Augustin, *Tal om Ungdomens uppfostran til Krigsmän*, Stockholm, 1743.

BIBLIOGRAPHY

Engman, Max, *St Petersburg och Finland: Migration och influens 1703–1917*, Helsinki: Finska Vetenskaps-Societeten, 1983.

Grönroos, Henrik, "När Sveaborgsofficerarnas böcker såldes på auktion", in Kai-Inge Hillerud, Erica Ljungdahl and Magnus von Platen, *Bland böcker och människor: Bok- och personhistoriska studier till Wilhelm Odelberg den 1 juli 1983*, Uddevalla: Bohuslänningens Boktryckeri AB, 1983.

Gustafsson, Sofia, *Leverantörer och profitörer: Olika geografiska områdens och sociala gruppers handel med fästningsbygget Sveaborg under den första byggnadsperioden 1748–1756*, Helsinki: Suomen Tiedeseura, 2015.

Af Hällström, Magdalena, "Omgifven av sina Werk: Augustin Ehrensvärds gravsättning på Sveaborg 1783", in Sophie Holm and Magdalena af Hällström (eds), *Viapori: Linnoitus, lähiseutu ja maailma*, Helsinki: Ehrensvärd-Seura, 2012, pp. 261–78.

Hietala, Marjatta, Martti Helminen and Merja Lahtinen (eds), *Helsinki—Helsingfors: Historiallinen kaupunkikartasto*, Scandinavian Atlas of Historic Towns: New Series 2, Helsinki: Tietokeskus, 2009.

Kuisma, Markku, *Helsingin pitäjän historia III: Isostavihasta maalaiskunnan syntyyn, 1713–1865*, Vantaa: Vantaan kaupunki, 1991.

——, *Kansallinen voitto ja kapitalismin henki: Luonnostelmia maailmantalouden reunalta*, Helsinki: Siltala, 2024.

Lönnqvist, Bo, *Herrgårdar och rusthåll i Helsingforstrakten*, Helsinki: Schildt, 2009.

Nikula, Oscar, *Augustin Ehrensvärd*, Helsinki: Svenska Litteratursällskapet i Finland, 2010.

Nordenstreng, Rolf, "Finländsk svenska på 1700-talet", in *Förhandlingar och uppsatser (16): 1902*, Helsinki, 1903.

Odelberg, Wilhelm, *Viceamiral Carl Olof Cronstedt: Levnadsteckning och tidsskildring*, Stockholm: Söderström, 1954.

Parland-von Essen, Jessica, *Affärer, allianser, anseende: Konsten att tillhöra eliten i Helsingfors ca 1740–1820*, Helsinki: Schildts, 2010.

Reuter, Mikael, "Skatudden: Reuters ruta", *Hufvudstadsbladet*, 6 May 1998.

Salminen, Tapio, *Vantaan ja Helsingin pitäjän keskiaika*, Vantaa: Vantaan kaupunginmuseo, 2013.

Zetterberg, Seppo, *Viron historia*, Helsinki: Suomalaisen Kirjallisuuden Seura, 2007.

3. The Capital City

Alapuro, Risto, *Suomen älymystö Venäjän varjossa*, Helsinki: Tammi, 1997.

Alin, Taavetti and Risto Törrö, *C.L. Engel—Hemmet i Helsingfors, hjärtat i Berlin* / *C.L. Engel—Koti Helsingissä, sydän Berliinissä*, Helsinki: Schildts, 2012.

Åström, Sven-Erik, *Samhällsplanering och regionsbildning i Kejsartidens Helsingfors: Studier i stadens inre differentiering 1810–1910*, Helsinki: Statens Humanistiska Kommission, 1957.

Blomstedt, Yrjö, *Johan Albrecht Ehrenström: Kustavilainen ja kaupunginrakentaja*, Helsingin kaupungin julkaisuja 14, Helsinki: City of Helsinki, 1963.

Engel, C. L., *Kirjeet* / *Brev* / *Briefe 1813–1840*, Mikael Sundman (ed.), Helsinki: Helsinki-seura, 1989.

Engman, Max, *St Petersburg och Finland: Migration och influens 1703–1917*, Helsinki: Finska Vetenskaps-Societeten, 1983.

Eronen, Jarmo, "Venäjän ja Suomen välinen kauppa autonomian ajalla", in Svante Kuhlberg (ed.), *Venäläiset kauppiaat Helsingin historiassa*, Helsinki: Helsingin venäläinen kauppiasyhdistys, 2002.

Hietala, Marjatta, Martti Helminen and Merja Lahtinen (eds), *Helsinki—Helsingfors: Historiallinen kaupunkikartasto*, Scandinavian Atlas of Historic Towns: New Series 2, Helsinki: Tietokeskus, 2009.

Hirn, Sven, *Kameran edestä ja takaa: Valokuvaus ja valokuvaajat Suomessa 1839–1870*, Helsinki: Suomen valokuvataiteen museon säätiö, 1972.

Johnsson, Raoul and Ilkka Malmberg, *Kauhia Oolannin sota: Krimin sota Suomessa 1854–1855*, Helsinki: John Nurmisen Sääti, 2013.

Juntunen, Alpo, *Sveaborg 1808–1918: Helsingin suoja ja Pietarin etuvartio*, Jyväskylä: Docendo, 2017.

BIBLIOGRAPHY

Kalleinen, Kristiina, *Valtioaamun aika: Suomen suuriruhtinaskunta 1809–1863*, Helsinki: Gaudeamus, 2023.

Klinge, Matti, *Ylioppilastalo: Helsingin yliopiston ylioppilaskunnan kiinteistöjen vaiheita*, 2nd edition, Helsinki: Helsigin yliopiston ylioppilaskunta, 1990.

——, *Huvudstaden: Helsingfors och Finska staten 1808–1863*, trans. Torsten Edgren, Helsinki: Otava, 2012.

Lindberg, Carolus and Gabriel Rein, "Stadsplanering och byggnadsverksamhet", in Ragnar Rosén, Eino Jutikkala and Eirik Hornborg (eds), *Helsingfors stads historia III, första bandet*, Helsinki: 1950.

Luntinen, Pertti, *The Imperial Russian Army and Navy in Finland 1808–1918*, Helsinki: Suomen Historiallinen Seura, 1997.

Markkanen, Tapio, "Helsingin tähtitorni: klassisten tähtitornien esikuva", in Henrik Meinander (ed.), *Unioninakseli: Pääkaupungin läpileikkaus*, Helsinki: Teos, 2012.

Meinander, Henrik (ed.), *Unioninakseli: Pääkaupungin läpileikkaus*, Helsinki: Teos, 2012.

Minard-Törmänen, Nathanaëlle, *An Imperial Idyll: Finland in Russian Travelogues (1810–1860)*, Helsinki: Societas Scientiarum Fennica, 2016.

Nakhimovsky, Isaac, *The Holy Alliance: Liberalism and the Politics of Federation*, Princeton, NJ: Princeton University Press, 2024.

Nivala Merja, Simo Määttä and Tero Halonen (eds), *Helsingin ja isänmaan puolesta: J. A. Ehrenströmin kirjeenvaihto C. J. Walleenin ja R. H. Rehbinderin kanssa 1814–1826*, Entisaikain Helsinki XXI, Helsinki: Helsinki-Seura, 2024.

Paavolainen, Pentti, *Nuori Bergbom: Kaarlo Bergbomin elämä ja työ 1843–1872*, Helsinki, 2013.

——, *Arkadian arki: Kaarlo Bergbomin elämä ja työ 1872–1887*, Helsinki, 2014.

Palmén, E. G., *Helsingfors 1800–1900: Byggnadsverksamhet och tomtvärde*, Helsinki: Yrjö Weilin, 1907.

Paunonen, Heikki, *Suomen kieli Helsingissä: Huomioita Helsingin puhekielen historiallisesta taustasta ja nykyvariaatiosta*, Helsinki: Helsingin yliopiston suomen kielen laitos, 1995.

——, "Vähemmistökielestä varioivaksi valtakieleksi", in Kaisu Juusela and Katariina Nisula (eds), *Helsinki kieliyhteisönä*, Helsinki: Helsingin yliopisto, Suomen kielen ja kotimaisen kirjallisuuden laitos, 2006.

——, *Sloboa Stadissa: Stadin slangin etymologiaa*, Jyväskylä: Docendo, 2016.

Pekkala-Koskela, Eea (ed.), *Yliopiston Helsinki: University Architecture in Helsinki*, Helsinki: Sanomaprint, 1989.

Perälä, Seppo; "Helsingin venäläissyntyinen kauppiaskunta vuosina 1809–79", in Åström, Sven-Erik et al. (eds), *Entisaikain Helsinki VIII*, Helsinki: Helsinki Seura—Helsingfors Samfundet, 1970.

Schauman, August, *Från sex årtionden I Finland: Levnadsminnen I-II, Ny illustrerad upplaga*, Helsinki: Schildts, 1922.

Tommila, Päiviö, *Helsinki Kylpyläkaupunkina 1830–1850: luvuilla*, Helsinki: Helsinki Seura, 1955.

Villstrand, Nils Erik, *Furstar och folk i Åbo 1812*, Stockholm: Atlantis, 2012.

Wrede, Johan, *Världen enligt Runeberg: En biografisk och idéhistorisk studie*, Helsinki: Society of Swedish Literature in Finland, 2005.

4. Industry and Independence

Aho, Juhani, *Helsinkiin*, Helsinki: WSOY, 1889.

——, *Yksin*, Helsinki: WSOY,1890.

——, *Hajamietteistä kapinaviikoilta: Kootut teokset, täydennysosa II*, Helsinki: WSOY, 1961.

Alanco, Jan and Riitta Pakarinen, *Foto Signe Brander: Valokuvia Helsingistä ja helsinkiläisistä 1907–1913 / Fotografier av Helsingfors och Helsingforsbor 1907–1913*, Helsinki: Helsingin Kaupunginmuseo, 2009.

Åström, Sven-Erik, *Helsingfors stads historia IV, andra bandet*, Helsinki: City of Helsinki, 1956.

Bell, Marjatta and Hietala, Marjatta, *Helsinki, The Innovative City:*

Historical Perspectives, Helsinki: Suomalaisen Kirjallisuuden Seura, 2002.

Byckling, Liisa, *Keisariajan kulisseissa: Helsingin venäläisen teatterin historia 1868–1918*, Helsinki: SKS Kirjat, 2009.

Castrén, Gunnar, "Helsingfors som kulturcentrum", in Ragnar Rosén, Eino Jutikkala and Eirik Hornborg (eds), *Helsingfors stads historia III, andra bandet*, Helsinki: City of Helsinki, 1950.

Elmgren, Ainur, "'Tataarit pois!'—Suomen tataarien uskonnolliset ja yhteiskunnalliset oikeustaistelut", in Miriam Attias and Panu Artemjeff (eds), *Historiat ja väestösuhteet*, Helsinki: Bookea, 2024.

Engman, Max, *St Petersburg och Finland: Migration och influens 1703–1917*, Helsinki: Finska Vetenskaps-Societeten, 1983.

Eronen, Jarmo, "Venäjän ja Suomen välinen kauppa autonomian ajalla", in Svante Kuhlberg (ed.), *Venäläiset kauppiaat Helsingin historiassa*, Helsinki: Helsingin venäläinen kauppiasyhdistys, 2002.

Estlander, Bernhard, *Elva årtionden ur Finlands historia, 2 uppl.*, Helsinki: Söderström, 1929.

Ganivet, Angel, *Suomalaiskirjeitä Helsingistä vv. 1896–1897*, trans. Kaarle Hirvonen, Porvoo: WSOY, 1964.

Hakaniementori: Kaupunkirakenne- ja ympäristöhistoriaselvitys, Urban Environment Publications 2021:8, Helsinki: Kaupunkimittausosasto, 2021.

"Helsingin raitiotielinjat", available on raitio.org (in Finnish, accessed 16.05.2025).

Hietala, Marjatta, *Services and Urbanization at the Turn of the Century: The Diffusion of Innovations*, Helsinki: Suomen Historiallinen Seura, 1987.

Hirn, Sven, *Kameran edestä ja takaa: Valokuvaus ja valokuvaajat Suomessa 1839–1870*, Helsinki: Suomen valokuvataiteen museon säätiö, 1972.

Howard, Jeremy (ed.), *Architecture 1900: Stockholm, Helsinki, Tallinn, Riga, St Petersburg*, Tallinn: Museum of Estonian Architecture, 2003.

Hultin, Tekla, *Päiväkirjani kertoo 1914–1918 / II*, Helsinki: Sanatar, 1938.

Jalava, Marja, "Rietas vai viaton Havis Amanda: Taideteos julkisen

BIBLIOGRAPHY

tilan keskiössä", in Henrik Meinander (ed.), *Unioninakseli—pääkaupungin läpileikkaus*, Helsinki: Teos, 2012.

Juntunen, Alpo, *Sveaborg 1808–1918: Helsingin suoja ja Pietarin etuvartio*, Jyväskylä: Docendo, 2017.

Kalha, Harri, *Tapaus Havis Amanda: Siveellisyys ja sukupuoli vuoden 1908 suihkulähdekiistassa*, Helsinki: Suomalaisen Kirjallisuuden Seura, 2008.

Kiiski, Venla, *Tekla Hultin, poliitikko*, Jyväskylä: Studia historica Jyväskyläensia, 1978.

Kolbe, Laura, *Brändö: Drömmen om en bättre framtid*, trans. Carl-Gustav Zilliiacus, Helsinki: Helsingfors stadsmuseum, 1990.

Kolbe, Laura and Nyström, Samu, *Helsinki 1918: Pääkaupunki ja sota*, Helsinki: Minerva, 2008.

Lackman, Matti, *Suomen vai Saksan puolesta? Jääkäreiden tuntematon historia*, Helsinki: Otava, 2000.

Luntinen, Pertti, *The Imperial Russian Army and Navy in Finland 1808–1918*, Helsinki: Suomen Historiallinen Seura, 1997.

Mäki, Heli and Jenni Korjus (eds), *Railways as an Innovative Regional Factor*, Helsinki: University of Helsinki, 2009.

Moisala, U. E., Kauko Rahko and Oiva Turpeinen, *Puhelin ja Puhelinlaitokset Suomessa 1877–1977*, Turku: 1977.

Moorhouse, Jonathan, Michael Carapetian and Leena Ahtola-Moorhouse, *Helsinki Jugendstil Architecture 1895–1915*, Helsinki: Otava, 1987.

Muir, Simo, "Juutalaisten tie tsaari alamaisista Suomen kansalaisiksi" in Miriam Attias and Panu Artemjeff (eds), *Historiat ja väestösuhteet*, Helsinki: Bookea, 2024.

Nieminen, Jarmo (ed.), *Helsinki ensimmäisessä maailmansodassa: Sotasurmat 1917–1918*, Helsinki: Gummerus, 2015.

Nikula, Riitta, *Yhtenäinen kaupunkikuva 1900–1930: Suomalaisen kaupunkirakentamisen ihanteista ja päämääristä, esimerkkeinä Helsingin Etu-Töölö ja uusi Vallila*, Helsinki: Societas scientarium Fennica, 1981.

Nyström, Samu, *Poikkeusajan kaupunkielämäkerta: Helsinki ja helsinkiläiset maailmansodassa 1914–1918*, Helsinki: University of Helsinki, 2013.

Pöyhönen, Jaakko, "Voimaa koneisiin, valoa kaduille ja asuntoihin", in Kirsi Ahonen, Marjaana Niemi and Jaakko Pöyhönen, *Tietoa, taitoa, asiantuntemusta: Helsinki eurooppalaisessa kehityksessä 1875–1917, osa 3, Henkistä kasvua, teknistä taitoa*, Helsinki: Suomen Historiallinen Seura, 1992.

Suominen-Kokkonen, Renja, "Naisarkkitehti vuosisadanvaihteen suomalaisessa arkkitehtuurimaisemassa—Wivi Lönn", in Pirjo Lyytikäinen, Jyrki Kalliokoski and Mervi Kantokorpi (eds), *Katsomuksen ihanuus: Kirjoituksia vuosisadanvaihteen taiteista*, Helsinki: Suomalaisen Kirjallisuuden Seura, 1996.

——, "Wivi Lönn", *Biografiskt lexikon för Finland/2: Ryska tiden*, available at https://blf.fi/artikel.php?id=3438.

Tanner, Väinö, *Näin Helsingin kasvavan*, Helsinki: Tammi, 1947.

Turpeinen, Oiva, *Suuriruhtinaan Suomi: [3] Pietarin rata, rajamaasta maailmalle*, Helsinki: 2004.

Tweedie, Mrs Alec, *Through Finland in Carts*, London: Thomas Nelson & Sons, 1898.

Upton, Anthony F., *The Finnish Revolution 1917–1918*, Minneapolis: University of Minnesota Press, 1980.

Vettenniemi, Erkki, *Suomi terrorin tukikohtana: Kuinka Lenin tuhosi Venäjän suomalaisten suosiollisella avustuksella*, Helsinki: SKS Kirjat, 2019.

Waris, Heikki, *Työläisyhteiskunnan syntyminen Helsingin Pitkänsillan pohjoispuolelle: 1*, Helsinki: [Heikki Waris] 1932.

Waris, Heikki, *Työläisyhteiskunnan syntyminen Helsingin Pitkänsillan pohjoispuolelle: 2*, Helsinki: Historiallisia tutkimuksia 1934.

Zakharova, Larissa, "The Telephone in Russia before 1917", in *Encyclopédie d'historie numérique de l'Europe* [online], ehne.fr/en/node/12497 (accessed 16.05.2025).

5. *The Heart of the Republic*

Aho & Soldan [Film Production Company], Newsreel "Torielämää Helsingissä vuonna 1933", available on Yle's Living Archive, https://yle.fi/elavaarkisto (in Finnish, accessed 18.05.2025).

BIBLIOGRAPHY

Alapuro, Risto, *Akateeminen Karjala-Seura: Ylioppilasliike ja kansa 1920- ja 1930-luvulla*, Helsinki: Tekijä, 1973.

Grotenfelt, Georg, Juha Ilonen and Wilhelm Helander (eds), *Kaupungin piirteet / Stadens prägel / Outlining a City,* Helsinki: AtlasArt, 2017.

Häggman, Kai, Teemu Keskisarja and Markku Kuisma, *1939*, Helsinki: WSOY, 2019.

Julkunen, Martti, *Talvisodan kuva: Ulkomaiset sotakirjeenvaihtajat Suomessa v. 1939–1940*, Helsinki: Weilin Göös, 1975.

Jutikkala, Eino, "Bakgrunden till Helsingfors stads historieverk", in Eino Jutikkala et al. (eds), *Helsingfors stads historia V, tredje bandet*, Helsinki: City of Helsinki, 1967.

Kuisma, Markku, Anna Finnilä, Teemu Keskisarj and Minna Sarantola-Weiss, *Crazy Days, Amazing Years: Stockmann 1862–2012*, trans. Kristian London, Helsinki: Siltala, 2012.

Lähteenmäki, Maria, *Mahdollisuuksien aika: Työläisnaiset ja yhteiskunnan muutos 1910–30-luvun Suomessa*, Helsinki: Suomen Historiallinen Seura, 1995.

Meinander, Henrik, *Finland 1944: Krig, samhälle, känslolandskap*, Helsinki: Söderströms, 2009.

—, *Nationalstaten: Finlands svenskhet 1922–2015*, Helsinki: Svenska Litteratursällskapet, 2016.

Nikula, Riitta, *Yhtenäinen kaupunkikuva 1900–1930: Suomalaisen kaupunkirakentamisen ihanteista ja päämääristä, esimerkkeinä Helsingin Etu-Töölö ja uusi Vallila*, Helsinki 1981.

Niska, Algoth, *Mina äventyr*, Helsinki 1931.

Nuorteva, Jussi and Päivi Happonen (eds), *Viapori—Suomenlinna: Kolmen valtakunnan linnoitus 1748–2021 / Sveaborg: Tre riken—en fästning 1748–2021*, Helsinki: Kansallisarkisto, 2021.

Rosén, Ragnar et al. (eds), *Helsingfors stads historia V, första bandet*, Helsinki: City of Helsinki, 1964.

—, *Helsingfors stads historia V, andra bandet*, Helsinki: City of Helsinki, 1965.

Sarje, Kimmo, *Sigurd Frosteruksen modernin käsite: Maailmankatsomus ja arkkitehtuuri*, Helsinki: Valtion taidemuseo, 2000.

Schildt, Göran, *Alvar Aalto: The Early Years*, New York: Rizzoli, 1984.

Sipilä, Seppo, Raine Haikarainen and Hannu-Matti Wahl (eds), Malmi—Helsingin lentoasema: 70 vuotta suomalaista ilmailua, Helsinki: Minerva, 2008.

Uusitalo, Kari (ed.), *Suomen kansallisfilmografia 1: 1907–1935*, Helsinki 2002.

——, *Suomen kansallisfilmografia 2: 1936–1941*, Helsinki 2002.

Vala, Katri, *Kootut runot*, Porvoo: WSOY, 1977.

Vasara, Erkki, "Helsingin kahdet olympiakisat", in Otto Mattsson and Milka Sunell (eds), *Pääkaupungin kuva: Luentoja Helsingin historiasta*, Helsinki: Helsingin kaupunginmuseo, 2000.

Waltari, Mika, *Surun ja ilon kaupunki*, Helsinki: WSOY, 1936. Swedish translation in Rosén, Ragnar et al. (eds), *Helsingfors stads historia V, andra bandet*, Helsinki: 1965.

Waris, Heikki, *Työläisyhteiskunnan syntyminen Helsingin Pitkänsillan pohjoispuolelle: I*, Helsinki: 1932.

——, "Huvudstadssamhället", in Rosén, Ragnar et al. (eds), *Helsingfors stads historia III, andra bandet*, Helsinki: 1950.

6. Cold War Climates

Helander, Vilhelm and Mikael Sundman, *Vems är Helsingfors? Rapport från innerstaden 1970*, Helsinki: Holger Schildts, 1970.

Johansson, Eva, *Drömmen som gick i kras—Alvar Aaltos centrumplan för Helsingfors 1959–1972: Bakgrund, utformning och bemötande i en samtida kontext*, Turku: Åbo Akademi University Press, 2018.

Kaelble, Hartmut, *A Social History of Europe, 1945–2000: Recovery and Transformation after Two World Wars*, trans. Liesel Tarquini, Oxford: Berghahn Books, 2013.

Kervanto Nevanlinna, Anja, *Helsingfors stads historia efter 1945: Del 4, Krafterna som byggde Helsingfors 1945–2010*, Helsinki: Suomalaisen Kirjallisuuden Seura, 2014.

Klinge, Matti, *Kadonnutta aikaa löytämässä: Muistelmia 1936–1960*, Helsinki: Siltala, 2012.

Kolbe, Laura, Jari Kupila and Samu Nyström, *Helsinki 1952: Kansainvälistyvä pääkaupunki*, Helsinki: Minerva, 2022.

Kortteinen, Matti, *Lähiö. Tutkimus elämäntapojen muutoksesta*, Helsinki: Otava 1982.

Kyösola, Satu and Satu Laaksonen, "Lähettäkää kiireesti jokin ranskalainen! Ranskalaisen elokuvan kultaiset vuodet Suomessa 1930—1960-luvuilla", in Outi Merisalo and Sini Sovijärvi (eds), *Ranska Helsingissä vuodesta 1890 / La France à Helsinki depuis 1890*, Helsinki: Artemisia Edizioni, 2023.

Laakkonen, Simo, Sari Laurila, Pekka Kansanen and Harry Schulman, (eds), *Näkökulmia Helsingin ympäristöhistoriaan. Kaupungin ja ympäristön muutos 1800- ja 1900-luvuilla*, Helsinki: Edita, 2001.

Meinander, Henrik, *Samtidigt: Finland och omvärld 1968*, Helsinki: S&S, 2019.

——, *Tikkanens linje: Tidsbilder 1967–1972*, Helsinki: S&S, 2021.

Mustonen, Pertti, *Kaupungin sielua etsimässä: Kertomus Helsingin kaupunkisuunnittelusta Bertel Jungista nykyaikaan*, Helsinki: Helsingin kaupunginsuunnitteluvirasto, 2010.

Niskanen, Mikko, *Lapualaismorsian*, 1967, available on Yle's Living Archive, https://yle.fi/elavaarkisto (in Finnish, accessed 18.05.2025).

Nuorteva, Jussi and Päivi Happonen (eds), *Viapori—Suomenlinna: Kolmen valtakunnan linnoitus 1748–2021 / Sveaborg: Tre riken—en fästning 1748–2021*, Helsinki: Kansallisarkisto, 2021.

Paunonen, Heikki, *Suomen kieli Helsingissä: Huomioita Helsingin puhekielen historiallisesta taustasta ja nykyvariaatiosta*, Helsinki: Helsingin yliopiston suomen kielen laitos, 1995.

——, "Vähemmistökielestä varioivaksi valtakieleksi", in Kaisu Juusela and Katariina Nisula (eds), *Helsinki kieliyhteisönä*, Helsinki: Helsingin yliopisto, Suomen kielen ja kotimaisen kirjallisuuden laitos, 2006.

Raevuori, Antero, *Viimeiset oikeat olympialaiset: Helsinki 1952*, Jyväskylä: Ajatus, 2002.

Saisio, Pirkko, *The Red Book of Farewells*, trans. Mia Spangenberg, Helsinki: Two Lines Press, 2023.

Schulman, Harry, Panu Pulma and Seppo Aalto, *Helsingfors stads historia efter 1945: Del 2, Planering och byggande, sociala problem, sport*, Helsinki: Edita, 2002.

Turpeinen, Oiva, Timo Herranen and Kai Hoffman, *Helsingfors stads historia efter 1945: Del 1, Befolkning, stadsplanering och boende, näringsliv*, Helsinki: Edita, 2002.

7. The Northern European Metropolis

"Air Quality in the Helsinki Metropolitan Area and Elsewhere", Helsinki Region Environmental Services Authority HSY, available on https://www.hsy.fi/en/ (accessed 18.05.2025).

Clark, Peter (ed.), *The European City and Green Space: London, Stockholm, Helsinki and St Petersburg*, London: Routledge, 2006.

Hein, Carola, "Port Cities", in Peter Clark (ed.), *The Oxford Handbook of Cities in World History*, Oxford: Oxford University Press, 2013.

Helimäki, Jussi (ed.), *Lumoava Helsinki: 200 luontoelämystä*, Helsinki: Edita, 2017.

Helsinki Facts and Figures 2024, Helsinki: City Executive Office, 2024.

"Ilmastonmuutos pääkaupunkiseudulla", vol.1, Helsinki: Finnish Meteorological Institute, 2023.

Joutsiniemi, Anssi, "Helsinki on maantieteensä ja hallintonsa vanki", vol.1, *Arkkitehti*, 2024.

Kyösola, Satu and Satu Laaksonen, "Lähettäkää kiireesti jokin ranskalainen! Ranskalaisen elokuvan kultaiset vuodet Suomessa 1930—1960-luvuilla", in Outi Merisalo and Sini Sovijärvi (eds), *Ranska Helsingissä vuodesta 1890 / La France à Helsinki depuis 1890*, Helsinki: Artemisia Edizioni, 2023.

Lahti, Juhani, Kristiina Paatero and Eija Rauske (eds), *Rantaviivoja: Asuinalueita veden äärellä*, Helsinki: Suomen arkkitehtuurimuseo, 2012.

Melosi, Martin V., "The Urban Environment", in Peter Clark (ed.), *The Oxford Handbook of Cities in World History*, Oxford: Oxford University Press, 2013.

Söderström, Panu, Harry Schulman and Mika Ristimäki (eds), *Pohjoiset suurkaupungit: Yhdyskuntarakenteen kehitys Helsingin ja Tukholman metropolialueilla*, Helsinki: 2014.

INDEX

Aalto University, 128
Aalto, Alvar, 174, 180, 230–31
Academic Karelia Society (AKS), 185
Academic Male Voice Choir, 98
Age of Sail (c. 1571–1862), 24
Agrarian League, 216
agriculture, 9, 122, 216
Aho & Soldan, 195
Aho, Juhani, 139–40, 142, 163
air pollution, 231–3, 266
airports, 180, 219
Åland Islands, 104, 108, 120, 160
alcohol, 55, 59, 103, 140–41, 188–9
aldermen, 30
Aleksanterinkatu, Helsinki, 25, 116, 169, 178, 191, 194
Alexander I, Emperor of Russia, 68, 71, 73, 74–5, 77, 78, 82, 83, 84, 101, 115
Alexander II, Emperor of Russia, 108, 111–16, 169–70
Alexander III, Emperor of Russia, 93
Alexander Nevsky Church, Suomenlinna, 119
Alexander Theatre, Helsinki, 120
Alexandra, Empress consort of Russia, 95
Alku, 134
Allegro Service, 259
Allied Control Commission, 209, 220, 242
Allmänna Promenaden, Helsinki, 98
Alppila, Helsinki, 126, 203, 231, 238
Ämmässuo, Espoo, 232
Amsterdam, Netherlands, 41
Anders de Bruce, 51
Anderson, Amos, 243
Animal Park, Helsinki, 176

Anna Karenina (1967 film), 240
Arabianranta, Helsinki, 254
Arabic, 258
   architecture, viii, ix, 13–14,
     25–6, 27, 53, 173–5,
     252–7
   Aalto buildings, 174, 231
   Burgman House, 31–2, 36,
     39, 53
   Empire style, 1, 81, 84, 86,
     87, 88, 90, 190
   Enemmistö movement,
     229–30
   functionalism, 175, 177, 180,
     195, 231
   grid plans, 19, 25, 38, 79, 83,
     144
   Jugend style, 133, 142–5,
     148, 243
   Jung's planning (1908–46),
     211
   manor houses, 47, 55, 63–4
   neo-Baroque, 144
   neo-Classical, 172, 175
   neo-Gothic, 130
   neo-Renaissance, 130
   paint colour rules, 87
   redevelopment (1810–25),
     73–5, 79–87
   redevelopment (1990s), 252
   stone houses, 31–2, 36, 39,
     52, 53, 54
   Töölönlahti redevelopment
     plans, 173–5, 231
   wooden buildings, 13, 26, 27,
     38, 87

   working-class housing,
     130–35, 175
Argelander, Friedrich, 85–6
Arkadia Hill, Helsinki, 172, 174
Arkadiankatu, Helsinki, 117,
   215
Armfeldt, Carl Gustaf, 36
Armfelt, Gustav Mauritz, 74–5,
   78, 79
artisans, 14, 28, 46, 47, 54, 58
Ateneum, Helsinki, 148
Atheneum, Helsinki, 144
Augustin Ehrensvärd, 50
Austria, 68, 169
aviation, 180, 219

baby boom (1945–60s), 214–15
Baltic Sea, vii, 1, 2, 12
Baltic Sea Fleet, 150, 159
Baltic Sea trade, 4–7, 9, 11, 12,
   23, 41–2, 49
   tar, 8, 23–4, 27
Baltic states, 172, 196
Bank of Finland, 114, 198
barnacle geese, 263
baths, 96–7, 176
Battle of Bomarsund (1854),
   104, 105, 110, 120
Battle of Helsinki (1713), 35–7,
   42, 56
Battle of Helsinki (1918), 162–3,
   165
Battle of Narva (1700), 34
Battle of Poltava (1709), 34
Battle of Tampere (1918), 161
Bauakademie, Berlin, 81

Belgium, 4
Bell, Alexander Graham, 128
Belle Époque (1871–1914), 142
Bergbom, Emilie and Kaarlo, 117–18
Berlin, Germany, 81, 128, 210
Biedermeier, 87
bilingualism, 135–6, 186, 217
birds, 263, 266
Black Death (1346–53), 3, 29
Black Sea Fleet, 104
Blomqvist, Arthur, 154
von Blücher, Wipert, 204
blue-green algae, 265
Bobrikov, Nikolay, 146, 149
Bolsheviks, 153–5, 157, 158–61, 183
Bomarsund Fortress, Åland, 104, 105, 110, 120
Book House, Helsinki, 231
Borgström, Henrik, 96, 100, 176
Bornholm, Denmark, 50
Brahe Field, Helsinki, 176
Brahe, Per, 18, 19–20, 22
Brander, Signe, 130–32
Brezhnev, Leonid, 247
brothels, 139
Bruges, Belgium, 4
Bucharest, Romania, 169
Budapest, Hungary, 210
Bulevardi, Helsinki, 80, 87, 120, 143, 243
Bulgarin, Faddei, 85
burgher guard, 64–5
burghers, 17, 30, 56, 57–8, 64–5, 67, 114

Burgman, Hans, 30
Burgman, Petter, 30
Burgman, Torsten, 30–32, 36, 39, 53
burn beating, 9
butter, 8, 151
Byström, Anders, 59

Cable Factory, Helsinki, 254
Café Ursula, Helsinki, 218
cafés, 97
capital city status, 74–5, 77, 90
capitalism, 3, 112
carbon neutrality, 262
cars, 212, 227–8, 230–31
cats, 263
cattle farming, 9
censorship, 101, 103, 152, 155, 200, 238
Central Library, Helsinki, 173
Central Park, Helsinki, 176
Central Station, Helsinki, 88, 144, 154, 174, 177, 178, 194, 206, 229
Centre Party, 216
Charles IX, King of Sweden, 15–16, 17
Charles X, King of Sweden, 23
Charles XI, King of Sweden, 33
Charles XII, King of Sweden, 33–8
Charles XIV, King of Sweden, 78
childbirth, 60
Christian II, King of Denmark, 141

Christianity
  churches, *see* churches
  clergy, 13–14, 17, 32, 101, 114
  congregations, 32–3
  Lutheranism, 1, 5–6, 14, 28, 71, 80, 93, 102, 170, 253
  Orthodox Church, 1, 83, 89–90, 111, 119, 170
Christina, Queen of Sweden, 18–19
Christina Church, Helsinki, 27
Christophori, Bertil, 14
Church of St Lawrence, Helsinki, 9
Church of the Holy Spirit, Helsinki, 27, 36
churches, 13–14, 27, 32–3, 39
  Alexander Nevsky Church, 119
  Christina Church, 27
  Church of St Lawrence, 9
  Church of the Holy Spirit, 27, 36
  German Church, 94, 228
  Helsinki Cathedral, 1
  Holy Trinity Church, 119
  Kallio Church, 144
  St John's Church, 1, 130, 228
  St Nicholas's Church, 80, 84, 95, 120, 130, 141
  Ulrika Eleonora Church, 39, 65
  Uspenski Cathedral, 1, 36, 119–20, 141
cinema, *see* film

Citizens' Square, Helsinki, 173, 252
City Museum, Helsinki, 190
City of Sorrow and Joy, The (Waltari), 192
civil society, 112, 123, 137
Civil War (1918), 82, 149, 159–63, 165–8, 186–7, 201
Clarke, Edward Daniel, 52–3
class, *see* social class
clergy, 13–14, 17, 32, 101, 114
climate, 2, 3, 264–6, 269–70
clothing, 31–2
Coca-Cola, 223–4
coffee, 151
Cold War (1947–91), 224, 238–9, 241–9, 251
  Finlandisation, 238, 241–4, 246
  Helsinki Accords (1975), 231, 245–8
Collier's, 199
communism
  Communist Party of Finland, 171, 187, 193, 202, 235, 237, 242
  Red Guards, 149, 154–68, 186–7
Conference on Security and Cooperation in Europe, 231, 245–8
Constantinople, 169
contact mines, 106
Continuation War (1941–4), 198, 202–8, 214, 234, 243
coppersmiths, 58

Count's War (1534–6), 6
County Governor's residence, 22, 31, 39, 53, 65
courts, 32
Creutz, Ernst Johan, 22–3, 26, 39
crime, 261
Crimean War (1853–6), 98, 104–11, 120
Cron Printzen Gustaf Adolph, 50–51
Cronstedt, Carl Olof, 69, 70–71
Culture House, Helsinki, 231
customs warehouse, 53
cyanobacteria, 265
Cygnaeus, Fredrik, 103
Czechoslovakia, 169

Dammert, Ingrid Maria, 59
Danton, Georges, 158
declaration of independence (1917), 158
deer, 263
Denmark
  Count's War (1534–6), 6
  Great Northern War (1700–21), 33
  Kalmar Union (1397–1523), 5, 141
  Napoleonic Wars (1803–15), 68
  Northern War (1655–60), 23
Diet of the Estates, 112–16, 172
Diet of Porvoo (1809), 71–3, 82, 115
Disabled War Veterans' Association, 224

disease epidemics, 3, 12, 28, 29, 60, 67, 167
dogs, 263
Dorpat, Estonia, 4
Dutch merchants, 7, 12, 13
Dutch Republic (1588–1795), 41
dyes, 31

East Germany (1949–90), 245
Ebeneserkoti, Helsinki, 144–5
economy
  Republic era (1919–), 168–9, 182–3, 187–8, 212, 225–6, 235, 244, 251–2
  Russian era (1809–1917), 77, 99–100, 122, 125–6
  Swedish era (1150s–1809), 4–7, 9, 11, 12, 23, 41–2, 49–57
Edelfelt, Albert, 141–2
Edison Cinema, Helsinki, 205
education, 137, 259
Eerikinkatu, Helsinki, 134
Ehrenström, Johan Albrecht, 60–63, 79–84, 87, 181
Ehrensvärd, Augustin, 45, 46, 47, 56, 57, 65–6
eight-hour workdays, 157
Eira, Helsinki, 143
Ekman, Anna Gustafva, 60
Eläintarha, Helsinki, 176
Eläintarhanlahti Bay, Helsinki, 144
Elanto, 135
elections, 112, 133, 135, 146–7, 149, 157, 181–2, 226

electricity, 122, 127–8
Empire style, 1, 81, 84, 86, 87, 88, 90, 190
Enemmistö, 229–30
Engel, Carl Ludwig, 81–8, 97, 102, 116, 181, 234
English language, 223, 258, 259–61
Enlightenment (c. 1685–1815), 61
Enso-Gutzeit, 231
Eric XIV, King of Sweden, 15
Erottaja, Helsinki, 80, 178
fire station, 130
Esplanadi, Helsinki, 64, 80, 181
Esplanadin Puisto, Helsinki, 25, 116, 235, 252, 265
Espoo, Finland, 128, 213, 217, 232, 239, 257, 262
Espoon tulli, Helsinki, 64
Estlander, Bernhard, 137
Estnässkatan, see Vironniemi
Estonia
Danish period (1219–1346), 4–5
German occupation (1941–4), 204, 210
Republic, First (1920–40), 169, 196
Republic, Third (1991–), 249
Russian period (1710–1917), 34, 37, 43, 49, 81, 90, 96, 144
Soviet period, First (1940–41), 202

Soviet period, Second (1944–91), 249
Swedish period (1561–1710), 12, 14–15, 23, 26, 34, 249
Teutonic period (1346–1561), 7, 9
Estonia Theatre, Tallinn, 144
Estonian language, 258
Etelä-Esplanadi, Helsinki, 161
Etelä-Häme, Helsinki, 92, 143
Eteläranta, Helsinki, 218
Etu-Töölö, Helsinki, 143, 172, 194, 215
European Union (EU), 249, 251–2, 267

F/A-18 Hornets, 249
factories, 125–6, 132, 142, 171, 254
famines, 26
1315–17: 3
1696–97: 27, 28–9
1866–68: 122
fauna, 263–4, 266
Federley, Alex, 190
ferries, 218, 249, 255, 267
film, 148, 187, 194–6, 205, 240–41
financial services, 225
Finland
Republic of Finland (1919–), see Republic of Finland
Russian Grand Duchy (1809–1917), viii, 42, 48, 61, 71–120, 121–55

INDEX

Swedish rule (1150s–1809),
  see under Sweden
Finlandia Hall, Helsinki, 174,
  231, 248
Finlandisation, 238, 241–4, 246
Finnish Broadcasting Company,
  238
Finnish Civil War (1918), 82,
  149, 153, 159–63, 165–8,
  186–7, 201
Finnish Employers'
  Confederation, 218
Finnish language
  Republic era (1919–), 184–6,
    216–17, 239, 257–60
  Russian era (1809–1917),
    91–3, 101, 113–19,
    123–4, 135–40
  Swedish era (1150s–1809),
    28, 90
Finnish Literature Day, 118
Finnish Literature Society,
  100–101, 216
Finnish National Theatre,
  Helsinki, 144
Finnish People's Delegation, 149
Finnish People's Democratic
  League, 226, 231
Finnish Rural Party, 216
Finnish Society of Sciences and
  Letters, 101
Finnish Swedish Heritage Day,
  186
Finno, Jaakko, 14
fires, 26
  1570: 12

1654: 26, 27, 269
1808: 31, 53, 72–3
1855: 107
First World War (1914–18), viii,
  144, 150–53, 157, 168
Fish Harbour, Helsinki, 255
fish, 5, 8, 9, 49
flags, 166, 200
flora and fauna, 263–4, 266
Flower Day, 103
Ford, Gerald, 247
Forsius, Henrik, 29
Forsius, Sigfrid Aronus, 15
Forsman, Georg, 114
Fort George, Inverness, 45–6
four estates, 17, 112
France, 44, 46
  Crimean War (1853–6), 104,
    107, 109, 110
  Helsinki Accords (1975), 247
  Napoleonic Wars (1803–15),
    viii, 42, 66, 68–71, 77–9,
    82
  Revolution (1789–99), 67–8,
    158
Franzén, Frans Mikael, 84
Frederick I, King of Sweden, 39
Fredrik Posse, 51
Freemasonry, 61
French language, 61, 94–5, 259
French New Wave, 241
von Frenckell, Erik, 221, 223
Frosterus, Sigurd, 179
functionalism, 175, 177, 180,
  195
Furst Menschikoff, S/S, 96

Gallen-Kallela, Akseli, 141, 142
gambling, 223
gardeners, 58
gas lighting, 127
Gävle, Sweden, 49
Gellhorn, Martha, 199–200
general strike (1905), 133
Generalguvernören von Rosen, 50
German Church, Helsinki, 94,
    228
German Empire (1871–1918)
    Bolsheviks, relations with,
        154
    electricity in, 128
    Finnish Civil War (1918),
        120, 158, 160–63, 165–6,
        168
    First World War (1914–18),
        150, 155, 157, 168
    Jäger Movement, 153
    trade with, 125
    Treaty of Brest-Litovsk
        (1918), 159, 160
German language, 12, 13, 28, 94,
    125, 259
German merchants, 12, 13, 94
Germany
    Democratic Republic
        (1949–90), 245
    Empire (1871–1918), see
        German Empire
    Federal Republic (1949–),
        218, 245
    Nazi era (1933–45), 196,
        202–7, 210
Gesellius, Herman, 143

Giscard d'Estaing, Valéry, 247
Glass Palace, Helsinki, 177–8
globalisation, 122–3, 259
Godard, Jean-Luc, 240
Goddess of Justice, 116
von der Goltz, Rüdiger, 165
Göta Canal, 44
Gothenburg, Sweden, 19, 45, 49
Government Palace, Helsinki,
    84, 234
grammar schools, 137
Granatenhjelm, Fredrik, 62
Grand Duchy of Finland
    (1809–1917), viii, 42, 48, 61,
        71–120, 121–55
    censorship in, 101, 103, 152
    civil service, 183
    Crimean War (1853–6),
        104–11
    Diet of the Estates, 71–3, 82,
        112–16, 138, 172
    First World War (1914–17),
        viii, 144, 150–53
    governor-generals, 94–5
    Helsinki reconstruction
        (1810–25), 73–5, 79–87
    housing in, 123, 130–35
    industry in, 125–6, 136, 212
    language in, 101, 113–19,
        123–5, 135–40
    nationalism in, 100–101,
        102–4, 113, 116, 137–42,
        148
    Parliament, 133, 146–50, 172
    railways in, 121–2, 137, 144
    Russian migration, 88–94, 99

Russification programmes
(1899–1917), 124, 138,
146, 152, 155
social reforms (1863–1906),
111–12
technology in, 127–9
theatre in, 116–18, 120
water supply in, 126–7
working class in, 130–37
Great Britain (1707–1800), 68,
69, 71
Great Famine (1315–17), 3
Great Northern War (1700–21),
33–8, 42, 56
Great Square, Helsinki, 25, 27,
53, 65
Green League, 226, 262
grid plans, 19, 25, 38, 79, 83, 144
Guards' Barracks, Helsinki, 82,
130, 219, 234
Gustav I, King of Sweden, 5–8,
10–12, 17, 19, 41–2, 191
Gustav II, King of Sweden,
16–18, 191
Gustav III, King of Sweden, 57,
61, 64–7, 74, 79, 115
Gustav IV, King of Sweden, 67,
69, 79

Hakaniemi, Helsinki, 130, 254
Hakaniemi Market Square,
Helsinki, 131, 133–4, 154,
202, 241
Halkola, Kristiina, 241
Häme, Finland, 19, 22, 26, 73,
123, 182, 214, 216

Hämeenlinna, Finland, 53, 73
Hämeentie, Helsinki, 25, 53–4,
88, 131, 132
Hamina, 40, 49, 66
Hanko, Finland, 160, 161
Hanseatic League (c. 1159–
1669), 4, 6, 14, 49
Harbig, Rudolf, 202
hares, 263
Hats, 42–4, 45
Havis Amanda, Helsinki, 145–6,
147
hawthorn, 264
heating, 232
Heikinkatu, Helsinki, 178, 179,
195
Heimola, Helsinki, 148, 149
Helander, Vilhelm, 230
Helsinga rapids, 5
Helsinge socken, 9
Helsinge, 92
Helsingeland, Finland, 9
Helsingfors Dagblad, 113, 138–9
Helsingfors Morgonblad, 100–101
Helsingfors, 92
Helsingin Jyry, 161
Helsingin Sanomat, 138, 148,
177, 221, 223, 228, 248
Helsingin Uutiset, 113
Helsinginkatu, Helsinki, 144
Helsinki Accords (1975), 231,
245–8
Helsinki Cathedral, 1
Helsinki Day, 8
Helsinki Finnish Real Lyceum,
135

Helsinki Lyceum, 100
Helsinki Monitoring Groups, 246
Helsinki Rural Municipality, 211–13, 219
Helsinki University of Technology, 219
Helsinki Voluntary Fire Brigade, 148
Helsinki-Malmi Airport, 180
Helsinki-Seura, 191
Helsinki-Vantaa Airport, 219
Helsinkiin (Aho), 139–40
Hemingway, Ernest, 199
Hermanni, Helsinki, 131, 162, 175
herons, 266
Herttoniemenranta, Helsinki, 254
Herttoniemi, Helsinki, 212
Herttoniemi Manor, Helsinki, 71
Hertzberg, Rafael, 189–90
Hietalahdenkatu, Helsinki, 134
Hietalahti, Helsinki, 228, 241
Hietaniemi Cemetery, Helsinki, 201, 236
Hietaniemi, Helsinki, 28
Hitler, Adolf, 196
Hoffers, Eugen, 130
Holy Trinity Church, Helsinki, 119
homosexuality, 241
Honecker, Erich, 247
Hotel Fennia, Helsinki, 144
Hotel Kämp, Helsinki, 199

Hotel Torni, Helsinki, 209
Hotel Vaakuna, Helsinki, 178
House of the Estates, Helsinki, 114–15, 173, 194
House of the Nobility, Helsinki, 114, 148
'house Russkis', 242–3
housing
  Republic era (1919–), 175, 210–11, 232, 253, 260–61
  Russian era (1809–1917), 86–7, 123, 130–35
  Swedish era (1150s–1809), 13, 26, 27, 31–2, 36, 38, 39, 52, 53, 54
Hufvudstadsbladet, 113, 163, 177
Hultin, Tekla, 148–9, 162
human rights, 246, 247, 248
hydroplanes, 180

ice age, 2, 8
Ice Hall, Helsinki, 236
Ignatius, Andreas, 28
Ikonen, Ansa, 187
immigration, *see under* migration
Imperial Alexander University, 83–4, 100–102, 116, 118–19, 137
Imperial Palace, Helsinki, 165, 169
Independence Day, 236
industry, 125–6, 187–8, 212, 225, 254
Ingria, 33, 34
Ingrian War (1610–17), 33
insurance, 225

INDEX

Inverness, Scotland, 45–6
Iron House, Helsinki, 231
Ischora, 95
Isosaari, Helsinki, 167
Itäinen Heikinkatu, Helsinki, 178, 179, 195

Jäähalli, Helsinki, 236
Jacobite uprising (1745–6), 46
Jäger Movement, 153
Jäntti, Toivo, 177
Järnefelt family, 140
Järvenpää, Finland, 140
Jätkäsaari, Helsinki, 188, 255
Jews, 93–4, 152, 184, 253
John III, King of Sweden, 15
judicial system, 32, 112
Jugend style, 133, 142–5, 148, 243
Jung, Bertel, 211

Kaisaniemenkatu, Helsinki, 178
Kaisaniemi, Helsinki, 98, 206
Kaivohuone, Helsinki, 96, 97
Kaivopuisto, Helsinki, 96–8, 176, 194, 204, 218, 244
Kajaani, Finland, 166
Kalasatama, Helsinki, 1, 20, 255–6
Kalastajatorppa, Munkkiniemi, 247
Kalevala, 101, 146
Kalevalankatu, Helsinki, 241
Kalevankatu, Helsinki, 169
Kaljaasi Auroran Kuja, Kalasatama, 256

Kallio, Helsinki, 130, 131, 132, 142, 176, 203
Kallio, Kyösti, 235
Kallio, Oiva, 174
Kallio Church, Helsinki, 144
Kalmar Union (1397–1523), 5, 141
Kamppi, Helsinki, 94, 200, 229, 252–3
Kansalaistori, Helsinki, 173, 252
Kapteeni Sundmanin Katu, Kalasatama, 256
Käpylä Sports Park, Helsinki, 176–7
Käpylä, Helsinki, 175, 219
Karelia, 33, 34, 197, 207, 214, 215
Karjalan Liitto, 215–16
Karl X, King of Sweden, *see* Charles X
Kasaberg, Helsinki, 45
Katajanokka, Helsinki, 21, 24, 36, 53, 82, 119, 156, 167, 180, 188, 254
Katri Valan puisto, Helsinki, 193
Kauhajoki, Finland, 198
Kaunas, Lithuania, 169
Kauniainen, Finland, 145, 217
Kaupunginlahti, Helsinki, 24, 25, 27, 53
Kearsarge, USS, 268
Kehä III, Helsinki, 255
Kekkonen, Urho, 166, 168, 236, 238, 242, 243–4, 246, 247, 248
Kela, 231

Kenen Helsinki? (Helander and Sundman), 230
Kerberos, 180
'Kesäilta laitakaupungissa' (Vala), 193
Keskuskatu, Helsinki, 231
KGB, 242–3
Kiasma, Helsinki, 173
Kiasma Museum of Contemporary Art, Helsinki, 252
King's Avenue plan, 173–4, 181, 253
Kingdom of Finland (1918–19), 168
Kirjatalo, Helsinki, 231
kiva kaveri, 92–3
Kivi, Aleksis, 117–18
Kleineh, Louis, 97
Kliininen instituutti, Helsinki, 102
Klinge, Matti, 224
Kluuvi, Helsinki, 24–5
Kluuvinlahti, Helsinki, 54, 80, 86, 88, 148
Koivisto, Mauno, 242
Kolehmainen, Hannes, 221
Kolmikulma, Helsinki, 205
Kontula, Helsinki, 212
Konung Gustaf III, 51
Korkeasaari, Helsinki, 176
Korkeavuorenkatu, Helsinki, 203
kotiryssät, 242–3
Koulupuistikko Park, Helsinki, 228

Kronstadt, St Petersburg, 72, 96, 105, 106, 108, 161
Kruununhaka, Helsinki, 21, 100
Kruunuvuorenranta, Helsinki, 256
Kruunuvuorenselkä, 36
Kuhlberg, Johan, 55–6
Kukanpäivä, 103
Kulosaari Manor, Helsinki, 47
Kulosaari, Helsinki, 145, 171, 211, 212
Kulttuuritalo, Helsinki, 231
Kumtähden kenttä, Helsinki, 103
Kuninkaansaari, Helsinki, 105, 257
Kuninkaansaari, Helsinki, 267
Kuopio, Finland, 139, 182
Kustaanmiekka Strait, 1, 45–6
Kuusela, Armi, 221
Kyläsaari, Helsinki, 232

Laajasalo, Helsinki, 212, 255, 256
Lake Päijänne, 233
Lake Saimaa, 99
Lake Tuusula Artistic Community, 140
Länsimetro, 262
Läntinen Heikinkatu, Helsinki, 178, 195
Läntinen Viertotie, Helsinki, 143
Lapinlahti Hospital, Helsinki, 102
Lapland War (1945), 210
Lappeenranta, Finland, 99
Lapua Movement, 171

Lapua, Finland, 171
Lapualaismorsian (1967 film),
240
Lasipalatsi, Helsinki, 177–8, 235
Latvia, 26, 34, 90, 169, 172, 196,
202
Lauantaiseura, 100–101
Lauttasaari, Helsinki, 106, 212
Le Moine, Erik Wilhelm, 54
Lea (Kivi), 117–18
lead bottle tops, 232
Lebensraum, 196
Lenin, Vladimir, 153–5, 157,
158, 238
Lenininpuisto, Helsinki, 238
Liberal People's Party, 226
Lighthouse, Kalasatama, 256
lighting, 127
Liisankatu, Helsinki, 141
lilac, 264
Lindegren, Yrjö, 177
Lindgren, Armas, 143, 144
Lindqvist, Gustav, 72–3
literature, 139–40, 192–4, 241
Lithuania, 169, 172, 196, 202
livestock, 263
Livonia, 34
Livonian War (1558–83), 13
London Olympics Games (1948),
222
London, England, 128, 208
Lönn, Wivi, 144–5
Loviisa, Finland, 44, 49, 161
Lübeck, 6
Lunatic Asylum, *see* Lapinlahti
Hospital

Lutheranism, 1, 5–6, 14, 28, 71,
80, 93, 102, 170, 253

'Maamme', 100, 103
Madrid Conference (1980–83),
248
magazines, 192
magistrates' courts, 32
Maiden of Finland, 116
Majakka, Kalasatama, 256
Majority, The, 229–30
Makkaratalo, Helsinki, 229–30
Malmgård Manor, Pernaja, 22
Malminkatu, Helsinki, 94
Mannerheim, Gustaf, 165–6,
168, 198–9, 201, 224, 234–5
Mannerheimintie, Helsinki, 25,
143, 144, 173, 175, 195, 235,
248
Mäntsälä rebellion (1932), 171
manual labourers, 14, 28, 131,
132, 134
Marjatan talo, Helsinki, 193
Market Square, Helsinki, 1, 53,
80, 82, 95, 156, 170, 194,
195, 235
marriage, 32
Married Woman, A (1964 film),
240
Marshall Plan (1948), 220, 224
Martin, Elias, 62–3
May Day, 241
Mechelin, Leo, 94, 114–15, 116
Meilahti, Helsinki, 175, 176,
243
memento mori, 14

mercantilism, 3, 4, 5, 6, 8, 12, 30, 43, 51, 58
merchants, 4, 7, 8, 10, 12–13, 14, 16, 23, 30, 40, 54–7
    Dutch, 7, 10, 12, 13
    German, 12, 13, 94
    houses, 54
    Jewish, 93–4
    Revaler, 43
    Russian, 7, 10, 37, 88–94
    Russo-Swedish War (1700–21), 35, 39
    Russo-Swedish War (1741–3), 49
    shipping companies, 49–53
    Suomenlinna construction, 46–7
Merihaka, Helsinki, 254
Messuhalli, Helsinki, 219
metal industry, 126, 136, 152, 225, 226
metro system, 227–9, 262
middle class, 123, 135, 171, 182, 183, 186, 226, 227
midwives, 60
migration
    Republic era (1919–), 182–3, 214–18, 239, 257–61
    Russian era (1809–1917), 88–94, 123
    Swedish era (1150s–1809), 8, 9, 29–30
Mikkeli, Finland, 199, 215
military complexes, 82
Minä ja ministeri (1934 film), 194

Ministry of Defence, 234
Miss Universe, 221
Molotov–Ribbentrop Pact (1939), 196
mortality rates, 59–60
Moscow Armistice (1944), 207, 242
Moscow, Russia, 121, 208
municipal elections, 135, 157, 181–2, 226
Munkkiniemi, Helsinki, 247
Munkkisaari, Helsinki, 188
Munkkivuori, Helsinki, 212
Museum of Contemporary Art, Helsinki, 173
music, 140–41, 240
Musiikkitalo, Helsinki, 173, 252
Myllypuro, Helsinki, 212

Napoleon I, Emperor of the French, 68, 72, 78, 82
Napoleonic Wars (1803–15), viii, 42, 66, 68–71, 77–9, 82
Narinkka blocks, 88
Narinkka Square, Helsinki, 115, 253
Narva, Estonia, 4
national anthem, 100, 103
National Archives, 114
National Coalition Party, 149
National Library of Finland, 84
National Museum, Helsinki, 143
National Theatre, Helsinki, 144
nationalism, 100–101, 102–4, 113, 116, 137–42, 148
Naval Barracks, Helsinki, 82, 234

Nazi Germany (1933–45), 196, 202–7, 210
neo-Baroque architecture, 144
neo-Classical architecture, 172, 175
neo-Gothic architecture, 130
neo-Renaissance architecture, 130
Nervanderinkatu, Helsinki, 170–71
Neva River, viii, 35, 37, 72
Nevsky Prospekt, St Petersburg, 37, 85
New Wave, 241
newspapers, 95, 113, 138–9, 192
Nicholas I, Emperor of Russia, 84, 95
Nicholas II, Emperor of Russia, 146, 147, 155
Nihti, Helsinki, 256
Nikolainkatu, Helsinki, 88, 169
Niska, Algoth, 189
Niskanen, Mikko, 240
Nobel, Immanuel, 106
nobility, 17, 51, 54–5, 60–61, 64, 73, 114
manor houses, 55, 63–4
Nokia, 251
Nordmann, Petrus, 190
Norrland, Finland, 9
North Atlantic Treaty Organization (NATO), 245, 267–8
North Harbour, Helsinki, 27, 65, 73
North Sea, 3, 4, 49

Northern War (1655–60), 23
Norway
  Kalmar Union (1397–1523), 5, 141
  Napoleonic Wars (1803–15), 78
novels, 139–40, 192
November Uprising (1830), 95
Novgorod, Russia, 4
Nurmi, Paavo, 176, 220, 221
Nya Teatern, Helsinki, 117, 118
Nyen, 19, 34
Nyland, see Uusimaa
Nyländska Jaktklubbens hamn (Edelfelt), 141–2
Nylund, Felix, 191

Observatory Hill, Helsinki, 54, 130
Observatory, Helsinki, 45, 54, 85–6, 102, 130
Old Church Park, Helsinki, 28, 29, 60
Old Finns, 93, 138, 145, 149
Old Student House, Helsinki, 237
Olympic Games
  1912 Stockholm, 189, 221
  1940 Helsinki (cancelled), 174, 175, 177, 180
  1948 London, 222
  1952 Helsinki, 180, 218–24
Olympic Stadium, Helsinki, 174, 177, 202
Oodi, Helsinki, 173, 252
Opera House, Helsinki, 175

Orko, Risto, 194
Orthodox Church, 1, 83, 89–90, 111, 119, 170
Östergötland, Sweden, 79
Ostrobothnia, Finland, 18, 19, 35, 159, 171, 198
Ostrobothnia student nation, 153
Otaniemi, Helsinki, 219
Ottoman Empire (1299–1922), 34, 66, 104, 108
'Our Land', 100, 103
Oxenstierna, Axel, 18

Paasikivi, Juho Kusti, 221, 235, 242
Paasitorni, Helsinki, 133–4, 157–8, 159, 162
Pacius, Fredrik, 100
Padise Abbey, Estonia, 4
painters, 54, 62, 86, 141
Päivälehti, 138–9, 148
Palme, Olof, 247
Palo, Tauno, 187
Paluu (Vala), 193
paper industry, 168
Paris, France, 128
Paris Peace Treaty (1947), 220
Parliament, 133, 146–50, 152, 172
  establishment (1906), 133
  independence (1917), 157, 158
  Stump Parliament (1918), 168
Parliament Act (1906), 133

Parliament House, Helsinki, 172, 174, 230, 235, 252–3
Pärssinen, Hilja, 149
Pasila Station, Helsinki, 253
Pasila, Helsinki, 131
Peasant March (1930), 171
peasantry, 5, 6, 7, 9, 17
Pénaud, Charles, 110
People's Delegation, 160
Pernaja, Finland, 22
Peter I, Emperor of Russia, 34, 35, 41
Peter the Great's Naval Fortress, 150
Pihjalanmäki, Helsinki, 212
Piper's Park, Suomenlinna, 63
Pitkäsilta Bridge, Helsinki, 80, 83, 86, 88, 142
  Battle of Helsinki (1918), 162
  north of, 130–37
Plague Park, Helsinki, 28, 29, 60
plague, 3, 12, 28, 29, 60
poetry, 192–4
Pohjois-Haaga, Helsinki, 212
Pohjoisesplanadi, Helsinki, 97, 141, 199, 231
Pohjolankatu, Helsinki, 175
Poland
  Northern War (1655–60), 23
  Russian War (1830–31), 95
  Second World War (1939–45), 210
  Swedish War (1600–29), 16, 17, 18
pollution, 231–3, 266

Polytechnic Institute, 128
population
    Republic era (1919–), 175,
        182, 212–18, 252, 257
    Russian era (1809–1917), 90,
        123, 131
    Swedish era (1150s–1809), 2,
        3, 9, 23, 26, 48–9
Porkkalanniemi, Finland, 50,
    209, 220, 225
Pörssitalo, Helsinki, 149
Portugal, 51, 68
Porvoo, Finland, 8, 10, 16, 18,
    22, 40, 49, 65
Postitalo, Helsinki, 127, 178,
    235
Prague, Czechoslovakia, 169
Pro Helsingfors Foundation, 191
Progress Party, 149
prohibition (1919–32), 188–9
prostitution, 139
Protestantism, 94, 123
Prussia (1701–1918), 68, 150
public sector, 225
public transport, see
    transportation
Punavuori, Helsinki, 134
Puotinharju, Helsinki, 227, 229

Raa-Winterhjelm, Charlotta,
    118
rabbits, 263
Railway Square, Helsinki, 144
railways, 121–2, 137, 144, 253,
    258–9
Räsänen, Maria, 136

rats, 263
Rauma, Finland, 8, 10
Rautatalo, Helsinki, 231
real Finn movement, 179, 185–6
reconstruction (1810–25), 73–5,
    79–87
Red Book of Farewells, The
    (Saisio), 241
Red Guards, 149, 156, 157,
    158–68, 186–7
rental properties, 260–61
Republic of Finland (1919–), 48,
    168
    architecture in, 229–31,
        252–7
    baby boom (1945–60s),
        214–15
    class in, 226–7
    Cold War (1947–91), 224,
        238–9, 241–9, 251
    Continuation War (1941–4),
        198, 202–8, 214, 234, 243
    economy, 168–9, 182–3,
        187–8, 212, 225–6, 235,
        251–2
    establishment (1919), 168
    EU membership, 249, 251–2,
        267
    film in, 187, 194–6, 240–41
    history in, 189–92
    industry in, 187–8, 225, 254
    language in, 184–6, 216–17,
        239, 257–61
    Lapland War (1945), 210
    Lapua Movement (1929–32),
        171

literature in, 192–4, 241
monuments in, 234–5
NATO accession (2023), 249,
    267–8
Olympic Games (1952),
    218–24
pollution in, 231–3
prohibition (1919–32),
    188–9
Ritavuori assassination
    (1922), 171
shipping in, 254–6
transportation in, 227–9
water supply, 233
Winter War (1939–40),
    197–202, 204, 215–16
Restaurant Lehtovaara, 215
restaurants, 97–8, 188
Return, The (Vala), 193
Reuterholm, Gustaf Adolf, 79
Reval, Estonia, 4, 7, 12, 14–15,
    23, 26, 34, 43, 49, 90, 96, 249
see also Tallinn
Riga, Latvia, 26, 34, 90, 169,
    210
Riksdag, 14, 16, 40, 42, 56, 64
Ritavuori, Heikki, 170–71
roads, 212, 227–8
roe deer, 263
Roman Empire (27 BCE–CE
    395), 2
Romania, 169, 202
Röö, Erik, 59
Rotbraut-Pleyer, Barbara, 221–2
Royal Academy of Turku, 18, 75,
    84, 101

Runeberg, Johan Ludvig, 64,
    100, 103
Ruoholahti, Helsinki, 134, 254
Russia
    Bolshevik period (1917–22),
        159, 160, 168, 187
    Empire (1721–1917), *see*
        Russian Empire
    Russian Federation (1991–),
        238, 258–9, 267–8
    Soviet period (1922–91), *see*
        Soviet Union
    Tsardom (1547–1721),
        11–12, 13, 33–8, 42, 266
Russia, vii–viii, 3, 4
Russian Baltic Sea Fleet, 150,
    159
Russian Black Sea Fleet, 104
Russian Empire (1721–1917),
    viii, 39, 49, 61, 66, 266
    Crimean War (1853–6), 98,
        104–11, 120
    Finland colony (1809–1917),
        see Grand Duchy of
        Finland
    Napoleonic Wars (1803–15),
        viii, 42, 66, 68–71, 77–9
    Ottoman War (1787–92), 66
    Polish War (1830–31), 95
    Revolution (1905), 133
    Revolution (1917), viii,
        153–5, 157, 158
    Swedish War (1741–3), 42–3,
        45, 46, 49
    Swedish War (1788–90), 42,
        66–8

Swedish War (1808–9), 42,
66, 68–71
Russian Federation (1991–), 238,
258–9, 267–8
Russian language, 88–94, 99,
119, 124, 170, 258–9
Russian Orthodox Church, 1, 83,
90, 111, 119, 170
Russian Revolution (1917), viii,
153–5, 157, 158
Russification, 124, 138, 146, 152,
155
Russo-Japanese War (1904–5),
146
Russo-Swedish Wars
1554–57 Russo-Swedish War,
11–12
1610–17 Ingrian War, 33
1700–21 Great Northern
War, 33–8, 42, 269
1741–43 Russo-Swedish War,
42–3, 45, 49
1788–90 Russo-Swedish War,
42, 66–8
1808–09 Finnish War, 42,
66, 68–71
Ryti, Risto, 198

Saaremaa, Estonia, 50
Saarinen, Eliel, 143, 173, 181,
211, 253
Saimaa Canal, 99
Saisio, Pirkko, 241
salmon, 8
salt, 51
Santahamina, Helsinki, 7, 19,

21, 105, 106, 107, 151, 167,
219, 256–7
Saturday Club, 100–101
Sausage House, Helsinki, 229–30
Savonia, 14
Savonius, Samuel, 14
Schauman, August, 88, 111, 113
Schmidt, Helmut, 247
schools, 137, 259
sea eagles, 266
seals, 9
Second World War (1939–45),
ix, 193, 197–208, 209–10,
235
Continuation War (1941–4),
198, 202–8, 214, 234,
243
Lapland War (1945), 210
Winter War (1939–40),
197–202, 204, 215–16
Sederholm House, Helsinki, 53,
190
Sederholm, Hedvig Catharina,
57
Sederholm, Johan, 50–51, 53,
55–7
Senate building, Helsinki, 80,
83, 99, 161
Senate Square, Helsinki, 39, 80,
83, 85, 88, 115
Alexander II statue, 108,
111–16, 169–70
German victory parade
(1918), 162
Government Palace, 234
Sederholm House, 53, 190

Senate building, 80, 83, 99, 161
St Nicholas's Church, 84, 120
student protests (1967), 236–7
Ulrika Eleonora Church, 39
University of Helsinki, 207
Senate, 75, 80, 82, 99, 128–9, 158, 159, 160, 165, 166
Sergel, Johan Tobias, 66
servants, 14, 28, 30, 123
Seurahuone, Helsinki, 97
Sevastopol, Crimea, 104, 105, 108
Seven Years' War (1756–63), 47
sex; sexuality, 32, 240, 241
shipping, 50–53, 77, 254–6
containerisation, 254–5
steam ships, 95–6, 122
Sibelius, Aino, 140
Sibelius, Jean, 140–41, 142
Sigismund III, King of Sweden, 15–16, 17
Silcke, Sven, 40
Siltasaarenkatu, Helsinki, 144
Siltasaari Workers' House, 133–4, 157–8, 159, 162
Siltasaari, Helsinki, 54, 142, 144, 162
Siltavuori, Helsinki, 45
Sirén, Johan Sigfrid, 172
Smolny, St Petersburg, 160
Snellman, Johan Vilhelm, 114
Snellmaninkatu, Helsinki, 88, 169
social class, 130–37, 186, 226–7

Social Democratic Party, 133, 134, 153–4, 155–9, 187, 226, 229
socialism, 133, 155–6
Somalians, 258
Sompasaari, Helsinki, 264, 256
Sörnäinen, Helsinki, 19–20, 21, 127, 130, 131, 144, 162, 193, 255, 264
Sörnäisten rantatie, Helsinki, 154
South Harbour, Helsinki, 1, 24, 53, 80, 165, 218, 231
Soviet Union (1922–91), 187, 209, 224–5, 235, 238, 241–9, 251
disarmament talks (1969–72), 245
dissolution (1991), 246, 248, 267
Finlandisation, 238, 241–4, 246
Finnish War, First (1939–40), 197–202, 215–16
Finnish War, Second (1941–4), 198, 202–8, 214, 234
German invasion (1941), 202
Helsinki Accords (1975), 231, 245–8
Helsinki Olympics (1952), 219
Korea Airlines shootdown (1983), 248
Molotov–Ribbentrop Pact (1939), 196

Porkkalanniemi withdrawal (1955–6), 225
Stalin's death (1953), 224–5
Spain, 50, 52
Spanish flu (1918–20), 167
Spåre, Erik, 11
spas, 96–7, 176
sports, 176–7
Olympic Games, 174, 175, 177, 180, 189, 218–24
St John's Church, Helsinki, 1, 130, 228
St Nicholas's Church, Helsinki, 80, 84, 95, 120, 130, 141
St Petersburg, Russia, viii, 19, 35, 37, 41, 72, 84, 85, 90, 168–9, 183
First World War (1914–17), 150
Kronstadt, 72, 96, 105, 106, 108, 161
rail links to, 121, 122, 258–9
Revolution (1917), 155, 157
water purification plant, 267
Ståhlberg, Kaarlo Juho, 149–50, 168, 171, 211, 234, 235
Stalin, Joseph, 158, 196–7, 200, 207, 224–5, 241, 242
State and Revolution, The (Lenin), 154–5
steam ships, 95–6, 122
Stjernvall, Fredrik, 73–4
Stock Exchange Building, Helsinki, 149
Stockholm, Sweden, 23, 25, 26, 34, 49, 90, 96, 218, 261–2

Olympic Games (1912), 189, 221
Stockmann, Georg Franz, 178
Stockmann department store, 178–9, 192, 194
Storfursten, S/S, 96
Strasbourg, France, 128
streetlamps, 127
Student House, Helsinki, 116
student movement, 236–7, 240–41
student nations, 153
Stump Parliament (1918), 168
Summer Evening on the Edge of Town' (Vala), 193
Sundman, Mikael, 230
Sunn, Carl Magnus, 55–6
Suomalainen, Kari, 223
Suomen Kuvalehti, 192
Suomenlinna, Helsinki, 1, 44–9, 51, 54, 61–3, 64, 65, 77, 79, 92, 170, 269
Alexander Nevsky Church, 119
Civil War (1918), 163, 167, 168
Crimean War (1853–6), 105–11
First World War (1914–18), 150, 151
flora, 264
migration and, 90–91
Russo-Swedish War (1788–90), 67
Russo-Swedish War (1808–09), 69–71, 85, 88

Suometar, 113
surnames, 170, 185
Surun ja ilon kaupunki
(Waltari), 192
Susisaari, Helsinki, 44, 45
Suurkatu, Helsinki, 25, 27, 30,
31, 53, 56, 59, 65
Svartholm Sea Fortress,
Loviisa, 44
Sveaborg, *see* Suomenlinna
Svecoman movement, 119
Svenska Teatern, Helsinki, 117,
186
Svinhufvud, Pehr Evind, 235
Sweden, viii, 4, 191–2, 266
bicameral legislature
introduced (1866), 112
Charles IX's reign (1604–11),
16
Charles X's reign (1654–60),
23
Charles XI's reign (1660–97),
33
Charles XII's reign (1697–
1718), 33–8
Christina's reign (1632–54),
18–22
Count's War (1534–6), 6
Crimean War (1853–6), 109
Great Northern War (1700–
21), 33–8, 42, 56
Gustav I's reign (1523–60),
5–8, 10–12, 17, 19, 41–2,
191
Gustav II's reign (1611–32),
16–18, 191

Gustav III's reign (1771–92),
57, 61, 64–7, 74, 79, 115
Gustav IV's reign (1792–
1809), 67–9
Helsinki Accords (1975), 247
Ingrian War (1610–17), 33
Kalmar Union (1397–1523),
5, 141
Livonian War (1558–83), 13
migration to, 218, 239
NATO accession (2024), 267
Polish War (1600–29), 16,
17, 18
Russian Wars, *see* Russo-
Swedish Wars
Second World War (1939–
45), 202
Sigismund III's reign (1592–
9), 15–16
Stockholm Olympics (1912),
189, 221
War of Liberation (1521–3),
5
Swedish language
Republic era (1919–), 184–6,
217, 239, 257–8, 260
Russian era (1809–1917),
91–2, 99, 119, 123, 135,
163, 181–2
Swedish era (1150s–1809),
9–10, 21, 28, 89, 90–91
Swedish People's Party of
Finland (SPP), 181–2, 226
Swedish Royal Academy, 61
Swedish Theatre, Helsinki, 117,
186

sweets, 126
Switzerland, 153
Symposion (Gallen-Kallela), 141
synagogues, 94

Tähtitorninvuori, Helsinki, 54, 130
Taka-Töölö, Helsinki, 154, 175, 231
Tallberg, Julius, 191
Tallinn, Estonia, 4, 144, 169, 204, 210, 249
see also Reval
Tamminiemi, Meilahti, 243
Tammisaari, Finland, 8, 10
Tampere, Finland, 160, 161
Tanner, Väinö, 134–5, 136, 187, 200
tar, 8, 23–4, 27, 52
Tatars, 93, 152
Tavastians, 9, 13
taxation, 6, 11, 12, 13, 17, 18, 135, 149, 261
Tehtaankatu, Helsinki, 244
telephones, 128–9
Tenholantie, Helsinki, 144
terrorism, 261
Tervasaari, Helsinki, 27
textiles, 31, 125, 152
theatre, 116–18, 120
Thomasson, Gustaf, 136
Three Smiths statue, Helsinki, 191
Tilsit Treaties (1807), 68
timber, 8, 13, 24, 30, 37, 46, 47, 49, 51–2, 55, 125

tobacco, 93, 100, 126
Tokazier, Abraham, 177
Töölön kisahalli, Helsinki, 219
Töölönlahti, Helsinki, 25, 80, 97–8, 130, 154, 162, 173–5, 231, 252, 253
Topelius monument, Koulupuistikko Park, 228
Topelius, Zacharias, 117, 121
topography, 25–6
Torch Bearers, The, 193
tourism, 169, 178, 179, 180, 218, 220, 222, 240, 258–9, 265, 267
trade
Republic era (1919–), 168–9, 182–3, 225–6, 244
Russian era (1809–1917), 77, 99–100, 122, 125
Swedish era (1150s–1809), 4–7, 9, 11, 12, 23, 41–2, 49–57
trade unions, 186
transportation, 179–80, 212, 214, 227–9
aviation, 180, 219
cars, 212, 227–8, 230–31
Enemmistö movement, 229–30
ferries, 218, 249, 255, 267
metro, 227–9, 262
railways, 121–2, 137, 144, 253, 258–9
Treaty of Brest-Litovsk (1918), 160
Treaty of Tartu (1920), 168

Tsardom of Russia (1547–1721), 11–12, 13, 33–8, 42, 266
Tukiainen, Aimo, 235
Tulenkantajat, 193
Tuomarinkylä, Helsinki, 63
Turku Barracks, Helsinki, 82, 117, 127, 177–8, 234
Turku, Finland, 6, 16, 18, 73, 75, 78, 80, 87, 92, 96, 184
Royal Academy, 18, 75, 84, 101
Turuntie, Helsinki, 25, 64, 178
Tuusulanjärven taiteilijayhteisö, 140

Ukraine, 238, 259, 267–8
Ullanlinna, Helsinki, 50, 51, 53, 54, 80, 105, 111, 130, 144
Ulrika, Queen of Sweden, 39, 45
Ulrika Eleonora Church, Helsinki, 39, 65
Ulrikasborg, Helsinki, 45, 50, 85
Ulvila, Finland, 8, 10
Unioninkatu, Helsinki, 80, 83, 85, 86, 94, 102, 119, 144, 169
United Kingdom (1800–), 41
Crimean War (1853–6), 104, 107, 109, 111
migration to, 218
United States, 224
disarmament talks (1969–72), 245
Helsinki Accords (1975), 231, 245–8
Marshall Plan (1948), 220, 224

Second World War (1939–45), 205
University of Bonn, 86
University of Helsinki, 83–4, 100–102, 116, 118–19, 137, 176, 185, 207, 234
upper class, 117, 123, 171, 182, 186
Uspenski Cathedral, Helsinki, 1, 36, 119–20, 141
Uudenmaan Esikaupunki, Helsinki, 80
Uudenmaankatu, Helsinki, 87
Uusi Suometar, 113, 145–6
Uusi Ylioppilastalo, Helsinki, 144
Uusikaupunki, Finland, 34
Uusimaa, Finland, 4–5, 8, 10, 11, 19, 22, 23, 26, 51, 73, 91, 135, 182, 214
Uusimaa student nation, 153
Uusimaa Suburb, Helsinki, 80, 86–7
Uusimaa Yacht Club's Harbour, The (Edelfelt), 141–2

Vaasa, Finland, 159, 160, 165
Vala, Katri, 193–4
Vallgren, Ville, 145–6, 147
Vallila, Helsinki, 175
Vallisaari, Helsinki, 105, 151, 257, 267
Valtionrautatiet, 229
Vanhakaupunki, Helsinki, 131, 191, 254

Vanhankaupunginlahti, Helsinki, 54, 266
Vantaa, Finland, 213, 214, 257, 260
Vantaa River, 5, 7, 9, 21, 55, 126, 213, 233
'Vårt Land', 100, 103
Veikkaus, 223
Vennamo, Veikko, 216
Viapori, 92
Vienna, Austria, 169
Vietnam War (1955–75), 247
Viikki, Helsinki, 266
Viipurin Suomalainen Kirjallisuusseura, 216
Viking Age (800–1050), 3, 7
Vilhonvuori, Helsinki, 193
Villa Hakasalmi, Helsinki, 190
Virolainen, Johannes, 216
Vironniemi, Helsinki, 21–2, 24, 180
Vladivostok, Russia, 121
VMV 6 (1936 film), 194
voting rights, 112, 133, 135, 146–7, 149
VR Group, 229
Vuosaari, Helsinki, 20, 174, 211, 212, 232, 254–5
Vyborg, 6, 23, 30, 34, 66, 99, 182, 184, 215

Wahllund, Catharina, 97–8
Waltari, Mika, 192, 193, 194
War of the Hats (1741–3), 42–3, 45, 49
Waris, Heikki, 131

Warsaw, Poland, 169, 210
watchsmiths, 58
water mills, 55
water supply, 126–7, 233
Watergate scandal (1972–4), 247
Weckström, Johannes, 63–4
welfare state, 239
West Germany (1949–90), 218, 245
West Metro, 262
Westman, Ebba, 30, 31
Wetter, Abraham, 39
White Guards, 149, 153, 156, 158–60, 165–6, 170, 186–7, 201, 235
white-tailed deer, 263
widows, 58–9
Wiipurin Korsetti, 215
Wijnblad, Carl, 63
Wikholm, Fredrik, 58
Winter War (1939–40), 197–202, 204, 215–16
Wladimirinkatu, Helsinki, 169
women
  childbirth, 60
  suffrage, 146–7, 149
  widows, 58–9
wooden buildings, 13, 26, 27, 38, 87
Workers' House, Helsinki, 133–4, 157–8, 159, 162
Workers' Party, 133
working class, 130–37, 175, 186–8, 200, 226, 227
World of Wonders, Helsinki, 148

von Wright, Magnus, 86
Wulff, 155

Yiddish, 93
Yksin (Aho), 140
Young Finns, 137–42, 148, 149, 162, 168

Yusupova, Zinaida, 97

Zarkhi, Aleksandr, 240
Zátopek, Emil, 222
Zátopková, Dana, 222
Zhdanov, Andrei, 209, 242
zoo, 176